Repositioning Reference

Repositioning Reference

New Methods and New Services for a New Age

Laura Saunders, Lillian Rozaklis,
and Eileen G. Abels

ROWMAN & LITTLEFIELD
Lanham • Boulder • New York • London

Published by Rowman & Littlefield
A wholly owned subsidiary of The Rowman & Littlefield Publishing Group, Inc.
4501 Forbes Boulevard, Suite 200, Lanham, Maryland 20706
www.rowman.com

Unit A, Whitacre Mews, 26-34 Stannary Street, London SE11 4AB

British Library Cataloguing in Publication Information Available

Library of Congress Cataloging-in-Publication Data

Saunders, Laura, 1975-
Repositioning reference : new methods and new services for a new age / Laura Saunders, Lillian Rozaklis, and Eileen G. Abels.
pages cm
Includes bibliographical references and index.
ISBN 978-0-8108-9322-1 (hardcover : alk. paper) -- ISBN 978-0-8108-9211-8 (pbk. : alk. paper) -- ISBN 978-0-8108-9212-5 (ebook)
1. Reference services (Libraries) 2. Reference services (Libraries)--Information technology. 3. Reference librarians--Effect of technological innovations on. 4. Organizational change. I. Rozaklis, Lillian, 1978- II. Abels, Eileen G. III. Title.
Z711.S275 2015
025.5'2--dc23
2014030444

Printed in the United States of America

Contents

List of Illustrations

Preface

For years now we have heard predictions and even declarations of the end (or death) of reference. With Internet access and nearly ubiquitous mobile devices making information so easily accessible, many libraries and information organizations have seen numbers of reference questions dwindle, causing some pundits to go so far as to question the relevance of libraries and specifically of reference services. To compete in the twenty-first century, librarians and information professionals can no longer provide the same long-standing services in new ways. Rather, reference librarians and information professionals are being pressured to reimagine their services in innovative ways to meet the demands and expectations of their users. Efforts to date include implementing new models of reference service, reorganizing staff, introducing completely new positions, and setting new priorities. In essence, reference services are experiencing a paradigm shift. These changes to service delivery models and positions entail a new and ever-growing set of competencies that information professionals are expected to master.

Repositioning Reference: New Methods and New Services for a New Age examines the transformations in reference services and the role of the reference librarian, exploring the impact of rapid developments in technology as well as changes to information-specific services in nonlibrary sectors. The book is unique from other books on reference services in that it recognizes and documents novel approaches for initiating reference services growth and examines the ways that librarians are using both traditional and contemporary skills in new ways. An additional unique component of this book is its inclusion of the sources consulted for an environmental scan for reinventing reference services and the results of that scan, so that the reader can implement a scan. The authors offer access to a living blog and invite readers to learn of innovative initiatives and to contribute to the contents of the blog in order to inspire each other. This book may be used as a textbook by library and information sciences (LIS) educators, whose courses and learning experiences prepare aspiring librarians to lead the reference revolution, and by practicing librarians in diverse settings who want to be change agents.

Chapter 1 begins with the historical development of reference over more than one hundred years of technological advances, including the impact of changes in elementary and higher education on library services. Starting with the seminal paper by Samuel Green, this chapter then traces the evolution of services and the shift from collecting and organizing materials to a focus on connecting users with information. The authors also examine the changing definitions of reference services over time and provide an overview of the various models of reference service delivery. This chapter concludes with an analysis of the user's perspective on information seeking and an overview of professional competencies for current reference practice.

Chapter 2 provides an in-depth analysis of the competitive pressures facing reference librarianship, from rapid technological advancement to declining numbers of reference questions, and the accessibility of expert information online. It also looks at evolving user preferences for finding information, including the fact they rarely turn to reference librarians for assistance. These external pressures raise questions about the cost-effectiveness of the traditional "sit and wait" model of the reference desk. Next, this chapter considers some of the ways in which reference services have evolved to meet these changes in user expectations, including embedded librarianship and research consultations and an increased focus on instruction and creation of content to facilitate information seekers' self-help behaviors.

The third chapter of this book moves the discussion forward by considering the implications of the changes described in chapters 1 and 2 on the position of reference librarianship. The authors describe some new areas of responsibility and job functions increasingly included in reference positions, as well as some completely new positions that are emerging as reference services are reorganized and job areas reprioritized. Next, this chapter examines the new competencies and skills areas related to these changes, with a focus on technology skills, soft skills, and content areas, such as instruction and data management. The authors also consider how some of the changes in reference might impact the fundamental philosophies that guide reference practice. Finally, this chapter concludes with a look at the implications of new responsibilities and competencies on LIS education.

The theme of this book is the need for reference librarians and information professionals to envision and implement innovative services to meet the demands of changing user expectations and external competitive pressures. Chapter 4 provides descriptions of libraries and information organizations that have done just that, with examples ranging from proactive reference chat services to personal librarians to self-help reference tools. In a series of mini–case studies, this chapter offers an overview of innovative reference services and analyzes the factors that led to the development of the service and enabled its success. This chapter also looks at innovations beyond reference in libraries and information settings broadly. Finally, this chapter concludes by outlining next steps for professionals wanting to engage in innovations in reference.

Environmental scanning is an effective method for librarians and information professionals to position themselves to take advantage of opportunities for innovation. Chapter 5 introduces the readers to the process of environmental scanning, which involves scanning relevant literature and news outlets in order to monitor trends and inform decision making. While environmental scanning allows librarians and information professionals to keep abreast of trends in the field, this chapter also offers an overview of SWOT analysis, a process of internal assessment to identify strengths and weaknesses so the organization can position itself to take advantage of opportunities and minimize threats posed by new trends. Chapter 5 provides a table that identifies a number of innovative services and traces them back to the trends that inspired them and the news outlets that identified those trends, thereby offering a snapshot of an environmental scan.

The transformations described in chapters 1 through 5 signal major changes in the field of reference and in libraries and information organizations broadly. Acknowledging that change can be difficult; chapter 6 provides several models for change management and change leadership. This chapter pays special attention to staffing issues and considers how to overcome resistance to change and get staff on board with new ideas and services. This chapter also reviews the competencies and qualifications for reference services that emerged from the previous chapters and explores the implications of these changes for LIS education. Finally, this chapter introduces *Unbound: Library Futures Unfettered*, the living blog that accompanies this book. *Unbound* will continue to provide readers with inspiration and examples after they have completed the book, and it also provides a platform for readers to contribute their own ideas and share experiences with reference service innovations. The chapter concludes with a call to action for readers to use the tools and examples provided to spur their own innovations and then share their experiences for others to build on.

Repositioning Reference: New Methods and New Services for a New Age identifies untapped opportunities for reference services and librarians, details entrepreneurial solutions for energizing the profession and engaging library user communities, and prescribes means for evaluating technologies and service models for reference services. Through the creative and innovative ideas of librarians and information professionals across the field, reference is experiencing a rebirth. If these same librarians and information professionals acknowledge the constant nature of change in the field and continue to adapt in response to change, then reference—by whatever name—should continue to be relevant and valuable. The new incarnations of reference services described in or inspired by this book might look quite different from those of the past. However, this book demonstrates that, as was famously the case with Mark Twain, the death of reference has been greatly exaggerated.

ONE

The Evolution of Reference Services

Reference services exist to assist users in navigating and using the wide range of available information resources to answer a question or fulfill an information need. While the format and model of the service can vary widely, reference is often considered a core service, and nearly every type of library offers some dedicated support for finding, retrieving, and evaluating information. Despite its current position as a central service, reference is actually a relatively new development in the long history of libraries, and its future depends heavily on how librarians structure the service to meet the demands and expectations of a user base that has unprecedented access to massive amounts of information through simple and intuitive mechanisms for finding information. This chapter examines the evolution of reference services across different types of libraries and information organizations, including public, academic, and special libraries, as well as archives, and looks at the definitions and competencies that have been associated with this service over time.

HISTORY OF REFERENCE

Libraries as collections of recorded knowledge have existed for millennia. Historically, however, staff in these institutions largely focused on collecting, organizing, and preserving the materials in these collections. Direct interaction with users was fairly limited, and users were expected to search for materials on their own. The development of reference services in American public libraries largely mirrored developments in education.[1] To begin with, as Americans gained greater access to public education in the nineteenth century, literacy rates increased. The increase in education meant that young people needed access to materials to complete homework and assignments, while increased literacy meant that

1

more people wanted books for reading. These developments coincided with the establishment of public libraries both to support public education and to supply the communities with reading materials. Before long, library staff realized that simply providing access to the resources within the library was not enough. Those people who came to the public library for reading materials did not necessarily know how to use a library and would turn to the librarian for help in finding and choosing books or other resources.[2]

The birth of reference services in the United States is usually associated with the publishing of "Personal Relations between Librarians and Readers" by Samuel Green of the Worcester Public Library. In this article, he explained that, while some scholars and well-educated users will be able to use library resources without assistance, most users of public libraries require help to find what they need. He acknowledged that librarians will have to field questions in a variety of subjects and that, even when they are not experts in a certain subject, librarians can use their knowledge of classification and authority to help users find information more quickly and effectively than they would on their own.[3]

Reference services in academic libraries evolved around the same time and largely mirrored developments in higher education.[4] In the eighteenth and nineteenth centuries, academic libraries such as those at Harvard were open very limited hours and restricted borrowing to senior members of the college. These restrictions reflected the fact that the curriculum of colleges and universities at the time was largely based on recitation and did not require students to access library materials.[5] Toward the start of the twentieth century, American colleges and universities began to adopt an empirical-based curriculum, or German model, which required students to do outside research and consult texts beyond those considered part of the classical canon.[6] As increasing numbers of students began to use the academic library, the library staff recognized that students often had difficulty navigating the collections and finding information. At first, some librarians offered help, but such assistance was not a regular part of their job description or expectations. Over time, libraries began to designate staff members to help users and to offer instruction in using such tools as the card catalog. Eventually these duties were coordinated into the modern reference position.[7]

Special libraries are information organizations found in companies, not-for-profit organizations, government agencies, or professional associations as well as subject-focused units in public and academic libraries.[8] The tagline of the Special Libraries Association (SLA), "Connecting People and Information,"[9] communicates clearly the importance of reference services in these libraries and in many ways is the focus of this type of library. Special libraries in the different settings emerged at different times, starting as early as 1787.[10] Special libraries focus on services for their users, including searching for information and packaging that information for use to resolve a specific information need. Special libraries developed selective dissemination of information (SDI) services to keep their users abreast of developments in their fields.[11] The focus of special libraries has, for the most part, been on the user and the provision of information rather than on the collection.

While the purpose of reference in archives is similar to that in libraries, its history and development are somewhat more complex. As in libraries, reference in archives is considered a central service that provides an "essential link" between archival documents and the user.[12] Both the Academy of Certified Archivists (ACA)[13] and the Society of American Archivists (SAA)[14] identify reference as a core area of practice. In a way reference is inherent in archives services. Closed stacks means that users cannot directly interact with the collection but must request assistance from the archivist in retrieving items. In addition, archives generally operate under a number of rules around access and use of items that may not be familiar to users, so most archives visits begin with an orientation in which the archivist explains policies and procedures. Finally, the nature of archival documents and their organization often lead to "difficulty identifying potential sources to meet reference queries" on the part of the user, leading to further need of support from the archivist.[15] Indeed, a 2004 survey of archivists indicates that a large portion of their time (19.9 percent) is spent on reference and access-related services.[16] Nevertheless, because archival documents are generally unique and often delicate, reference services typically come second to preservation of the collection—if not in overall importance than in order of attention.[17] Perhaps for that reason there appears to be a lack of attention to reference in the archival literature and even in archival education in the past decades, making the history of reference in archives somewhat challenging to trace.[18]

REFERENCE: A QUESTION OF DEFINITIONS

So what exactly is reference, and what does a reference librarian do? In his seminal article, Green identified four components of reference work:

1. Instruct the reader in the ways of the library
2. Assist readers in solving their inquiries
3. Aid the reader in the selection of good works
4. Promote the library within the community

Of course, at the time that Green was writing, both libraries and their resources existed only in physical formats and so reference work at that time centered on direct transactions between users and librarians. Librarians helped users to navigate, learn about, and use materials that were housed in the library and to find resources related to their information needs. Other early definitions of *reference work* are similarly focused. The

American Library Association (ALA) proffered its first definition of *reference* in 1943, describing it as "that phase of library work which is directly concerned with assistance to readers in securing information and in using the resources of the library in study and research."[19] In Samuel Rothstein's history of reference, he emphasizes the role of personal assistance in reference and also stresses that reference rooms and reference books are not integral to the definition of the service but are only tools used in providing the service.[20]

Rothstein's distinctions between the service and tools foreshadow later definitions of *reference*, which go beyond those direct interactions to include indirect reference services, such as collection development and maintenance and the preparation of pathfinders or other guides to resources.[21] Currently, the Reference and User Services Association (RUSA), a division of the American Library Association, offers separate definitions for *reference transactions* and *reference work*:

- *Reference Transactions* are information consultations in which library staff recommend, interpret, evaluate, and/or use information resources to help others to meet particular information needs. Reference transactions do not include formal instruction or exchanges that provide assistance with locations, schedules, equipment, supplies, or policy statements.
- *Reference Work* includes reference transactions and other activities that involve the creation, management, and assessment of information or research resources, tools, and services. *Creation and management of information resources* includes the development and maintenance of research collections, research guides, catalogs, databases, web sites, search engines, etc., that users can use independently, in-house or remotely, to satisfy their information needs.
- *Assessment activities* include the measurement and evaluation of reference work, resources, and services.[22]

Certainly, there are many common threads in these definitions. For instance, nearly all of the frameworks center on the direct and individual assistance of the librarian in support of a user's search for information, as well as the importance of trained and dedicated staff to provide such assistance. However, there is also some evidence of debate and differences of opinion. In fact, the variety and complexity of the many definitions led Lanell Rabner and Suzanne Lorimer to conclude that the "library profession has grappled both with constructing a definition of reference and creating tools to measure and evaluate reference services for the past 75 years."[23] For instance, librarians have struggled over time to differentiate what comprises a "reference" question versus other kinds of queries.

As front-line service people, reference librarians have to handle all kinds of questions, from in-depth research queries to questions about the location of the bathroom or help with photocopies. In tracking their activities for reporting or staffing purposes, librarians want to separate out those requests that require some specialized knowledge of information sources or searching from basic directional and technical questions that would not require a professional's assistance. Current guidance from the National Information Standards Organization (NISO) indicates that information requests within reference include only an "information contact that involves the knowledge, use, recommendations, interpretation, or instruction in the use of one or more information sources by a member of the library staff,"[24] indicating that librarians should not consider directional or equipment questions that do not require their specialized knowledge as part of their statistics.

Even those questions that can be categorized as "reference" questions can be further broken down. Reference service definitions of the 1980s and 1990s made distinctions for many different types of information requests, including readers' advisory, ready reference, directional transactions, fact-finding transactions, and catalog transactions.[25] David A. Tyckoson elaborates on some of the categories in frequent use today.[26] For instance, reader's advisory centers on making specific recommendations to users based on their reading history and their particular likes and dislikes. Ready reference refers to questions with known, factual answers, which often lend themselves to that category of sources that have traditionally made up the reference collection, such as dictionaries, encyclopedias, and almanacs. Similarly, bibliographic verification involves helping users track down a particular item, such as a book or journal article, often starting with incomplete citations. On the other hand, research consultations result from in-depth questions, tend to involve recommendations on search pathways and resources, and may result in a collection of relevant materials rather than a single factual answer. Such classification of questions can be useful to librarians for many reasons. To begin with, each type of question requires a different set of sources and a different knowledge base to best answer it. Once the librarian understands the type of query, she can better plan her search strategy and decide where to concentrate her efforts. In addition, some questions, such as research consultations and reader's advisory, usually involve more time to answer. When faced with multiple questions at once, it can be helpful for librarians to triage questions so as to answer quick questions first and have the necessary time to spend with those who need in-depth research. Tracking numbers of and time spent on different types of questions can also help managers in planning coverage for reference services.

Instruction, whether in formalized classroom and workshop settings or more informally through point-of-need interactions, is an integral part of reference service. Although David A. Tyckoson notes that historically there has been some lack of consensus over the amount of emphasis to put on instruction over direct provision of answers,[27] virtually every definition of *reference* beginning with Green includes some component of instruction in the use of library sources. The importance of instruction relates to the adage "Give a man a fish and he eats for a day; teach a man to fish and he eats for life." In other words, if a librarian simply provides a user with an answer, then that user will still be dependent on the librarian for help with future inquiries. If, on the other hand, the librarian shows the user how to use the resources and find answers on their own, then that user can become more self-sufficient and self-directed with future information needs. One approach to reference, then, is for the reference librarian to explain the search process to the user as they work through it, including instruction on the structure and use of information resources and guidance on the evaluation of sources.[28] Of course, the success of the instruction depends in part on the receptivity of the user, which is discussed in more depth later in this chapter. Also, the emphasis on instruction might vary by information setting. For instance, school and academic libraries often include instruction as part of their mission, and in fact, giving students answers could be considered cheating in some cases. On the other hand, librarians in a corporate library might be expected to gather and deliver information rather than offering to teach employees how to use resources. Public libraries probably have the most variability. Public librarians likely will offer to teach users how to use resources, but the users are by no means required to engage and might have an expectation that they will be provided with answers instead.

Beyond one-on-one instruction during reference transactions, many reference librarians also engage in more formal instruction, which can include workshops, in-class or class-integrated instruction, or standalone courses. Indeed, as information literacy, or the ability to find, evaluate, and use information efficiently and effectively, becomes widely recognized as a crucial competency in a knowledge economy, librarians are finding themselves increasingly called upon to help people develop the necessary skills.[29] Employers in academic libraries increasingly expect librarians to engage in instruction,[30] and librarians themselves indicate that instruction is an integral part of their identity,[31] bearing out Lisa Janicke Hinchliffe's claim that instruction is a "fundamental function of librarianship."[32] While the lines between *reference* and *instruction* seem to be blurred in practice, the current RUSA definition specifically states that formal instruction is not considered a reference transaction nor does it include formal instruction explicitly under the broader umbrella of reference work.[33]

FORMATS AND MODELS OF REFERENCE SERVICES

A number of reference definitions exist. Though changing definitions reflect how the service has evolved to incorporate changing technologies and user expectations, the core service model has persisted over time. Traditionally, reference transactions not only depended on direct in-person contact between librarian and user, but they also tended to center on a single physical location: the reference desk. In this original model, libraries had a dedicated desk that was usually located near a physical collection of noncirculating reference resources and was staffed by a professional librarian whose job it was to field questions from users as needed. This model remained the dominant form of reference service well into the twentieth century, despite a number of limitations. From the librarian's perspective, the reference desk was not always the most effective or efficient use of time. During slow periods, librarians might staff the desk for hours without taking any questions. Further, because the desk was a visible and central point of contact, users would often use it as a general concierge desk, approaching with directional and technical questions that did not require a professional's expertise. Some librarians felt that such situations were not the best use of their time. On the other hand, at busy times, users would have to wait in line, and the librarian might not be able to devote as much time as necessary to in-depth or complex questions.

One model for alleviating some of the issues with the traditional reference desk is through a tiered model, also known as the Brandeis model after the university that first developed it in 1991.[34] In tiered service, the reference desk becomes a first-stop information desk. This service point is often staffed by paraprofessionals or student workers who field and screen questions as they come in. Certain ready-reference and fact-based questions as well as all directional and basic equipment questions are answered at the information desk, while more complex research questions are referred to professional librarians. The information desk staff are trained in the reference interview and in how to determine whether a question should be answered or referred. The advantages of the tiered service is that it frees professional librarians to devote their time to where it is most needed and allows them to deal with questions that require their particular expertise. The drawback is that users may not appreciate being referred from one service point to another, and if a librarian is not immediately available, they might be asked to make an appointment for a later time. If the question is time sensitive or returning at another time is inconvenient, then users might not be satisfied with tiered service.

Another drawback to the traditional reference desk model, whether tiered or not, is that it puts the onus on the user to approach the desk and ask for help. In other words, the user has to recognize that they need help, be able to articulate that need, and understand that the reference librarian is available to help. Approaching the reference desk and asking for help can be intimidating for many people. Early on, librarians realized that some people will avoid asking questions because they think they are bothering the librarian, they believe they should be able to find the answer on their own, or they have experienced bad customer service at the desk in the past.[35] In response, many librarians have argued for a more proactive variation of reference, sometimes called roving reference, in which the librarian is not tethered to the reference desk but moves through the library space and approaches the user to offer help. Some libraries have gone even further, taking librarians out of the library altogether and establishing reference outposts in places like campus centers, community events, academic departments, and student unions.[36] Although Martin P. Courtois and Maira Liriano point to the 1980s and 1990s as the time that roving reference began to be practiced widely, it is not a new concept.[37] Green advocated for such personal assistance in 1876, contending that "one of the best ways of making a library popular is to mingle freely with its users, and help them in every way" and further suggested that providing such assistance should be the "whole work" of a librarian.[38] Similarly, Joseph A. Boissè and Carla Stoffle suggested having librarians venture out into public places to promote the library and extend services, asking "why not have floating information librarians stationed in airports, supermarkets, and department stores (to name a few)."[39]

Other changes in reference have been influenced by changing technologies. Richard E. Bopp and Linda C. Smith offer a timeline of technologies, beginning with the typewriter in the 1890s, each of which has had some impact on how librarians store, retrieve, and share information in the provision of reference services.[40] In particular, technologies like the telephone, e-mail, chat, and Skype have enhanced librarians' ability to reach different kinds of users and further reduce reliance on a physical reference desk. Remote reference began with the telephone and greatly expanded the library's reach. Previously, libraries had largely served just their local communities, but telephone reference allowed them to field calls from virtually anyone, anywhere. In addition to consulting with people from large distances, the phone also allowed homebound users or those with mobility issues to receive the same service as those who were able to physically visit the library. As a result, the library's user base grew, and in fact, some large libraries established telephone reference centers to handle the volume of incoming phone calls.[41] Although they are essentially taken for granted now, telephone reference services still comprise a major part of overall reference service.

Needless to say, more recent technological developments, such as mobile devices, have further impacted reference. As the Internet and the web became more widespread and accessible, many libraries added e-mail reference to their suite of services. Like phone reference, e-mail allows the librarians to reach a wider audience; however, it lacks the immediacy of the telephone. Depending on staffing and policies, users might wait a day or more for an answer to their questions. At one point, the Library of Congress informed users to expect a two-week wait for e-mail questions. On the other hand, e-mail offers some advantages, including the fact that librarians can embed links and attach documents to e-mails, which gives the users a tangible path to the information they needed and a record of the transaction that they could save and reference.

Chat software and instant-messaging services allow libraries to provide online reference services with the same immediacy of phone reference as they engage in synchronous conversations with users. Many different options exist for this form of virtual reference, including using free platforms, such as Facebook or Google, to proprietary software that offers sophisticated functionality, such as screen sharing, application sharing, and page pushing. Some libraries are also engaging in text-messaging reference services, offering an even more streamlined approach. Like with phone reference, chat services extend library services to the homebound, distance learners, and others who cannot or do not want to physically visit the library to have their information needs addressed. Not only do chat and virtual reference services eliminate the physical barriers of the reference desk, but there is also some evidence that they might reduce some of the psychological barriers as well. There is evidence that users might be more comfortable asking questions that are personal, sensitive, or embarrassing in nature through a virtual service, perhaps because those services generally afford some measure of anonymity.[42]

Virtual reference services have become as ubiquitous as the telephone, with libraries and information settings of every type offering some variation of the service to allow users to contact them remotely. In most places, these virtual reference services are treated as an additional layer of service. The chat, text messaging, and other forms of remote reference usually supplement the traditional in-person service, which still forms the core in most places. However, some libraries are beginning to rethink this approach and are either reducing or eliminating the reference desk in favor of online services supplemented by on-call librarians. In fact, Scott Kennedy argues that "staffing a reference desk is no longer practical, cost-effective, or user-driven" and that the "librarian is less and less an in-person guide; today she is more likely to be a virtual guide, an invisible guide . . . leading not only through occasional mediated actions, but also, and perhaps more importantly, through facilitative actions conceived of and performed apart from any determinable time or space."[43]

Another model of reference service incorporates technological changes along with better understanding of pedagogical and learning theories to create online and physical spaces that allow for dynamic interaction and integrated access to resources. Often termed the *information* or *learning commons*, this model is currently very popular, especially in academic libraries. In this incarnation, librarians reorganize space and facilities to support group and collaborative study, access to various software and technical applications for creating multimedia presentations, and access to a range of staff with varying expertise to support user activities.[44]

REFERENCE FROM THE INFORMATION SEEKER'S PERSPECTIVE

Most of the changes and developments in reference have been made in response to the perceived needs and expectations of library users. So what do we know about when and how users currently use reference services? For the last few decades, most libraries have seen the numbers of reference questions declining, often dramatically. As personal computers, Internet access, and mobile devices became more widespread, and as search engines became more intuitive, fewer people found it necessary to turn to the library to answer questions. As a result, most libraries saw the number of reference questions being fielded at the desk falling drastically, with some academic libraries reporting declines ranging from 33 to 63 percent.[45] This trend is explored further in chapter 2, but it is worth noting that the declining numbers spurred questions about the relevance of libraries in general and reference desks in particular.[46] Library directors increasingly find themselves being called on by stakeholders to defend their value and justify their existence in the face of these statistics.

Librarians argue that the numbers do not tell the whole story. Rachel Applegate notes that the level of decrease in questions varies widely by institution type, and some academic libraries are actually seeing increases in numbers of questions.[47] Others suggest that Internet access has actually increased the numbers of reference questions, as users struggle to find, sort through, and evaluate the abundance of information.[48] Also, many libraries continue to track online reference questions separately from those asked in person. Although in-person reference questions were declining, librarians were seeing increases, sometimes exponential ones, in the numbers of e-mail, chat, and text questions they were receiving.[49] When virtual reference services were still in their infancy, some librarians argued that the questions they received varied depending on whether they were asked online or face to face, with users generally asking ready-reference questions remotely, while in-person reference questions tended to be more complex and take more time to answer. However, research suggests that users ask all types of questions in all formats, but the proportions of question type might vary.[50]

While it is certainly true that reference librarians continue to answer all types of questions in many different formats, it is also true that users are not turning to the library for the vast majority of their information needs. When they do access library resources and services, they seem to favor speed, convenience, and self-service, even over quality of information. To begin with, although a digital divide still exists, the vast majority of Americans has some form of Internet access and uses the Internet to find information and answer questions. According to the Pew Research Center, 70 percent of adults age eighteen and older in the United States have high-speed broadband access at home, while 56 percent own a smartphone.[51] These technologies put vast amounts of information at the user's fingertips, greatly reducing the perceived need for a library, as users can search for, retrieve, and use information without an intermediary. Use of the web to find information is virtually ubiquitous, with 92 percent of American adults reporting that they use the web to search for information and more than half (six in ten) saying they engage in such searching on a daily basis.[52] Not a single respondent to OCLC's "Perceptions of Libraries" study reported beginning an information search on the library website.[53] In fact, after searching the Internet, users turn to professionals, friends and family, and newspapers and magazines before consulting a librarian. When asked where they go to find information if faced with a particular problem from a set of scenarios, only 13 percent of respondents claim to go to the public library.[54]

These trends appear to hold true for academic libraries. For several years, Ithaka S+R has been surveying higher-education faculty to understand trends in their research and teaching habits, including their discovery and use of materials to support research and teaching.[55] Overall, the reports are dismal, showing progressive declines in faculty use of library resources, as well as declining perceptions of the continued importance and relevance of their campus libraries. Of the various roles the library could play in supporting teaching and research, by far respondents see the main role of the library as buyer, with eight in ten responding that the most important role of the library is purchasing and paying for the resources they need for teaching and research.[56]

The second most important role of the library, according to these respondents, is to serve as a gateway or starting point for research. Indeed, 80 percent of respondents indicate that the library is a very important source of journal articles and scholarly monographs, and these respondents indicate that peer-reviewed journals and scholarly monographs are the two most important resources for their research and teaching. Nevertheless, since 2003, the surveys have found that faculty increasingly start their research online, either with scholarly or general resources, while fewer and fewer begin with the library in either its physical or online format. In fact, freely available online resources are the second largest source of materials for these faculty members, after proprietary databases. That said, the report did find a slight increase from 2009 to 2012 in the use of the library catalog, which the researchers contribute in part to the integration of single interface discovery systems and increased marketing on the part of the library.

With regard to reference sources and services, fewer than half (40 percent) say that traditional reference sources, such as bibliographies and handbooks, are very important to them. While the survey does not ask specific questions about reference services, it does ask whether the library "provides active support that helps to increase the productivity of my research and scholarship," which might include the type of service usually provided by reference librarians, such as answering questions and finding relevant literature.[57] From 2009 to 2012, the number of faculty agreeing with that statement fell somewhat, although the total agreeing is still over 50 percent. As the statistics relating to where faculty start their searches for materials show, very few consult with librarians when engaging in research. Perhaps most ominously, the report indicates that a small but growing number of faculty, around 20 percent, believe that libraries will become much less important over time and that resources for library buildings and staff should be redirected elsewhere. It is worth noting that there were variations, sometimes significant ones, in faculty perceptions and use of the library by discipline. A *Library Journal* article summarized those differences, pointing out that more than two-thirds of respondents in the humanities rated all the roles of the library aside from that of actively supporting research as very important, compared to fewer than half of scientists.[58] Likewise, about half of humanities professors still believe reference collections and resources are very important to their work, while only about one-third of scientists do.[59]

College students do not differ greatly from faculty or the general public in their overall use of the library. Although research suggests that many college students experience anxiety when faced with library research[60] and report "being challenged, confused, and frustrated by the research process, despite the convenience, relative ease, or ubiquity of the Internet,"[61] they rarely turn to a librarian for help.[62] Like their counterparts on the faculty or in the general population, they also do not start their research at the library but rather with the general web[63] or with course readings and library databases.[64] According to research conducted by the Project on Information Literacy, 80 percent of undergraduates say they "rarely" or "never" ask a librarian for help, turning instead to instructors, classmates, and even parents first.[65]

For most people, choosing the Internet over the library is likely a question of immediacy and convenience. As Jim Rettig notes, early search technologies, such as print indexes and mainframe databases like DIALOG, required librarians to act as search intermediaries, while web databases put the search directly in the hands of the user.[66] Web resources are available 24/7, and the simple interface and natural language searching popularized by such search engines as Google have changed user expectations about how searching works. Users assume they will be able to interact directly with information systems and expect those systems to be intuitive. Based on their experience with search engines on the web, most users now rely on basic keyword searches, often limited to just one or two words per query, even when more sophisticated search interfaces and subject searching are offered.[67]

Librarians and information professionals might argue that such searches are ineffective or that searchers are likely missing quality information, but most people are generally confident in their search skills and satisfied with the results that they get. According to the Pew Internet and

American Life Project, 91 percent of people who use search engines for information say that they always or almost always find what they want, and over half (56 percent) say they are very confident in their search abilities. Further, 73 percent of respondents say that most of the information they find is trustworthy, with two-thirds claiming that search engines are fair and unbiased sources of information.[68] Regardless of whether the average Internet user's perceptions of their own abilities or evaluation of their success is accurate, most people do not perceive a need to ask for help fulfilling their information needs.

Convenience, including both speed and ease of access, is another important factor for users, often motivating them to select a resource that is "good enough," even when they realize there might be other, perhaps better, resources available.[69] College students will often turn to the Internet over library resources because of the speed with which they can find and access information, compared with using library resources.[70] According to the Ithaka survey, almost half of faculty respondents "indicated that they 'often' or 'occasionally' simply give up and look for a more easily accessed resource" when they want access to materials that their library does not provide.[71] Convenience might also relate to the level of difficulty of using a resource. Some users find the library catalog or online databases difficult or confusing to use, especially compared with the straightforward nature of Google-style search engines.[72]

It is worth noting that, despite the gloomy statistics and perceptions, many users still value the library. In 2010, OCLC found that use of the public library was up from previous years, especially for economically impacted Americans, and that these users see increased value in libraries and librarians. Much of the perceived value, however, seems to rest on access to such resources as books, computers, and free Wi-Fi over services provided by librarians.[73] Similarly, the Pew Research Center identified generation Y (adults between the ages of eighteen and twenty-nine) as one of the heaviest user groups of public libraries. Further, this group was among the most likely to predict returning to the library in the future for information needs.[74] Younger Americans believe that it is important for libraries to be staffed by librarians as well as stocked with books and are more likely than older adults to seek assistance from a librarian or information professional.[75]

There is also some evidence to suggest that, while searchers are generally confident in their abilities to find and evaluate credible information, they value information from the library and librarians and believe it to be more trustworthy. J. Patrick Biddix, Chung Joo Chung, and Han Woo Park found that college students "preferred the library for projects because they believed the information was vetted, or pre-accepted, by virtue of being housed in an academic library."[76] OCLC confirms that college students generally find information from the library to be at least as trustworthy, if not more so, than what they find on the web. The study also found that about 24 percent of college students do consult with a librarian to cross-reference material when they are unsure of its trustworthiness.[77] These findings suggest that libraries do still have some relevance and perhaps a chance to increase that relevance with their younger users if they can determine how to identify and continue to meet user needs and expectations.

COMPETENCIES FOR REFERENCE LIBRARIANS

Part of the success of the reference service depends upon the skills and abilities of the staff members to fulfill the requirements of that position. What, exactly, are the competencies that a reference librarian needs? One difficulty in defining reference work and hence reference competencies arises from the fact that, in their quest to connect users with information, reference librarians engage in a wide range of activities, many of which go beyond or are tangential to the basic question-answering service that originally defined reference. As a result librarians need a host of skills and qualities to successfully fill this multifunction position, ranging from subject knowledge to a host of technical skills to communication and interpersonal skills.

In addition to offering the basic definitions of reference transaction and reference work, RUSA also offers frameworks for core reference competencies. The "Professional Competencies for Reference and User Services Librarians" are organized around five competency areas—access, knowledge base, marketing/awareness/informing, collaboration, and evaluation and assessment of resources and services—each with associated goals and strategies.[78] For instance, RUSA defines *access* as "competencies related to coping with user information overload, recognizing the importance of user time and convenience, and removing barriers to service." Related to access, the guidelines indicate that the librarian should demonstrate responsiveness in developing and organizing a collection and set of services that meets users' needs and by engaging with the user in a welcoming way. Under *knowledge base*, RUSA identifies seven areas it considers crucial for reference librarians. These are:

1. The structure of information resources in areas of knowledge central to primary users;
2. Knowledge of basic information tools, including online catalogs, search systems, databases, websites, journals and monographs in both printed and electronic formats, videos, and sound recordings;
3. Information-seeking patterns and behaviors of primary users;
4. Communication principles involving interaction with users, both in person and through other channels;
5. The influence of technology on the structure of information;
6. Copyright and intellectual property law; and

7. Information competency standards.

The guidelines go on to emphasize the importance of continuous learning for reference librarians, encouraging them to engage in environmental scanning as one method for keeping abreast of new trends and resources, a technique discussed in depth in chapter 5. The guidelines stress the importance of communication in various formats, including the ability to reach out to the community and to work with colleagues within the profession. Finally, RUSA notes that reference librarians should understand the basic strategies and methodologies for evaluating and assessing their service and resources for informed decision making.

In addition to its *Professional Competencies*, RUSA also offers a set of behavioral guidelines that expand upon the interpersonal and communication skills crucial to reference work.[79] This document highlights the need for reference librarians to be approachable, demonstrate interest in their users, and engage in active listening. This document has been revised several times, most recently in 2011, and as such incorporates specific points about behaviors for remote reference. The *Professional Competencies*, on the other hand, have not been updated since 2003, making them over a decade old. While they still offer a solid baseline of skills and qualities, they do not reflect some of the technological changes that have impacted reference since that time.

The Association of College and Research Libraries (ACRL) does not offer standards for reference librarians per se, but it has published a set of competencies for instruction librarians, an area often overlapping with reference. These standards suggest that instruction librarians should have knowledge of instructional design and information literacy, as well as strong presentation and teaching skills.[80] Interestingly, in its "Standards for Libraries in Higher Education," ACRL does not mention reference services at all but does include a section related to the librarian's education role, with an emphasis on collaboration with faculty and instruction in the discovery, access, and effective use of information, perhaps signaling a shift in focus from mediated reference services to instruction.[81] Similarly, the Association of Research Libraries (ARL) does not include reference as an area of focus but in a recent report claims that many member libraries have eliminated or reduced in-person reference desks in favor of research consultations and more formal instruction.[82] The report emphasizes support of faculty in interdisciplinary research, as well as instructional support and outreach as key areas for librarians.

The Special Library Association also offers "Competencies for Information Professionals of the 21st Century."[83] These competencies do not address reference services specifically; however, three of the four professional competencies relate directly to the provision of information services to clients: managing information resources, managing information services, and applying information tools and technologies. In these competencies, applied scenarios for information professionals are described and include: "work with clients on projects"; tailor "information services to better meet the specific needs and usage patterns of clients"; and provide "curricula educating clients in information literacy, Internet usage, and locating and interpreting information sources." Specific types of special librarianship mention reference skills, either directly or indirectly, in their competency statements, including, among others, law librarians,[84] health sciences librarians,[85] and art librarians.[86] The Society of American Archivists includes reference and access, or the "policies and procedures designed to serve the information needs of various user groups,"[87] as core knowledge to be addressed in archival studies. This indicates that archivists need to understand user behavior and technology and engage in instruction and evaluation.

Research and reviews of the library and information sciences literature uncover a host of additional competencies required, or highly desired, of reference librarians. Needless to say, technology has heavily impacted reference work, and librarians need to master sophisticated search strategies and be familiar with a range of online sources of information. They also need to be comfortable with various software and be able to move across different platforms. Reviews of job ads for academic reference librarians confirm the increasingly central role that technology plays in reference work. Specific technical skills and knowledge include the ability to create web pages or web guides, assist and instruct users in the use of technology, and facilitate social networking and Web 2.0 applications.[88] In some cases, reference librarians might also be expected to work with data sets and learning objects and develop access systems.[89] As reference work continues to shift online, librarians also need to master online communication, including chat conventions and online etiquette,[90] as well as the tools and applications for providing those services.[91]

While technology skills are highly important, many traditional and "soft" skills are considered equally important, if not more so. Collection development is still considered a core area for reference librarians, although building and managing an electronic collection also requires an ability to negotiate contracts and manage vendor relations.[92] Instruction has long been a part of reference work, but teaching responsibilities are becoming even more central to most reference positions.[93] Indeed, in academic libraries, reference and instruction are virtually synonymous, with more than 90 percent of job postings for reference librarians including some instruction. Librarians involved in instructional roles are expected to have an understanding of pedagogy and learning styles, as well as strong public speaking and presentation skills.

As libraries compete with other information service providers for users' attention and with other community or academic departments for limited budget money, marketing and outreach or advocacy are increasingly important.[94] In order to engage the community and raise the profile of the library, reference librarians need to understand their communities' needs and expectations, as well as their habits and preferences for receiving information. Librarians need to be willing and able to participate in community events and to take advantage of traditional and new media to promote library events and services to users. Robert Detmering and Claudene Sproles found just under half of reference job ads include responsibilities related to marketing and promotion, leading them to suggest that this has become a core area.[95]

Related in part to external competition are emerging responsibilities in the areas of evaluation and assessment. As noted earlier, declining numbers have spurred stakeholders to question the viability and relevance of libraries and information settings. In turn information professionals, including reference librarians, are being called on to gather and analyze data to assess their services, demonstrate progress toward goals, and hold themselves accountable to those stakeholders.[96]

Soft skills—interpersonal and intrapersonal skills as opposed to subject or technical knowledge—appear to be among the most important. Michael Stephens argues that soft skills are crucial, listing communication, initiative, continuous learning, and sensitivity as essential for librarians.[97] Studies of practitioners and library employers tend to confirm Stephens's claims. In a nationwide survey, more than 90 percent of practicing reference librarians indicated that customer service, verbal communication, listening, and approachability are important competencies. Each of these areas is associated with the traditional reference interview, in which the librarian negotiates a user's question to uncover the full and underlying information need. In addition to selecting those individual skills, more than three-quarters of respondents selected the reference interview as important for librarians to master.[98] In fact, results from focus groups of library and information setting employers suggest that, while technical skills are important and even assumed to some degree, employers might put more emphasis on soft skills, such as customer service and communication skills, when making hiring decisions. As one participant noted, technical skills can usually be learned on the job, but interpersonal skills are more difficult to teach.[99]

CONCLUSION

Despite its relatively short existence, reference has a rich history. Over time, librarians have worked to identify and respond to changes in users' expectations and patterns of behavior, as well as new technologies. As a result, the service has expanded to include additional duties ranging from collection development and management to instruction to technology troubleshooting and web design. In consequence, reference librarians have had to continuously cultivate new skills to fulfill their functions successfully. So far, though, most of the changes in reference seem to have been reactive responses to external changes in technology and its users. The basic model of reference as a mediated question-answering service still appears to be the basic paradigm, delivering the same service with some new tools and additional areas of responsibility overlaid on the old model. The question now is where reference needs to go next. As this chapter demonstrates, the relevance of the traditional reference desk has been called into question, but which model or models will replace it? Or must a new and completely revolutionary system be developed? The following chapters explore these questions as they examine how reference librarians are currently meeting new challenges and how they can use tools like environmental scanning to identify and respond to challenges and opportunities.

NOTES

1. Sharon Gray Weiner, "The History of Academic Libraries in the United States: A Review of the Literature," *Library Philosophy and Practice* 7, no. 2 (2005): 1–12, accessed August 14, 2013, http://web.ebscohost.com/ehost/pdfviewer/pdfviewer?vid=3&sid=93da8bcc-5bc1-4405-b73f-5f8ce49c069b%40sessionmgr114&hid=119.

2. David A. Tyckoson, "History and Functions of Reference Service," in *Reference and Information Services: An Introduction*, ed. Richard E. Bopp and Linda C. Smith (Santa Barbara, CA: Libraries Unlimited, 2011), 3–22.

3. Samuel Swett Green, "Personal Relations between Librarians and Readers," *American Library Journal* 1 (1876): 74–81.

4. Weiner, "History of Academic Libraries."

5. John M. Budd, *The Academic Library: Its Context, Its Purpose, and Its Operation* (Santa Barbara, CA: Libraries Unlimited, 1998).

6. Lester Goodchild and Harold Weschler, *The History of Higher Education* (Boston: Pearson Custom Publishing, 2008).

7. Samuel Rothstein, *The Development of Reference Services through Academic Traditions, Public Library Practice, and Special Librarianship* (Chicago: Association of College and Reference Libraries, 1955).

8. Ellis Mount, *Special Libraries and Information Centers: An Introductory Text* (Washington, DC: Special Libraries Association, 1995).

9. "Competencies for Information Professionals of the 21st Century," *Special Library Association*, June 2003, http://www.sla.org/about-sla/competencies.

10. Ibid., 7.

11. Ibid., 118.

12. Randall C. Jimerson, *Archives Power: Memory, Accountability, and Social Justice* (Chicago: Society of American Archivists, 2009), 314.

13. Cindy C. Smolovik, "Role Delineation Statement," *Academy of Certified Archivists*, 2008–2009, http://www.certifiedarchivists.org/get-certified/role-delineation-statement.

14. "Guidelines for a Graduate Program in Archival Studies," *Society of American Archivists*, accessed September 16, 2013, http://www2.archivists.org/gpas.

15. Randall C. Jimerson, "Archives and Manuscripts: Reference, Access, and Use," *OCLC Systems and Services* 19, no. 1 (2003): 13, doi:10.7560/IC49103.

16. "A*CENSUS Results," *Society of American Archivists*, accessed September 16, 2013, http://www2.archivists.org/sites/all/files/ACENSUS-Final.pdf.

17. Terence M. Eastwood, "Public Services Education for Archivists," *The Reference Librarian* 26, no. 56 (1997): 27–38.

18. See, for example, Susan L. Malbin, "The Reference Interview in Archival Literature," *College & Research Libraries* 58, no. 1 (1997): 69–80, accessed September 16, 2013, http://crl.acrl.org/content/58/1/69.full.pdf+html; and Ciaran B. Trace and Carlos J. Ovalle, "Archival Reference and Access: Syllabi and a Snapshot of the Archival Canon," *The Reference Librarian* 53, no. 1 (2012): 76–94, doi:10.1080/02763877.2011.596364.

19. American Library Association Committee on Terminology, *ALA Glossary of Library Terms* (Chicago: American Library Association, 1943).

20. Rothstein, *Development of Reference Services.*

21. Lanell Rabner and Suzanne Lorimer, comps., "Definitions of Reference Service: A Chronological Bibliography," *Reference and User Services Association*, accessed August 15, 2013, http://www.ala.org/rusa/sites/ala.org.rusa/files/content/sections/rss/rsssection/rsscomm/evaluationofref/refdefbibrev.pdf.

22. "Definitions of Reference," *Reference and User Services Association*, January 14, 2008, accessed August 15, 2013, http://www.ala.org/rusa/resources/guidelines/definitionsreference.

23. Rabner and Lorimer, "Definitions of Reference Service," 1–2.

24. "Information Services and Use: Metrics and Statistics for Library and Information Providers—Data Dictionary," *National Information Standards Organization*, March 26, 2013, http://www.niso.org/apps/group_public/download.php/11283/Z39-7-2013_metrics.pdf.

25. Rabner and Lorimer, "Definitions of Reference Service."

26. Tyckoson, "History and Functions."

27. David A. Tyckoson, "What Is the Best Model of Reference Service?" *Library Trends* 50, no. 2 (2001): 183–96, accessed August 15, 2013, https://www.ideals.illinois.edu/bitstream/handle/2142/8398/librarytrendsv50i2d_opt.pdf?sequence=1.

28. Lisa Janicke Hinchliffe, "Instruction," in *Reference and Information Services: An Introduction*, eds. Richard E. Bopp and Linda C. Smith (Santa Barbara, CA: Libraries Unlimited, 2011), 221–60.

29. "Information Literacy Competency Standards for Higher Education," *Association of College & Research Libraries*, accessed August 15, 2013, http://www.ala.org/acrl/standards/informationliteracycompetency.

30. Russell A. Hall, "Beyond the Job Ad: Employers and Library Instruction," *College & Research Libraries* 74, no. 1 (2013): 24–38, accessed August 15, 2013, http://web.ebscohost.com/ehost/pdfviewer/pdfviewer?vid=12&sid=158e9514-24d9-4bc7-82fc-b3b7a3dd2a5a%40sessionmgr114&hid=119.

31. Heidi Julien and Shelagh K. Genuis, "Librarians' Experiences of the Teaching Role: A National Survey of Librarians," *Library and Information Science Research* 33, no. 2 (2011): 103–11, doi:10.1016/j.lisr.2010.09.005.

32. Hinchliffe, "Instruction," 221.

33. "Definitions of Reference."

34. Virginia Massey-Burzio, "Reference Encounters of a Different Kind: A Symposium," *The Journal of Academic Librarianship* 18, no. 5 (1992): 276–86, accessed September 30, 2013, http://web.ebscohost.com/ehost/pdfviewer/pdfviewer?vid=7&sid=573101f4-e976-4e93-9d8f-803fe61a2737%40sessionmgr110&hid=121.

35. Mary Jane Swope and Jeffrey Katzer, "The Silent Majority: Why Don't They Ask Questions," *RQ* 12 (1972): 161–66.

36. See for example, Samantha Schmehl Hines, "Outpost Reference: Meeting Patrons on their Own Ground," *PNLA Quarterly* 72, no. 1 (2007): 12–26, accessed August 24, 2013, http://web.ebscohost.com/ehost/pdfviewer/pdfviewer?sid=0ed601f2-4b74-4ffa-aff6-0513aef85990%40sessionmgr104&vid=8&hid=108; Triveni Kuchi, Laura Bowering Mullen, and Stephanie Tama-Bartels, "Librarians without Borders: Reaching out to Students at a Campus Center," *Reference & User Services Quarterly* 43, no. 4 (2004): 310–17, accessed August 24, 2013, http://web.ebscohost.com/ehost/pdfviewer/pdfviewer?sid=0ed601f2-4b74-4ffa-aff6-0513aef85990%40sessionmgr104&vid=7&

hid=108; and Billie Moffett and Melissa Ziel, "Librarians on the Loose: Serving Patrons beyond the Building," *Refer* 29, no. 1 (2013): 15–18.

37. Martin P. Courtois and Maira Liriano, "Tips for Roving Reference: How to Best Serve Library Users," *College & Research Library News* 61, no. 4 (2000): 289–301.

38. Green, "Personal Relations," 80.

39. Joseph A. Boissè and Carla Stoffle, "Epilogue: Issues and Answers: The Participants' Views," in *The Information Society: Issues and Answers*, ed. E. J. Josey (Phoenix, AZ: Oryx Press, 1978), 115.

40. Richard E. Bopp and Linda C. Smith, *Reference and Information Services: An Introduction* (Santa Barbara, CA: Libraries Unlimited, 2011).

41. Karen Niemla, "Libraries and the Telephone: A Look Back and a Look Around," *CODEX (2150-086X)* 2, no. 2 (2012): 5–16, accessed August 25, 2013, http://web.ebscohost.com/ehost/pdfviewer/pdfviewer?sid=f4492048-c3c7-4178-be8c-cd944f1a0107%40sessionmgr104&vid=6&hid=108.

42. Samantha Thompson, "I Wouldn't Normally Ask This . . . : Or, Sensitive Questions and Why People Seem More Willing to Ask Them at a Virtual Reference Desk," *Reference Librarian* 51, no. 2 (2010): 171–74, doi:10.1080/02763870903579869.

43. Scott Kennedy, "Farewell to the Reference Librarian," *The Journal of Library Administration* 51, no. 4(2011): 323, 324, doi:10.1080/01930826.2011.556954.

44. Denise E. Agosto, Lily Rozaklis, Craig MacDonald, and Eileen G. Abels, "A Model of the Reference and Information Service Process: An Educator's Perspective," *Reference & User Services Quarterly* 50, no. 3 (2011): 235–44, accessed August 26, 2013, http://web.ebscohost.com/ehost/pdfviewer/pdfviewer?vid=6&sid=9621f023-be66-4d37-9625-04e84fd092a8%40sessionmgr115&hid=126.

45. Charles Martell, "The Absent User: Physical Use of Academic Library Collections and Services Continues to Decline 1995–2006," *The Journal of Academic Librarianship* 34, no. 5 (2008): 400–407, doi:10.1016/j.acalib.2008.06.003.

46. See, for example, Scott Carlson, "Are Reference Desks Dying Out? Librarians Struggle to Redefine—and in Some Cases Eliminate—the Venerable Institution," *Reference Librarian* 48, no. 2 (2007): 25–30, doi:10.1300/J120v48n02_06; and Sarah Barbara Watstein and Stephen Bell, "Is There a Future for the Reference Desk? A Point-Counterpoint Discussion," *Reference Librarian* 49, no. 1 (2008): 1–20, doi:10.1080/02763870802103258.

47. Rachel Applegate, "Whose Decline? Which Academic Libraries Are 'Deserted' in Terms of Reference Transactions?" *Reference & User Services Quarterly* 48, no. 2 (2008): 176–89, doi:10.5860/rusq.48n2.176.

48. Janet Murray and Cindy Tschernitz, "The Internet Myth: Emerging Trends in Reference Enquiries," *APLIS* 17, no 2 (2004): 80–88, accessed August 27, 2013, http://web.ebscohost.com/ehost/pdfviewer/pdfviewer?sid=675051be-9ccb-4527-8d38-ddacd20ac951%40sessionmgr12&vid=13&hid=14.

49. Kennedy, "Farewell to the Reference Librarian."

50. Joseph Fennewald, "Same Questions, Different Venue: An Analysis of In-Person and Online Questions," *Reference Librarian* 46, no. 95–96 (2006): 21–35, doi:10.1300/J120v46n95_03; and Susan Hurst and Matthew Magnuson, "School Libraries and Academic Libraries, What We Can Learn from Each Other," *Chat, E-mail, and IM Reference*, last modified May/June 2007, http://www.ala.org/aasl/aaslpubsandjournals/knowledgequest/kqwebarchives/v35/355/355hurstmagnuson.

51. Kathryn Zickuhr and Aaron Smith, "Home Broadband 2013: Trends and Demographic Differences in Home Broadband Adoption," *Pew Research Internet Project*, last modified August 26, 2013, http://www.pewinternet.org/Reports/2013/Broadband/Findings/Trends-and-demographic-differences.aspx.

52. Kristen Purcell, "Search and Email Still Top the List of Most Popular Online Activities," *Pew Research Internet Project*, August 9, 2011, http://www.pewinternet.org/Reports/2011/Search-and-email.aspx.

53. OCLC, "How Americans Use Online Sources and Their Libraries," *Perceptions of Libraries 2010*, accessed August 28, 2013, http://www.oclc.org/content/dam/oclc/reports/2010perceptions/howamericansuse.pdf.

54. Lee Rainie, Leigh Estabrook, and Evans Witt, "Information Searches That Solve Problems," *Pew Research Internet Project*, December 30, 2007, http://pewinternet.org/Reports/2007/Information-Searches-That-Solve-Problems.aspx.

55. "Research and Publications," *Ithaka S+R*, http://sr.ithaka.org/research-publications.

56. Roger C. Schonfeld and Ross Housewright, "US Faculty Survey 2012," *Ithaka S+R*, April 8, 2013, http://sr.ithaka.org/research-publications/us-faculty-survey-2012.

57. Ibid, 67.

58. Meredith Schwartz, Michelle Lee, and Bob Warburton, "Ithaka Survey: Humanities Faculty Love the Library; Scientists Less Enthusiastic," *Library Journal* 138, no. 8 (May 1, 2013): 8, accessed August 28, 2013, http://web.ebscohost.com/ehost/detail?vid=3&sid=70b2122e-d117-4916-aff3-15c16f0be0a4%40sessionmgr198&hid=108&bdata=JnNpdGU9ZWhvc3QtbGl2ZQ%3d%3d#db=lls&AN=87078753.

59. Schonfeld and Housewright, "US Faculty Survey 2012."

60. Nahyun Kwon, "A Mixed-Methods Investigation of the Relationship between Critical Thinking and Library Anxiety among Undergraduate Students in their Information Search Process," *College & Research Libraries* 69, no. 2 (2008): 117–31, accessed August 28, 2013, http://web.ebscohost.com/ehost/pdfviewer/pdfviewer?sid=70b2122e-d117-4916-aff3-15c16f0be0a4%40sessionmgr198&vid=6&hid=108.

61. Alison J. Head and Michael B. Eisenberg, "Finding Context: What Today's College Students Say about Conducting Research in the Digital Age," *Project Information Literacy Progress Report*, February 4, 2009, http://files.eric.ed.gov/fulltext/ED535161.pdf.

62. See, for example, Jee Yeon Lee, Woojin Paik, and Soohyung Joo, "Information Resource Selection of Undergraduate Students in Academic Search Tasks," *Information Research* 17, no. 1 (2012): 5, accessed October 3, 2013, http://web.ebscohost.com/ehost/detail?vid=3&sid=9621f023-be66-4d37-9625-04e84fd092a8%40sessionmgr115&hid=126&bdata=JnNpdGU9ZWhvc3QtbGl2ZQ%3d%3d#db=lls&AN=76620582; and Ruth Vondracek, "Comfort or Convenience? Why Students Choose Alternatives to the Library," *portal: Libraries and the Academy* 7, no. 3 (2007): 277–93, doi:10.1353/pla.2007.0039.

63. Rainie, Estabrook, and Witt, "Information Searches."

64. Alison J. Head, "Beyond Google: How Do Students Conduct Academic Research?" *First Monday* 12, no. 8 (2007), accessed August 28, 2013, http://www.uic.edu/htbin/cgiwrap/bin/ojs/index.php/fm/article/view/1998/1873.

65. Alison J. Head, "Project Information Literacy: What Can Be Learned about the Information-Seeking Behavior of Today's College Students?" in *Proceedings of the 2013 ACRL Conference: Imagine, Innovate, Inspire*, ed. Dawn Mueller (Chicago: ACRL, 2013), 472–82.

66. Jim Rettig, "The Reference Question—Where Has Reference Been? Where Is Reference Going?" *Reference Librarian* 48, no. 2 (2007): 15–20, doi:10.1300/J120v48n02_04.

67. Holly Yu and Margo Young, "The Impact of Web Search Engines on Subject Searching in OPAC," *Information Technology & Libraries* 23, no. 4 (2004): 168–80, accessed August 28, 2013, http://web.ebscohost.com/ehost/pdfviewer/pdfviewer?vid=5&sid=919a6690-c056-4938-8bde-5aca520ed75c%40sessionmgr115&hid=108.

68. Kristen Purcell, Joanna Brenner, and Lee Rainie, "Search Engine Use 2012," *Pew Research Internet Project*, March 9, 2012, accessed August 27, 2013, http://pewinternet.org/Reports/2012/Search-Engine-Use-2012.aspx.

69. Lynn Sillipigni Connaway, Timothy J. Dickey, and Marie L. Radford, "If It's Too Inconvenient, I'm Not Going after It: Convenience as a Critical Factor in Information-Seeking Behaviors," *Library & Information Science Research* 33, no. 3 (2011): 179–90, doi:10.1016/j.lisr.2010.12.002.

70. J. Patrick Biddix, Chung Joo Chung, and Han Woo Park, "Convenience or Credibility? A Study of College Student Online Research Behaviors," *The Internet and Higher Education* 14, no. 3 (2011): 175–82, doi:10.1016/j.iheduc.2011.01.003.

71. Schonfeld and Housewright, "US Faculty Survey 2012," 36.

72. Connaway, "If It's Too Inconvenient."

73. Cathy De Rosa, Joanne Cantrell, Matthew Carlson, Peggy Gallagher, Janet Hawk, and Charlotte Sturtz, *Perceptions of Libraries 2010: Context and Community* (Dublin, OH: OCLC, 2011), accessed August 28, 2013, http://www.oclc.org/content/dam/oclc/reports/2010perceptions/2010perceptions_all.pdf.

74. Rainie, Estabrook, and Witt, "Information Searches."

75. Kathryn Zickuhr, Lee Rainie, and Kristen Purcell, "Younger Americans' Library Habits and Expectations," *Pew Internet & American Life Project*, June 25, 2013, http://libraries.pewinternet.org/2013/06/25/younger-americans-library-services.

76. Biddix, Chung, and Park, "Convenience or Credibility?" 180.

77. De Rosa et al., *Perceptions of Libraries 2010*.

78. RUSA Task Force on Professional Competencies, "Professional Competencies for Reference and User Services Librarians," *Reference and User Services Association*, January 26, 2003, accessed August 28, 2013, http://www.ala.org/rusa/resources/guidelines/professional.

79. RASD Ad Hoc Committee on Behavioral Guidelines for Reference and Information Services, "Guidelines for Behavioral Performance of Reference and Information Service Providers," *Reference and User Services Association*, last updated May 28, 2013, http://www.ala.org/rusa/resources/guidelines/guidelinesbehavioral.

80. "Association of College and Research Libraries Standards for Proficiencies for Instruction Librarians and Coordinators," *Association of College & Research Libraries*, June 24, 2007, http://www.ala.org/acrl/standards/profstandards.

81. "Standards for Libraries in Higher Education," *Association of College and Research Libraries*, October 2011, http://www.ala.org/acrl/standards/standardslibraries.

82. Janice M. Jaguszewski and Karen Williams, *New Roles for New Times: Transforming Liaison Roles in Research Libraries* (Washington, DC: Association of Research Libraries, 2013), accessed September 30, 2013, http://www.arl.org/storage/documents/publications/NRNT-Liaison-Roles-final.pdf.

83. "Competencies for Information Professionals of the 21st Century," *Special Libraries Association*.

84. "Competencies of Law Librarianship," *American Association of Law Libraries*, last modified April 2010, http://www.aallnet.org/main-menu/Leadership-Governance/policies/PublicPolicies/competencies.html.

85. "Competencies for Professional Success: Executive Summary," *Medical Library Association*, accessed July 12, 2014, http://www.mlanet.org/education/policy/executive_summary.html#B.

86. Heather Ball, *Core Competencies and Core Curricula for the Art Library and Visual Resources Professions* (Oak Creek, WI: ARLIS/NA, n.d.).

87. "Reference and Access," *Society of American Archivists*, accessed October 3, 2013, http://www2.archivists.org/gpas/curriculum/reference-access.

88. Robert Detmering and Claudene Sproles, "Forget the Desk Job: Current Roles and Responsibilities in Entry-Level Reference Job Advertisements," *College and Research Libraries* 73, no. 6 (2012): 543–55, accessed August 29, 2013, http://web.ebscohost.com/ehost/pdfviewer/pdfviewer?sid=b59fa71d-97a8-40e5-9bb6-2b520a2e7f49%40sessionmgr110&vid=19&hid=124.

89. Jenny McCarthy, "Planning a Future Workforce: An Australian Perspective," *New Review of Academic Librarianship* 11, no. 1 (2005): 41–56, doi:10.1080/13614530500417669.

90. Lili Luo, "Toward Sustaining Professional Development: Identifying Essential Competencies for Chat Reference Service," *Library and Information Science Research* 30, no. 4 (2008): 298–311, doi:10.1016/j.lisr.2008.02.009.

91. Wendy Clark, "Reference Service 2.0 Revisited," *Refer* 26, no. 2 (2010): 11–16; and Lorri Mon and Ebrahim Randeree, "On the Boundaries of Reference Services: Questioning and Library 2.0," *Journal for Education for Library and Information Science* 50, no. 3 (2009): 164–75, accessed August 29, 2013, http://web.ebscohost.com/ehost/pdfviewer/pdfviewer?vid=22&sid=b59fa71d-97a8-40e5-9bb6-2b520a2e7f49%40sessionmgr110&hid=124.

92. Detmering and Sproles, "Forget the Desk Job."

93. Hall, "Beyond the Job Ad."

94. Jo Henry, "Death of Reference or Birth of a New Marketing Age?" *Future Voices in Public Service* 7, no. 1/2 (2011): 87–93, doi:10.1080/15228959.2011.572793.

95. Detmering and Sproles, "Forget the Desk Job."

96. Ibid.

97. Michael Stephens, "Essential Soft Skills: Office Hours," *Library Journal* 138, no. 3 (2013): 39, accessed January 13, 2014, http://lj.libraryjournal.com/2013/02/opinion/michael-stephens/essential-soft-skills.

98. Laura Saunders and Mary Wilkins Jordan, "Significantly Different? Reference Services Competencies in Public and Academic Libraries," *Reference and User Services Quarterly* 52, no. 3 (2013): 216–23, accessed August 29, 2013, http://web.ebscohost.com/ehost/pdfviewer/pdfviewer?sid=80f40ba4-8fdf-47e3-943e-ada8f2443d2f%40sessionmgr110&vid=6&hid=108.

99. Laura Saunders, "Professional Perspectives on Library and Information Science Education," *Library Quarterly* (forthcoming).

TWO

Competitive Pressures Facing Reference Services

As chapter 1 illustrates, while reference librarians have experimented with different models and added new layers of service over time, such as digital reference, the basic reference service has not changed fundamentally. The core definition of *reference* still centers on the question-answering component, or "finding needed information for the user or assisting the user in finding such information,"[1] and there is evidence that many librarians value their role as information providers as a basis of their professional identity.[2] Further, in many settings the physical reference desk still endures as the symbolic heart of the service. One study found a reference desk in just over two-thirds of academic libraries, and of those, 77.2 percent staff the desk with a professional librarian at least some of the time.[3]

However, debate about the efficiency, cost-effectiveness, and relevance of the reference desk has been ongoing since at least the 1980s, when Barbara J. Ford suggested librarians and information professionals "begin to think the unthinkable, exploring alternatives and possibly eliminating the reference desk."[4] Since that time, many libraries have seen the total number of reference transactions fall while information seekers increasingly turn to online sources, and various authors and researchers have questioned the wisdom of the physical reference desk as the central service point. To begin with, the reference desk is an inherently passive model, in which highly trained professionals sit and wait for users to approach with questions. Depending on the circumstances, librarians might spend much of their time at the desk without answering any questions. Even when users do approach the desk, reviews of transactions suggest that a majority of the questions asked do not require the expert knowledge of a professional librarian but could be answered by student workers and trained paraprofessionals.[5] In light of the evidence, Susan M. Ryan contends that staffing a physical reference desk with professional librarians is not cost-effective and that the professionals' time would be better spent on other activities, such as preparing and delivering instruction and engaging in research consultations.[6]

Christy R. Stevens suggests that the physical reference desk might have made sense as a service model at one time. Before the advent of the Internet, information seekers consulted the library with shorter and more fact-based ready-reference questions, and the reference desk was well designed to handle high volumes of these relatively quick reference transactions.[7] However, the immediate and ubiquitous access to information afforded by the Internet has changed people's behaviors and expectations and the role of the library and librarian as a premier source of information. In order to remain relevant in this highly connected world, librarians and information professionals will have to proactively create user-centered service models that are responsive to information seekers' needs and preferences. As user habits and expectations continue to evolve and technology further impacts both the information seeker and the reference service, librarians and information professionals need to consider an entirely new paradigm for service delivery rather than incremental changes and additions to the service.

The next sections examine statistical trends in the usage of library reference services and current understanding of information seekers' evolving behaviors and expectations, followed by a review of several different models and services being developed in response to new technologies and information seekers' evolving behaviors and expectations.

ANALYSIS OF REFERENCE USAGE STATISTICS

Interpreting the usage of library reference services is challenging because libraries and information organizations employ various methods to track reference transactions (e.g., electronic system versus hash mark on paper) and follow different procedures when recording the nature of the user's question (e.g., some librarians record the exact question posed, while other librarians record the category of the question, such as directional or research).[8] There is no accepted categorization of reference questions, so comparison among libraries is rarely possible. Adding to these challenges, some libraries count discreet questions, whereas other libraries use the library user as the unit of analysis, regardless of the number of questions the user posed during the interaction. Also, most libraries track and report in-person and electronic reference transactions separately. In addition, accounts of library reference activity presented in the research literature and popular press from the perspective of one library or librarian often highlight outliers in the data, obscuring conclusions about the extent of usage of reference services.[9]

Despite such challenges, data collected on reference activity in public and academic libraries point to a decrease in the number of transactions since the late 1990s, which is contrary to evidence that library site visits, program attendance, book borrowing, and usage of Internet-enabled computer terminals in those settings has remained strong. For this reason, it appears that Robert S. Taylor's articulation of information seeking from studies of special libraries users in the 1960s is appropriate in the modern context; that is, of the information seekers who visit a library, few will consult a librarian.[10] But how dramatic is the decline in reference usage, and what trends, if any, appear in digital reference usage statistics?

For academic libraries, statistics maintained by the Association of Research Libraries (ARL) demonstrate that the median number of reference transactions decreased by more than 40 percent from 1997 to 2003,[11] though statistics reported by other organizations show mixed results, with either an increase or a decrease in reference transactions. The Association for College and Research Libraries (ACRL) Summary Statistics, for example, detailed a 37-percent increase in academic library reference transactions between 1999 and 2005, while the Academic Library Survey of the National Center for Education Statistics reported a 25-percent decline in transactions between 1996 and 2004.[12] Rachel Applegate segmented the Academic Library Survey data, using survey responses from the period of 2002 to 2004, and found an overall 2.2-percent decline in reference transactions and that the decline per week and on a per-library and per-student basis was evident for all institution types.[13] Applegate's analysis of the data detected differences by library institution type, per Carnegie class; specifically, doctoral-level institutions—ARL members or not—saw distinctly larger drops in the number of reference transactions than other institution types.[14] Also, differences within ARL university libraries were apparent: between 1995 and 2006, law libraries experienced a 33-percent decrease in the number of reference transactions, compared to a 41-percent decrease for medical libraries and a 63-percent decrease for Ivy League libraries during that time.[15]

For public libraries, the results of the Public Libraries in the United States Survey administered by the Institute of Museum and Library Services (IMLS) found a 23.5-percent decrease in the number of reference transactions in public libraries between 2000 and 2009, with 194.6 reference transactions per 1,000 library visits in 2009.[16] More recently, from data collected on the average number of reference transactions in U.S. and Canadian public libraries, the annual survey results from the Public Library Data Service (PLDS) showed a 6-percent decline between 2010 and 2011, with an average of 155,719 reference interactions in 2011, as reported in its 2012 report.[17] Overall, OCLC reported that fewer informa-

Chapter 2

tion seekers are asking for research assistance in public libraries, noting a 28-percent decrease between 2005 and 2010.[18] And a national survey conducted in 2013 by the Pew Internet and American Life found that, of the 53 percent of Americans age sixteen or older who visited a library or bookmobile in the previous twelve months, 80 percent responded that they consider reference librarians to be a "very important" library service, but only 31 percent said they frequently get help from a librarian, while 7 percent self-reported never having consulted a librarian.[19]

Digital reference usage statistics show that a small number of questions are received at digital reference services and that those received are a small fraction compared to the number of transactions occurring at the physical reference desk.[20] At the Sims Memorial Library of Southeastern Louisiana University, fewer than two thousand digital reference interactions through the library's text messaging, chat, and e-mail reference services occurred each year between 2005 and 2010, though the authors note an increase in usage of text messaging and decrease in usage of the chat for reference during that time.[21]

Almost three-quarters of academic libraries[22] and approximately 61 percent of public libraries[23] supported some form of technology-mediated reference service for their users in 2012. Even with the option to consult a librarian using an online channel, some digital reference services have ceased operations due to reference traffic that never fully realized. Marie L. Radford and M. Kathleen Kern studied the discontinuation of nine chat-specific digital reference services—at academic and public libraries and consortia—and identified six reasons these services were discontinued. The researchers' analysis revealed that the low volume of questions received overall and for the target population was the most frequently cited reason for a library's discontinuation of their chat reference service.[24] Since the publication of Radford and Kern's research, QandA NJ, the statewide 24/7 digital reference service primarily serving the state of New Jersey, closed its digital reference service, with thought that the closure was in part because of the declining volume of digital reference questions received.[25]

INFORMATION SEEKERS CONSULT PEOPLE OTHER THAN LIBRARIANS

The previous section demonstrates that librarians in academic and public libraries have handled fewer in-person reference transactions from information seekers in recent years and that digital reference services have been underutilized despite their prevalence. These trends may appear counterintuitive because consulting other people when looking for information is an established information-seeking behavior.[26] Members of the general public consult such people as colleagues, friends and family, and experts (e.g., medical practitioners) for information, and undergraduate students turn to their peers or classmates, friends and family, and domain experts (e.g., instructors) during academic information seeking.[27] Librarians are the least frequently consulted people (among multiple categories of people) when undergraduate students look for information for their coursework.[28]

In contrast to digital or virtual reference services in libraries and information organizations, social question-and-answer (SQA) sites, such as Yahoo! Answers, Ask.com, Quora, or Google Helpouts, allow searchers opportunities to seek information from other individuals, including content experts. Virtual reference generally entails one librarian acting as the expert and pushing information and answers to one questioner. The librarian is usually the sole provider of answers, and those answers are assumed to be authoritative, given the librarian's expertise in searching and information sources. On the other hand, SQA sites provide a forum for interaction with both other individuals and the content. Once submitted, the questions "undergo algorithmic, economic, and social processing strategies designed to entice individuals to append useful answers, ratings, and comments, thus addressing the query and enriching the document."[29] Often, more than one answer is offered. The questioner can select an answer among the range of possibilities and can rate and comment on the answers provided. The interactions in the majority of SQA sites are visible to the public for information reuse at a later time, while interactions in digital or virtual reference services are contained in a closed environment, though possibly available for librarians to refer to during future reference interactions. The overall popularity of SQA sites is reflected in the fact that Yahoo! Answers is ranked fifth among the top ten social media websites tracked by Experian.[30]

Some research suggests that SQA sites might be setting new expectations for reference services in libraries and information organizations. Users of both virtual reference and SQA value credibility, authority, and relevance in the answers they receive, but in comparing librarian and user perceptions of virtual reference and SQA services, Chirag Shah and Vanessa Kitzie found that, while librarians focused on providing thorough and accurate answers with citations to sources, users tended to value the speed and social interactions offered by SQA,[31] and the founder of the SQA site Quora suggests that users are content with perceiving the truth or accuracy of answers to some questions through the lens of their personal experience.[32] While chat reference takes place in real time, few libraries offer a truly 24/7 service, which means users can only get immediate assistance during specific hours. Further, libraries vary widely in their response time for e-mail reference questions. Although SQA users post a question and have to wait for a response, they seem to have quick turnaround times. In fact, according to one study, 30 percent of SQA users received an answer within five minutes of posting a question, while

90 percent received an answer within one hour, although the answer selected as best was often one submitted later.[33]

Participants on SQA sites ask a wide range of questions, from fact finding to advice and opinion. Traditionally, while reference librarians might try to guide searchers to sources of information on any topic, they would not directly answer questions asking for opinion or personal advice. However, SQA sites may be influencing users to expect such service from librarians. In an analysis of questions submitted to the Internet Public Library (IPL), more than one thousand questions during a nearly three-year period were deemed "out of scope" by the librarians who received them. The reasons for rejecting the questions varied but included questions that asked for advice or opinions, required extended research, or might be inappropriate for a nonexpert to answer. In particular, librarians tended to reject questions that asked for personal rather than professional judgment, asked for the librarian to act for the user or to help the user decide on an action, or involved researching or contacting individuals.[34] As Lynn Westbrook notes, the user submitting the question likely believed it to be appropriate for the service, but the librarians interpreted it as somehow problematic, suggesting a "direct, substantive conflict between users' and IPL staffers' MM [mental model] of the reference transaction."[35] As such, she suggests that the boundaries between "appropriate" questions may be getting blurred, and librarians might have to adjust their own mental models while simultaneously managing their users' expectations of what virtual reference services can offer. Thomas A. Peters goes further and maintains that to meet the range of expectations for virtual reference services, "libraries, other organizations, and collaborative efforts involving individuals need to offer 24/7 services with rapid turnaround time (less than 10 minutes on average), a relaxed yet authoritative style, and an attitude that treats all questions with respect, including questions involving requests for opinions and advice."[36]

That said, information seekers' expectations do not focus exclusively on virtual or remote access and services. In fact, while library users do seem to rely increasingly on remote services, there is evidence that they also appreciate and sometimes even prefer face-to-face assistance. One study found that undergraduate students who do consult librarians prefer face to face over e-mail, telephone, and chat reference options.[37] Another study found that, even when other options were available, undergraduate students valued in-person research consultations because they could follow the librarian's process and collaborate with her. These undergraduate students felt that the face-to-face interaction actually contributed to their understanding.[38] Further, Amy Gratz and Julie Gilbert found that the heaviest users of the library website are also more likely to ask for help at the reference desk, suggesting that one service does not replace but only supplements the other.[39] As such, Amy VanScoy suggests combining virtual reference with a paging or on-call service to allow users to meet with a librarian in person as needed.[40]

Indeed, if librarians and information professionals in general, and reference librarians in particular, hope to remain relevant in the face of changing technologies and user expectations, there will need to be a paradigm shift not only in terms of service delivery but also in librarians' attitudes and philosophies surrounding those services. As Lynn Sillipigni Connaway, Timothy J. Dickey, and Marie L. Radford note, the "user once built workflows around the library systems and services, but now, increasingly, the library must build its services around user workflows."[41] The librarian is one of many alternative information sources in the crowded information environment, and the focus on the "library in the life of the user" to meet the user's needs and expectations is paramount.[42] Library services and systems need to be collaborative, offer both remote and local/physical support, and must entail access to information as well as value-added services in navigating, evaluating, synthesizing, and using a vast array of information sources and formats.

EVOLVING USER BEHAVIORS AND EXPECTATIONS

Many information seekers' behaviors and expectations are informed or driven by their interactions with technology, and research indicates that access to technology, data, and information continues to grow. Currently, 91 percent of American adults age eighteen and older own cell phones, while 56 percent report having a smartphone and another 34 percent own tablets.[43] Increasingly, people are using their mobile devices to access online information, with 57 percent of smartphone owners going online and 21 percent saying their smartphones are their primary source of Internet access.[44] Regardless of how they access the Internet, 91 percent of Americans report searching online, and more than half of Americans search for information online at least once a day. Google remains by far the most popular search tool.[45] The Internet, Wi-Fi, and mobile devices have raised expectations for ubiquitous and immediate access to information. Broadly speaking, David Bawden and Polona Vilar identify six areas of expectation for digital services, including the following capabilities:

1. Comprehensive—including everything
2. Accessible—everything available immediately
3. Immediate Gratification—speed of response
4. Followability of Data—seamless
5. Ease of Use—single interface
6. Multiple Formats—text, images, sound[46]

With simple interfaces and natural-language searching popularized by search tools like Google, information seekers have become accustomed to immediate results from simple queries. Further, searchers feel competent in their ability to find the information they need online. Indeed, 92 percent of Americans are confident in their search abilities, with more than half being very confident and only 8 percent lacking such confidence.[47] College students as a group are very comfortable with search engines, with 72 percent saying search engines are their first choice when they need information.[48] Information seekers' preferences for self-help and feelings of confidence are reflected in the fact that 91 percent of people report finding what they are looking for online either "always" or "most of the time." Further, searchers are overall satisfied with the results that they get. According to the Pew Research Center, 64 percent say they never find critical information to be missing from their search results.[49]

Because of the ease and apparent success with which information seekers search and access information online, they tend to get impatient with the complex and unintuitive organization and retrieval systems associated with library resources.[50] Studies of search success and failure rates show that users experience failed subject searches more often than failed keyword searches, which likely reinforces user preference for Google-style natural language searching.[51] The process of navigating to a subscription database, completing the authentication process, searching for an article, and then possibly having to follow a link resolver to obtain the full text or go to a physical shelf to retrieve the article is "time-consuming, complicated, and not intuitive to students raised in a point-and-click Google world."[52] Indeed, according to research on information retrieval systems, there is an inverse relationship between user effort and satisfaction. In other words, the more work an information seeker has to do to obtain relevant results from a database, they less likely they are to report satisfaction with that system.[53] There is some debate about how accurate searchers' self-perceptions are. Melissa Gross and Don Latham found that undergraduate students who tested with below-average information literacy skills believed themselves to be proficient searchers and that none of the students they tested scored in the advanced proficiency category. The authors point out that these students are unlikely to seek help even when their searches are unsuccessful because of their estimation of their abilities.[54]

Along with ease of search, information seekers have come to expect immediate and online full-text access to a full range of resources. As a result, users will often ignore resources that are only available to them in print or physical formats,[55] leading Jean Poland to suggest that, at least for some users, "information that is not on the Web and consequently not immediately available might as well not exist."[56] This reliance on what is readily available has prompted some researchers to speculate that searchers favor convenience over quality.[57] Indeed, along with quality and credibility, convenience or ease of use is ranked one of the most important considerations when users choose information sources.[58] While librarians might lament information seekers' choice of immediate access over potentially better-quality resources, Shawn V. Lombardo and Kristine S. Condic suggest that the users are not necessarily lazy but might be frustrated by the complex and inconvenient access structures of the library and thus choose what is available online to avoid having to navigate library resources.[59]

Prior to the era of digital transformation described earlier, ease of use and accessibility were factors known to be strong predictors of users' information-seeking behaviors.[60] In recent times, research has shown that these two factors influence usage and user perceptions of reference services to the extent that information seekers choose not to consult librarians because they believe that the reference interaction would require too much of their time[61] or require them to wait too long to receive a response from the digital reference service[62] or because they are restricted from posing questions due to limited or inconvenient reference service hours.[63] Numerous other factors are shown to influence the evolution of user behaviors and expectations. For instance, information seekers' understanding or awareness (or lack thereof) that libraries and information organizations offer reference services is an additional factor involved in their habits and preferences toward reference. While some studies have found that information seekers have high awareness of library reference services staffed with librarians providing information assistance,[64] other research has indicated otherwise. Studies have shown that members of the general public are unaware that librarians provide information assistance through reference services or what types of assistance are offered[65] and that undergraduate students are unaware that opportunities to consult librarians through digital reference services exist in their libraries.[66] Likewise, an additional factor is familiarity. For instance, the degree of satisfaction resulting from a prior experience with a librarian has been reported as an influence on an information seeker's decision to initiate contact with a reference service,[67] and undergraduate students have explained that their dissatisfaction from interacting with an unhelpful or unfriendly librarian has led them not to return to the reference desk.[68]

As is noted in the previous section, the popularity and sheer number of SQA sites, both general purpose and domain specific, and seeming success with natural-language searching has revived the notion that "everybody is an expert," and because of the proliferation of novel digital tools that directly connect information seekers to (potential) subject experts, librarians are not necessarily seen as such. For instance, undergraduate students turn to instructors—not librarians—because of the instructor's subject specialty[69] to gather ideas and recommendations about relevant information sources[70] and to get assistance with assessing the quality of information sources found in the library or on the web to align with course expectations.[71] Conversely, undergraduate students lack an understanding of librarians' educational backgrounds and expertise[72]; in their eyes, librarians roles are limited to circulation tasks[73] or offering directional support to help with navigating inside the library to locate materials or to assist with library technology.[74] When having had the opportunity to interact with librarians, undergraduate students shared that the most useful aspect is that librarians offer new perspectives and knowledge about digital information sources, selecting information sources, and locating journal articles and relevant information.[75]

The modern digital environment has made factors like ease of use, accessibility, awareness, familiarity, and expertise more pronounced than ever before and requires librarians and information professionals to conceive of novel systems considering information seekers' habits and preferences. The next section reviews some of the models and practices that have been implemented in response to changing user behaviors and expectations.

DIFFERENT MODELS AND SERVICES

While the physical reference desk still remains a staple across a range of libraries and information settings, many institutions are experimenting with different models of delivering reference services to leverage new technologies and meet evolving user expectations. One of the defining, and perhaps most problematic, characteristics of the traditional reference service is that it is a passive model. Both at the physical reference desk or through links and web forms on the library website, reference librarians wait to be asked a question. Not only does this model often result in professionals spending valuable time either not answering questions or fielding directional and technical questions that do not require their expertise, but it also puts the onus on the information seekers to understand the nature of the service, identify their own information needs, and overcome any physical or psychological barriers they may have to approach the desk and ask for assistance. Over time, librarians have developed some models and services that try to mitigate this burden and to extend their reach.

Embedded Librarianship

Embedded librarianship is applied in different ways and different settings but broadly describes a model in which librarians move out of the library and locate themselves in the physical or virtual space of their users, be that the classroom, online course management system, lab, office, or community organization. In one example, a librarian at the University of Michigan spends time at a local coffee shop and invites students to drop by for consultations.[76] The vast majority of writing on the topic, however, focuses on academic, and to some extent special or corporate, libraries. In an academic setting, embedded librarianship is most often associated with those librarians who are integrated into a course management system, where they build pathfinders and other learning objects, participate in discussion forums, and answer direct questions from students. These librarians might also collaborate with faculty on developing and delivering courses and assignments or even coteach courses. In corporations, embedded librarians might provide in-depth research for a research and development team or for grant proposals or engage in competitive intelligence research. Some librarians are assigned offices or hold office hours in their contact department, with estimates ranging from a few hours a week to more than 50 percent of the librarian's time being spent outside of the library.[77] The Welch Medical Library at Johns Hopkins University is implementing what it refers to as a distributed model, in which the physical plant is dissolved; books are stored off site; and librarians, now called informationists, are fully embedded into the departments they support.[78] While the bulk of embedding seems to take place in academic and special libraries, there are some examples of such services in public libraries. For instance, librarians in the Douglas County Libraries in Colorado spend four hours per week in the community, visiting women's shelters, schools, and other organizations to provide resources and services. Similarly, librarians from Deschutes Public Libraries in Oregon spend between one-quarter and one-third of their work week providing services off site.[79]

While answering questions, doing research, or offering literacy services and story hours sound like traditional library services, the difference with embedded librarianship is that the librarian is "in the spaces of their users and colleagues, either physically or through technology, in order to become a part of their users' culture."[80] Barbara I. Dewey compares embedded librarianship to embedded journalism, with the purpose being to integrate as fully as possible with the group being observed or served so as to understand as much as possible about their habits and practices. She notes that "embedding requires more direct and purposeful interaction than acting in parallel with another person, group, or activity" and thus should allow librarians a deeper understanding of their users, as well as greater opportunities to collaborate with them.[81] In this sense, embedded librarianship goes beyond the more traditional approaches to library services, which are usually supplemental to the user's other activities. In fact, a main objective and activity of embedded librarians is to develop strong relationships with their customers. Thus, while embedded librarians offer a range of services associated with reference, including answering ready-reference questions, engaging in in-depth research, and providing training and instruction, they will also attend department meetings and discipline-specific conferences to keep abreast of issues and trends of concern to their users.[82]

Michelle Lee describes this model as a "paradigm [that changed] from waiting behind a desk [to] actively seeking community problems and finding solutions."[83] By embedding in the information seeker's space and gaining a thorough understanding of their field, the librarian can develop a deeper understanding of and in some cases even anticipate individuals' needs. Further, close proximity and familiarity with the librarian and the type of support provided might make it easier for information seekers to ask questions and might promote collaboration. As David Shumaker notes, reference librarians still have valuable expertise to share with their users, but "we can only unlock that value when we establish the relationships that allow us to join their conversations—to identify their unexpressed information needs."[84] There is some evidence that embedding can be successful.

Starr Hoffman found that students enrolled in courses with embedded librarians expressed positive attitudes toward embedding, whether they ever interacted with the librarian or not.[85] However, the purpose of the program is to try to increase interactions with information seekers. Karen Malnati and Ronnie Boseman similarly found that students had mostly positive feelings toward embedded librarians, but in addition, students in courses with embedded librarians tended to spend more time interacting with the librarian than those in courses without an embedded librarian. Further, once those students became familiar with the librarian, they often sought that same librarian in later courses even if the librarian was not embedded in that course.[86] At Capella University there was a statistically significant 400-percent increase in reference questions among psychology students with the introduction of an embedded librarian in their courses. Further, researchers and the library found that the number of reference questions was positively correlated with the number of posts the librarian made to the course page, suggesting that librarian outreach and initiative is an important aspect of the embedded model.[87] With regard to public libraries, the National Network of Libraries of Medicine Greater Midwest Region partnered with thirty-one libraries to provide community outreach on health information topics. A survey of the participating institutions revealed positive impacts on the institutions and the public, including increased access to health information and improved community relationships.[88]

Research Consultations

In the research consultation model, librarians set aside extended and uninterrupted time, usually in an office or other private area, to meet with users for in-depth research assistance. In many cases, there is still a central service point, but it is often staffed by student workers or paraprofessionals who have been trained to handle basic questions and screen for questions that need the attention of a librarian. If a user does need more in-depth help, they might be referred to a librarian who is "on call," or they might make an appointment for a later time. While research consultations are still forms of mediated reference in which the user initiates the interaction and the librarian provides assistance in fulfilling an information need, "librarians scheduling appointments with students are better prepared to provide uninterrupted and individual attention focusing on the specific needs of just one student in ways that are not possible in a typical reference transaction."[89]

In general, research consultations involve a thirty-minute appointment in which the librarian will offer a range of services, including assistance with searching, help refining research topics, and assistance with selecting and evaluating information sources depending on the user's need. Users, or the student workers or paraprofessionals who refer them from the information desk, will usually fill out an intake form detailing the nature of the question so librarians can prepare for the consultation ahead of time. Often, the librarian will spend anywhere from fifteen minutes to one hour doing preliminary searching and preparing bibliographies, suggested sources, or other takeaways for the user.[90] In addition to offering value-added individualized attention, because the service is highly focused on the individual user's specific needs, the research consultation fits the millennial students' expectation that "everything in their world can be customized to suit them."[91] While the consultation model seems to be most popular in academic libraries, there are examples from the public library world as well. Vivian Reed describes public libraries in California that have implemented a tiered service, with paraprofessionals staffing a help desk and referring in-depth questions to an on-call librarian.[92] Similarly, the Skokie Public Library in Illinois offers a "Book a Librarian" program in which users can make appointments for assistance with information needs, such as genealogical research.[93] Research consultation has been a common service offered by special libraries.

Many academic and public librarians are reluctant to shift to a research consultation model, often fearing that it will undermine reference services and that users will not be properly referred by paraprofessionals or that they simply will not use the service. However, some institutions report success with these models. In one small study, a citation analysis of student research papers found a statistically significant difference in the quality of resource selection between students who engaged in individual consultations with librarians and those who did not. The students who had met with a librarian used sources that were ranked higher for relevance, currency, scope, and overall quality.[94] A survey study of students who were required to complete a research consultation as part of an English composition course revealed that students valued the service, felt less anxiety after their appointment, and indicated that they would use the service again.[95] Heather Ganshorn found a librarian consultation service to support health care practitioners with point-of-care questions both saved time and was more cost-effective. On average, it took librarians seven fewer minutes to answer these questions, which translated to a cost savings of between thirteen dollars and twenty dollars per question. Further, more than half of the health care practitioners in the study indicated that the service had a positive impact on their decision making.[96] At the same time, by using student workers and paraprofessionals to staff the service points, the research consultation model is usually structured in a way that frees the librarian from set shifts staffing the physical reference desk. In this way, librarians spend more time on questions that require their expertise but when not scheduled for appointments are able to focus their attention on other functions and services. As such, this model also makes more efficient and cost-effective use of the professional librarian's time.[97]

Instruction

As discussed in chapter 1, as librarians and information professionals shift attention away from the reference desk, many are spending more time on instruction. While reference librarians have always engaged in some level of one-on-one instruction at the reference desk, many librarians are now putting more time and emphasis into more formal kinds of instruction, including workshops, course-integrated sessions, and credit-bearing courses. Indeed, a review of academic library job postings over forty-four years reveals that instruction responsibilities have been increasing since the 1970s to the point that they are now considered a core part of the reference job.[98] Instruction in academic libraries tends to support the curriculum and specific assignments and is often integrated into courses, but academic librarians are not the only ones who offer instruction. In public libraries, librarians offer instruction on a wide range of topics depending on community interest and need, including job hunting, genealogical research, and consumer information. Instruction is perhaps even more integrated in archives reference because archives users nearly always have to engage in an orientation session before beginning their research.

Support for library instruction is underpinned in part by increasing attention to and support of information literacy as a core competency across all fields, education levels, and socioeconomic levels. The American Library Association (ALA) stresses the importance of information literacy to a democratic society, contending that people need access to information as well as the ability to critically evaluate and understand that information in order to make informed decisions on a wide range of political, health, and social issues. In its final report, the presidential committee formed by ALA to investigate information literacy maintains that information literacy is a "form of personal empowerment. It allows people to verify or refute expert opinion and to become independent seekers of truth."[99] Within higher education, the competencies associated with information literacy have been incorporated into the standards of the six regional accreditation associations[100] as well as standards set forth by the American Association of College and Universities in their "Liberal Education and America's Promise" (LEAP)[101] and the Lumina Foundation's Degree Qualifications Profile.[102]

Gabriela Sonntag and Felicia Palsson argue that by shifting focus to instruction, reference librarians are not changing the underlying goals of the reference service, but they are making better use of their time and expertise developing and delivering instruction rather than waiting at a desk for a question to be asked.[103] Librarians might anticipate some user questions in their library instruction sessions and will also field questions from participants. By handling these queries in a group setting, librarians can promote information-seeking and evaluation competencies to a larger and wider audience and avoid repeating this same content through one-on-one interactions at the reference desk.[104] As such, Bell suggests that library instruction comprises a form of "pre-emptive reference."[105] Many of the embedded models described earlier, especially those in academic institutions, are centered on library instruction as well as the traditional question-answering reference services.

Content Creation and Self-Service Models

Each of the models described so far involves direct interactions between information seekers and librarians and typically have the librarian at the center of that interaction. This focus aligns with the Reference and User Services Association (RUSA) definition of a *reference transaction*, which is based on such active exchanges.[106] However, there is also a trend toward creating systems and resources that would facilitate individuals' information seeking and discovery without direct involvement from a librarian, and indeed there is some suggestion that some information seekers might prefer such self-directed inquiry.[107] Such tools and resources can also be available to information seekers at times when the library is not open or a librarian is not immediately available. From this perspective, reference work includes not only those direct transactions with information seekers but also the "behind the scenes work of designing, organizing, and presenting information and resources in such a way that makes it possible for users to find information on their own."[108]

Pathfinders are one such resource that can "function as both a guide to the resources of a particular library and as a gateway to the wider literature of a subject field."[109] Also referred to as research or subject guides, pathfinders are compilations of resources—books, articles, websites, and subject and keyword suggestions—that users can use as a starting point when conducting research. Librarians build pathfinders on wide-ranging topics, from academic research to consumer and health information to job-hunting resources. In academic institutions, librarians will often create pathfinders tailored to specific courses or assignments. Pathfinders are not new; librarians have created guides for users as part of the reference service since the beginning. However, before the advent of the Internet, those guides were static, paper-based lists. Web-based guides can link users directly to resources and even be programmed to perform web or catalog searches that will keep the guide up to date with less direct maintenance on the part of the librarian.[110]

While research related to pathfinders and web guides is scarce, there is some suggestion that these resources have a positive impact. Through a review of literature and content analysis of guides, Sara Harrington concludes that pathfinders can introduce graduate students to advanced research concepts and resources in their fields and can be leveraged as a point of contact between student and librarian, which might lead to more in-depth consultations.[111] The ten most popular web guides at North Georgia College and State University, a campus of 5,800 students, were accessed 56,000 times in one year, signaling a high rate of usage. Librarians at the institution contend that the guides improve student research, but they have not actually evaluated the impact of the guides.[112] Finally, a survey of web guide users at George Washington University found that more than half of respondents rated the guides as either very or somewhat helpful.[113]

Pathfinders and web guides as described here are generally developed for direct use by information seekers. On the other hand, some librarians are experimenting with the creation of knowledge bases, or repositories of library-specific data, answers to frequently asked questions, and other types of communal knowledge that could be shared and accessed by reference librarians to improve services.[114] Scott Nicholson and R. David Lankes note that a regular reference transaction usually does not result in a tangible product, meaning that whatever knowledge is created during the interaction resides only with the people involved; however, digital transactions generate records that could be indexed and used for research, teaching, evaluation, and collaboration.[115] These stores of reference questions and answers can be both local, library-specific information and general-knowledge questions. Lynn L. Ralph and Timothy J. Ellis contend that knowledge bases could save time for the reference librarian, thereby freeing them to focus on more complex questions, reduce duplication of effort, and also result in quicker response time for library users. However, their research also showed little to no use of the knowledge base by reference librarians.[116]

Finally, while much library instruction centers on live, face-to-face sessions, librarians and information professionals are also developing vast arrays of self-paced tutorials and digital learning objects that can be accessed and used by information seekers at their convenience. Online tutorials can be developed for a specific question, course, or assignment, as a "demonstration of repeated skills-based questions . . . as discreet parts of some of our topic research guides, and as a way to embed information literacy skills in other academic courses."[117] Similarly, digital learning objects are "reusable succinct portions of self-contained information."[118] Katherine Stiwinter notes that online tutorials have been shown to be as effective as face-to-face, and because tutorials can be reused and embedded in multiple places, they help librarians reach more people and offer one answer to issues of scalability with library instruction programs.[119] Lori A. Mardis and Connie Jo Ury report that the majority of students exposed to online tutorials in an English composition class found the tutorials useful and would recommend that they be reused in other classes or tied into other assignments.[120]

MAINTAINING TRADITIONAL PERSPECTIVES AND SERVICES WILL NOT SUFFICE

The decline in traffic at physical reference desks in academic and public libraries is evident from reference usage statistics maintained by professional organizations, and the volume of reference interactions at digital reference services has been lackluster, despite the availability of some form of technology-mediated reference service provision in most library settings. Information seekers continue to utilize people other than reference librarians during information searches, and the steady rise of SQA sites and the level of user engagement and interaction on such sites present new challenges for libraries and librarians. Further, digital tools have changed information seekers' behaviors and will continue to impact their expectations and preferences. While librarians and information professionals have responded to these competitive pressures and factors influencing users' habits by implementing some changes to their suite of reference services, more work is needed to reconceptualize reference services in the face of competitive pressures and evolving user behaviors, tastes, and preferences. Maintaining traditional perspectives that have guided reference librarianship, along with minimal adaptation of existing services, is not enough. The next chapter investigates emerging librarian roles, competencies, and philosophies and touches upon implications for library and information science education.

NOTES

1. Charles A. Bunge, "Reference Services," *The Reference Librarian* 31, no. 66 (1999): 185–99, doi:10.1300/J120v31n66_17.

2. Amy Dianne VanScoy, "Practitioner Experiences in Academic Research Libraries: An Interpretative Phenomenological Analysis of Reference Work" (PhD diss., University of North Carolina, Chapel Hill, 2012), accessed November 18, 2013, http://search.proquest.com/docview/1024564087.

3. Dennis B. Miles, "Shall We Get Rid of the Desk?" *Reference & User Services Quarterly* 52, no. 4 (2013): 320–33, doi:10.5860/rusq.52n4.320.

4. Barbara J. Ford, "Reference beyond (and without) the Reference Desk," *College and Research Libraries* 47, no. 5 (1986): 491–94, accessed November 18, 2013, http://crl.acrl.org/content/47/5/491.full.pdf+html.

5. See, for example, Christy R. Stevens, "Reference Reviewed and Re-Envisioned: Revamping Librarian and Desk-Centric Services with LibStARs and LibAnswers," *The Journal of Academic Librarianship* 39, no. 2 (2013): 202–14, doi:10.1016/j.acalib.2012.11.006; and Marianne Stowell Bracke, Michael Brewer, Robyn Huff-Eibl, Daniel R. Lee, Robert Mitchell, and Michael Ray, "Finding Information in a New Landscape: Developing New Service and Staffing Models for Mediated Information Services," *College and Research Libraries* 68, no. 3 (2007): 248–67, accessed November 18, 2013, http://crl.acrl.org/content/68/3/248.full.pdf+html.

6. Susan M. Ryan, "Reference Transactions Analysis: The Cost-Effectiveness of Staffing a Traditional Academic Reference Desk," *The Journal of Academic Librarianship* 34, no. 5 (2008): 389–99, doi:10.1016/j.acalib.2008.06.002.

7. Stevens, "Reference Reviewed."

8. John V. Richardson and Matthew L. Saxton, *Understanding Reference Transactions: Turning an Art into a Science* (San Diego, CA: Academic Press, 2002).

9. See, for example, Reuven Blau, "Brooklyn Public Library Researchers Answered 3.5 Million Questions in 2013, Records Show," *New York Daily News*, March 26, 2014, accessed March 26, 2014, http://www.nydailynews.com/new-york/brooklyn-public-library-researchers-answered-3-5-million-questions-2013-records-show-article-1.1734547.

10. Robert S. Taylor, "Question-Negotiation and Information Seeking in Libraries," *College and Research Libraries* 29, no. 3 (1968): 178–94, http://hdl.handle.net/2142/38236.

11. Steve Coffman and Linda Arret, "To Chat Or Not to Chat—Taking Another Look at Virtual Reference, Part I," *Searcher* 12, no. 7 (2004), accessed February 16, 2014, http://www.infotoday.com/searcher/jul04/arret_coffman.shtml.

12. Charles Martell, "The Absent User: Physical Use of Academic Library Collections and Services Continues to Decline 1995–2006," *The Journal of Academic Librarianship* 34, no. 5 (2008): 400–407, doi:10.1016/j.acalib.2008.06.003.

13. Rachel Applegate, "Whose Decline? Which Academic Libraries Are 'Deserted' in Terms of Reference Transactions," *Reference & User Services Quarterly* 48, no. 2 (2008): 176–88, doi:10.5860/rusq.48n2.176.

14. Applegate, "Whose Decline?"

15. Martell, "Absent User," 404.

16. Kim A. Miller, Deanne W. Swan, Terri Craig, Suzanne Dorinski, Michael Freeman, Natasha Isaac, Patricia O'Shea, Peter Schilling, and Jennifer Scotto, *Public Libraries Survey: Fiscal Year 2009* (IMLS-2011-PLS-02) (Washington, DC: Institute of Museum and Library Services, 2011), http://www.imls.gov/assets/1/News/PLS2009.pdf.

17. Ian Reid, "The Public Library Data Service 2012 Statistical Report: Characteristics and Trends," *Public Libraries* 51, no. 6 (2012): 36–46, accessed February 28, 2014, http://publiclibrariesonline.org/2014/05/2013-plds; and Virgil E. Varvel Jr., "The Public Library Data Service 2011 Statistical Report Characteristics and Trends," *Public Libraries* 50, no. 5 (2011): 26–34, accessed February 28, 2014, http://www.ala.org/pla/sites/ala.org.pla/files/content/publications/plds/varvel_pl_50n5_sepoct11.pdf.

18. Cathy De Rosa, Joanne Cantrell, Matthew Carlson, Peggy Gallagher, Janet Hawk, and Charlotte Sturtz, *Perceptions of Libraries, 2010: Context and Community*, (Dublin, OH: OCLC, 2011), accessed March 2, 2014, http://www.oclc.org/content/dam/oclc/reports/2010perceptions/2010perceptions_all.pdf.

19. Kathryn Zickuhr, Lee Rainie, and Kristen Purcell, *Library Services in the Digital Age* (Washington, DC: Pew Internet and American Life Project, 2013), accessed February 26, 2014, http://libraries.pewinternet.org/files/legacy-pdf/ PIP_Library%20services_Report.pdf.

20. Pnina Shachaf, Lokman Meho, and Noriko Hara, "Cross-Cultural Analysis of E-Mail Reference," *The Journal of Academic Librarianship* 33, no. 2 (2007): 243–53, doi:10.1016/j.acalib.2006.08.010.

21. Beth Stahr, "Text Message Reference Service: Five Years Later," *The Reference Librarian* 52, nos. 1/2 (2010): 9–19, doi:10.1080/02763877.2011.524502.

22. Tai Phan, Laura Hardesty, and Jaime Hug, *Academic Libraries: 2012* (NCES 2014-038) (Washington, DC: U.S. Department of Education, National Center for Education Statistics, 2014), http://nces.ed.gov/pubs2014/2014038.pdf.

23. "The State of America's Libraries: A Report from the American Library Association, 2013," special issue, *American Libraries* (2013), accessed January 22, 2014, http://www.ala.org/news/sites/ala.org.news/files/content/2013-State-of-Americas-Libraries-Report.pdf.

24. Marie L. Radford and M. Kathleen Kern, "A Multiple-Case Study Investigation of the Discontinuation of Nine Chat Reference Services," *Library and Information Science Research* 28, no. 4 (2006): 521–47, doi:10.1016/j.lisr.2006.10.001.

25. Jenne, April 21, 2011 (1:22 p.m.), comment on Andy, "KIA for QandA NJ," *Agnostic, Maybe* (blog), *WordPress,* April 21, 2011, http://agnostic-maybe.wordpress.com/2011/04/21/kia-for-qanda-nj.

26. See, for example, Sylvia G. Faibisoff and Donald P. Ely, "Information and Information Needs," *Information Reports and Bibliographies* 5, no. 5 (1976): 2–16; and Heidi Julien and David Michels, "Source Selection among Information Seekers: Ideals and Realities," *Canadian Journal of Library and Information Science* 25, no. 1 (2000): 1–18, http://www.cais-acsi.ca/proceedings/2000/julien_2000.pdf.

27. See, for example, Soo Young Rieh, Brian Hilligoss, and Jiyeon Yang, "Toward an Integrated Framework of Information and Communication Behavior: College Students' Information Resources and Media Selection," *ASLIB Proceedings* 44, no. 1 (2007): 1–15, http://rieh.people.si.umich.edu/~rieh/papers/rieh_asist2007.pdf; and Jillian R. Griffiths and Peter Brophy, "Student Searching Behavior and the Web: Use of Academic Resources and Google," *Library Trends* 53, no. 4 (2005): 539–54, http:// hdl.handle.net/2142/1749.

28. Kyung-Sun Kim and Sei-Ching Joanna Sin, "Perception and Selection of Information Sources by Undergraduate Students: Effects of Avoidance Style, Confidence, and Personal Control in Problem-Solving," *The Journal of Academic Librarianship* 33, no. 6 (2007): 655–65, doi:10.1016/j.acalib.2007.09.012; and Ruth Vondracek, "Comfort and Convenience? Why Students Choose Alternatives to the Library," *portal: Libraries and the Academy* 7, no. 3 (2007): 277–93, doi:10.1353/pla.2007.0039.

29. Rich Gazan, "Social Q & A," *Journal of the American Society for Information Science and Technology* 62, no. 12 (2011): 2301–12, doi:10.1002/asi.21562.

30. "Social Media Trends," *Experian Marketing Services,* accessed November 24, 2013, http://www.experian.com/marketing-services/online-trends-social-media.html.

31. Chirag Shah and Vanessa Kitzie, "Social Q & A and Virtual Reference: Comparing Apples and Oranges with the Help of Experts and Users," *Journal of the American Society for Information Science and Technology* 63, no. 10 (2011): 2020–36, doi:10.1002/ asi.22699.

32. Quentin Hardy, "Quora and the Search for Truth," *Bits* (blog), *New York Times,* February 9, 2014, http://nyti.ms/1gal2Uu.

33. Gazan, "Social Q & A," 2307.

34. Lynn Westbrook, "Unanswerable Questions at the IPL: User Expectations of E-Mail Reference," *Journal of Documentation* 65, no. 3 (2009): 384, doi:10.1108/ 00220410910952393.

35. Ibid., 372.

36. Thomas A. Peters, "Left to Their Own Devices: The Future of Reference Services on Personal, Portable Information, Communication, and Entertainment Devices," *The Reference Librarian* 52, nos. 1/2 (2011): 88–97, doi:10.1080/02763877.2011.520110.

37. Corey M. Johnson, "Online Chat Reference: Survey Results from Affiliates at Two Universities," *Reference & User Services Quarterly* 43, no. 3 (2004): 237–47, http://www.jstor.org/stable/20864205; and Karen D. Sobel, "Promoting Library Reference Services to First-Year Undergraduate Students: What Works?" *Reference & User Services Quarterly* 48, no. 4 (2009): 362–71, doi:10.5860/rusq.48n4.

38. Trina J. Magi and Patricia E. Mardeusz, "Why Some Students Continue to Value Individual, Face-to-Face Instruction in a Technology-Rich World," *College and Research Libraries* 74, no. 6 (2013): 605–18, http://crl.acrl.org/content/74/6/605.full.pdf+html.

39. Amy Gratz and Julie Gilbert, "Meeting Student Needs at the Reference Desk," *Reference Services Review* 39, no. 3 (2011): 423–38, doi:10.1108/00907321111161412.

40. Amy VanScoy, "Page Us! Combining the Best of In-Person and Virtual Reference Service to Meet In-Library Patron Needs," *Internet Reference Services Quarterly* 11, no. 2 (2006): 15–25, doi:10.1300/J136v11n02_02.

41. Lynn Sillipigni Connaway, Timothy J. Dickey, and Marie L. Radford, "If It Is Too Inconvenient I'm Not Going after It: Convenience as a Critical Factor in Information-Seeking Behaviors," *Library and Information Science Research* 33, no. 3 (2011): 179–90, doi:10.1016/j.lisr.2010.12.002.

42. Douglas L. Zweizig, "With Our Eye on the User: Needed Research for Information and Referral in the Public Library," *Drexel Library Quarterly* 12, nos. 1/2 (1976): 48–58.

43. "Trend Data (Adults)," *Pew Research Internet Project*, accessed November 21, 2013, http://www.pewinternet.org/Static-Pages/Trend-Data-(Adults)/Device-Ownership.aspx.

44. Maeve Duggan and Aaron Smith, "Cell Internet Use 2013," *Pew Research Internet Project*, September 16, 2013, http://www.pewinternet.org/Reports/2013/Cell-Internet.aspx.

45. Kristen Purcell, Joanna Brenner, and Lee Rainie, "Search Engine Use 2012," *Pew Research Internet Project*, March 9, 2012, accessed November 21, 2013, http://pewinternet.org/Reports/2012/Search-Engine-Use-2012.aspx.

46. David Bawden and Polona Vilar, "Digital Libraries: To Meet or Manage User Expectations," *Aslib Proceedings* 58, no. 4 (2006): 347, doi:10.1108/00012530610687713.

47. Deborah Fallows, "Search Engine Users: Internet Users Are Confident, Satisfied, and Trusting, but They Are Also Unaware and Naïve," *Pew Internet and American Life Project*, January 23, 2005, accessed November 21, 2013, http://www.pewinternet.org/~/media//Files/Reports/2005/PIP_Searchengine_users.pdf.pdf.

48. Cathy De Rosa, Joanne Cantrell, Janet Hawk, and Alane Wilson, *College Students' Perceptions of Libraries and Information Resources: A Report to the OCLC Membership* (Dublin, OH: OCLC Online Computer Library Center, 2006), http://www.oclc.org/content/dam/oclc/reports/pdfs/studentperceptions.pdf.

49. Purcell Brenner, and Rainie, "Search Engine Use."

50. Lucy Holman, "Millennial Students' Mental Models of Search: Implications for Academic Librarians and Database Developers," *The Journal of Academic Librarianship* 37, no. 1 (2011): 19–27, doi:10.1016/j.acalib.2010.10.003.

51. Holly Yu and Margo Young, "The Impact of Web Search Engines on Subject Searching in OPAC," *Information and Technology Libraries* 23, no. 4 (2004): 168–80.

52. Bennett Claire Ponsford and Wyoma vanDuinkerken, "User Expectations in the Time of Google: Usability Testing of Federated Searching," *Internet Reference Services Quarterly* 12, nos. 1/2 (2007): 160, doi:10.1300/J136v12n01_08.

53. Azzah Al-Maskari and Mark Sanderson, "A Review of Factors Influencing User Satisfaction in Information Retrieval," *Journal of the American Society for Information Science and Technology* 61, no. 5 (2010): 859–68, doi:10.1002/asi.21300.

54. Melissa Gross and Don Latham, "What's Skill Got to Do with It? Information Literacy Skills and Self-Views among First-year College Students," *Journal of the*

American Society of Information Science and Technology 63, no. 3 (2012): 547–83, doi:10.1002/asi.21681.

55. David Stern, "User Expectations and the Complex Realities of Online Research Efforts," *Science and Technology Libraries* 22, nos. 3–4 (2002): 137–48, doi:10.1300/J122v22n03_11.

56. Jean Poland, "Adapting to Changing User Expectations" (paper 31, proceedings of the IATUL Conferences, Krakow, Poland, 2004), 1–5, http://docs.lib.purdue.edu/iatul/2004/papers/31.

57. Connaway, Dickey, and Radford, "If It Is Too Inconvenient."

58. José-Marie Griffiths and Donald W. King, "InterConnections: The IMLS National Study on the Use of Libraries, Museums and the Internet: Conclusions," *Institute of Museum and Library Services*, February 2008), accessed November 23, 2013, http://interconnectionsreport.org/reports/ConclusionsFullRptB.pdf.

59. Shawn V. Lombardo and Kristine S. Condic, "Convenience or Content: A Study of Undergraduate Periodical Use," *Reference Services Review* 29, no. 4 (2001): 327–38, doi:10.1108/EUM0000000006494.

60. William J. Paisley, "Information Needs and Uses," *Annual Review of Information Science and Technology* 3, (1967): 1–30.

61. See, for example, Pamela N. Martin and Lezlie Park, "Reference Desk Consultation Assignment: An Exploratory Study of Students' Perceptions of Reference Service," *Reference & User Services Quarterly* 49, no. 4 (2010): 333–40, http://digitalcommons.usu.edu/lib_pubs/91; and Virginia Massey-Burzio, "From the Other Side of the Reference Desk: A Focus Group Study," *The Journal of Academic Librarianship* 24, no. 3 (2010): 208–15, doi:10.1016/S0099-1333(98)90041-6.

62. Sharon Naylor, Bruce Stoffel, and Sharon Van Der Laan, "Why Isn't Our Chat Reference Used More: Findings of Focus Group Discussions with Undergraduate Students," *Reference & User Services Quarterly* 47, no. 4 (2008): 342–54, doi:10.5860/rusq.47n4.342.

63. Joel Cummings, Lara Cummings, and Linda Frederiksen, "User Preferences in Reference Services: Virtual Reference and Academic Libraries," *portal: Libraries and the Academy* 7, no. 1 (2007): 81–96, doi:10.1353/pla.2007.0004.

64. See, for example, Mary Jane Swope and Jeffrey Katzer, "The Silent Majority: Why Don't They Ask Questions?" *RQ* 12, no. 2 (1972): 161–66, http://www.jstor.org/stable/25825399; and Linda J. Durfee, "Student Awareness of Reference Services in a Liberal Arts College Library," *Library Quarterly* 56, no. 3 (1986): 286–302, http://www.jstor.org/stable/4308017.

65. May G. Kennedy, Laura Kiken, and Jean P. Shipman, "Addressing Underutilization of Consumer Health Information Resource Centers," *Journal of the Medical Library Association* 96, no. 1 (2008): 42–49, doi:10.3163/1536-5050.96.1.42.

66. Naylor, Stoffel, and Van Der Laan, "Why Isn't Our Chat Reference Used More."

67. Taylor, "Question-Negotiation."

68. See, for example, Swope and Katzer, "Silent Majority"; and Jody Fagan, "Students' Perceptions of Academic Librarians," *The Reference Librarian* 37 no. 78 (2002): 131–48, doi:10.1300/J120v37n78_09.

69. Barbara Fister, "The Research Processes of Undergraduate Students," *The Journal of Academic Librarianship* 18, no. 3 (1992): 163–69.

70. See, for example, Naylor, Stoffel, and Van Der Laan, "Why Isn't Our Chat Reference Used More"; and Ethelene Whitmire, "A Longitudinal Study of Undergraduates' Academic Library Experiences," *The Journal of Academic Librarianship* 27, no. 5 (2001): 379–85, doi:10.1016/S0099-1333(01)00223-3.

71. Alison J. Head and Michael B. Eisenberg, "Truth Be Told: How College Students Evaluate and Use Information in the Digital Age," *Project Information Literacy Progress Report*, November 1, 2010, accessed January 24, 2014, http://projectinfolit.org/images/pdfs/pil_fall2010_survey_fullreport1.pdf.

72. Joanne E. D'Esposito and Rachel M. Gardner, "University Students' Perceptions of the Internet: An Exploratory Study," *The Journal of Academic Librarianship* 25, no. 6

(1999): 456–61, doi:10.1016/S0099-1333(99)00078-6; Fagan, "Students' Perceptions," 2002; Cees-Jan de Jong, "Undergraduate Students' Perspectives on the Reference Transaction: A Pilot Study" (proceedings of the Annual Conference of the Canadian Association for Information Science, Toronto, Canada, 2006), 1–16, http://www.cais-acsi.ca/proceedings/2006/dejong_2006.pdf.

73. Sandra Jenkins, "Undergraduate Perceptions of the Reference Collection and the Reference Librarian in an Academic Library," *The Reference Librarian* 35, no. 73 (2001): 229–241, doi:10.1300/J120v35n73_01.

74. Ibid.

75. Martin and Park, "Reference Desk Consultation Assignment."

76. Scott Carlson, "Are Reference Desks Dying Out? Librarians Struggle to Redefine—and in Some Cases Eliminate—the Venerable Institution," *Reference Librarian* 48, no. 2 (2007): 25–30, doi:10.1300/J120v48n02_06.

77. Connaway, Dickey, and Radford, "If It's Too Inconvenient," 179.

78. Steve Kolowich, "Embedded Librarians," *Inside Higher Ed*, June 9, 2010, http://www.insidehighered.com/news/2010/06/09/hopkins.

79. Michelle Lee, "Reference on the Road," *Library Journal* 138, no. 18 (2013): 18–20, http://reviews.libraryjournal.com/2013/11/reference/reference-on-the-road.

80. Kathy Drewes and Nadine Hoffman, "Academic Embedded Librarianship: An Introduction," *Public Services Quarterly* 6, nos. 2/3 (2010): 75–82, doi:10.1080/15228959.2010.498773.

81. Barbara I. Dewey, "The Embedded Librarian: Strategic Campus Collaborations," *Resource Sharing and Information Networks* 17, nos. 1/2 (2004): 6, doi:10.1300/J121v17n01_02.

82. Stephanie J. Schulte, "Embedded Academic Librarianship: A Review of the Literature," *Evidence Based Library and Information Practice* 7, no. 4 (2012): 122–38, http://ejournals.library.ualberta.ca/index.php/EBLIP/article/view/17466/14483.

83. Lee, "Reference on the Road," 18.

84. David Shumaker, "Who Let the Librarians Out? Embedded Librarianship and the Library Manager," *Reference & User Services Quarterly* 48, no. 3 (2009): 240, http://blog.rusq.org/2009/05/29/who-let-the-librarians-out.

85. Starr Hoffman, "Embedded Academic Librarians Experiences in Online Courses: Roles, Faculty Collaboration, and Opinion," *Library Management* 32, nos. 6/7 (2011): 444–56, doi:10.1108/01435121111158583.

86. Karen Malnati and Ronnie Boseman, "Embedded Librarian Program Insights," *Community and Junior College Libraries* 18, nos. 3/4 (2012): 127–36, doi:10.1080/02763915.2012.792214.

87. Erika Bennett and Jennie Simning, "Embedded Librarians and Reference Traffic: A Quantitative Analysis," *Journal of Library Administration* 50, nos. 5/6 (2010): 443–457, doi:10.1080/01930826.2010.491437.

88. Jeffrey T. Huber, Emily B. Kean, Philip D. Fitzgerald, Trina A. Altman, Zach G. Young, Katherine M. Dupin, Jacqueline Leskovec, and Ruth Holst, "Outreach Impact Study: The Case of the Greater Midwest Region," *Journal of the Medical Library Association* 99, no. 4 (2011): 297–303, doi:10.3163/1536-5050.99.4.007.

89. Thomas L. Reinsfelder, "Citation Analysis as a Tool to Measure the Impact of Individual Research Consultations," *College and Research Libraries* 73, no. 3 (2012): 264, doi:10.5860/crl-261.

90. Megan S. Mitchell, Cynthia H. Comer, Jennifer M. Starkey, and Eboni A. Francis, "Paradigm Shift in Reference Services at the Oberlin College Library: A Case Study," *Journal of Library Administration* 51, no. 4(2011): 359–74, doi:10.1080/01930826.2011.556959.

91. Ibid., 367.

92. Vivian Reed, "Is the Reference Desk No Longer the Best Point of Reference?" *Reference Librarian* 48, no. 2 (2007): 77–82, doi:10.1300/J120v48n02_12.

93. "Book a Librarian," *Skokie Public Library*, accessed December 10, 2013, http://skokielibrary.info/s_info/book_librarian.asp.

94. Reinsfelder, "Citation Analysis."

95. Martin and Park, "Reference Desk Consultation Assignment."

96. Heather Ganshorn, "A Librarian Consultation Service Improves Decision-Making and Saves Time for Primary Care Practitioners," *Evidence-Based Library and Information Practice* 4, no. 2 (2009): 148–51, http://ejournals.library.ualberta.ca/index.php/EBLIP/article/view/6019.

97. Stevens, "Reference Reviewed."

98. Hanrong Wang, Yingqi Tang, and Carley Knight, "Contemporary Development of Academic Reference Librarianship in the United States: A 44-Year Content Analysis," *The Journal of Academic Librarianship* 36, no. 6 (2010): 489–94, doi:10.1016/j.acalib.2010.08.004.

99. "Presidential Committee on Information Literacy: Final Report," *Association of College and Research Libraries*, January 10, 1989, accessed December 13, 2013, http://www.ala.org/acrl/publications/whitepapers/presidential.

100. Laura Saunders, "Regional Accreditation Organizations' Treatment of Information Literacy: Definitions, Collaboration, and Assessment," *The Journal of Academic Librarianship* 33, no. 3 (2007): 317–26, doi:10.1016/j.acalib.2007.01.009.

101. "Liberal Education and America's Promise (LEAP): Essential Learning Outcomes," *Association of American Colleges and Universities*, accessed December 13, 2013, http://www.aacu.org/leap/vision.cfm.

102. "The Degree Qualifications Profile," *Lumina Foundation*, January 2011, accessed December 13, 2013, http://www.luminafoundation.org/publications/The_Degree_Qualifications_Profile.pdf.

103. Gabriela Sonntag and Felicia Palsson, "No Longer the Sacred Cow—No Longer a Desk: Transforming Reference Service to Meet 21st Century User Needs," *Library Philosophy and Practice* (2007), accessed December 10, 2013, http://www.webpages.uidaho.edu/~mbolin/sonntag-palsson.htm.

104. Stevens, "Reference Reviewed."

105. Steven J. Bell, "Who Needs a Reference Desk?" *Library Issues* 27, no. 6 (2007), accessed December 13, 2013, http://www.libraryissues.com/sub/LI270006.asp.

106. "Definitions of Reference," *Reference and User Services Association*, January 14, 2008, accessed August 15, 2013, http://www.ala.org/rusa/resources/guidelines/definitionsreference.

107. Alvin Hutchinson, "Creative Destruction in Library Services," *Issues in Science and Technology Librarianship* 73 (2013).

108. Stevens, "Reference Reviewed," 204.

109. Sara Harrington, "'Library as Laboratory': Online Pathfinders and the Humanities Graduate Student," *Public Services Quarterly* 3, nos. 3/4 (2007): 39. doi:10.1080/15228950802110445.

110. Ben Hunter, "Dynamic Pathfinders: Leveraging Your OPAC to Create Resource Guides," *Journal of Web Librarianship* 2, no. 1 (2008): 75–90, doi:10.1080/19322900802186694.

111. Harrington, "'Library as Laboratory.'"

112. Jonathon Miner and Ross Alexander, "LibGuides in Political Science: Improving Student Access, Research, and Information Literacy," *Journal of Information Literacy* 4, no. 1 (2010): 40–54.

113. Martin P. Courtois, Martha E. Higgins, and Aditya Kapur, "Was This Guide Helpful? Users' Perceptions of Subject Guides," *Reference Services Review* 33, no. 2(2005): 188–96, doi:10.1108/00907320510597381.

114. Lynn L. Ralph and Timothy J. Ellis, "An Investigation of a Knowledge Management Solution for the Improvement of Reference Services," *Journal of Information, Information Technology, and Organizations* 4 (2009): 17–38.

115. Scott Nicholson and R. David Lankes, "The Digital Electronic Warehouse Project: Creating the Infrastructure for Digital Reference Research through a Multidisciplinary Knowledge Base," *Reference & User Services Quarterly* 46, no. 3 (2007): 45–59, doi:10.5860/rusq.46n3.45.

116. Ralph and Ellis, "Investigation."

117. Debra Kimok and Holly Heller-Ross, "Visual Tutorials for Point-of-Need Instruction in Online Courses," *Journal of Library Administration* 48, nos. 3/4 (2008): 527–43, doi:10.1080/01930820802289656.

118. Lori A. Mardis and Connie Jo Ury, "Innovation—An LO Library: Reuse of Learning Objects," *Reference Services Review* 36, no. 4 (2008): 390, doi:10.1108/00907320810920360.

119. Katherine Stiwinter, "Using an Interactive Online Tutorial to Expand Library Instruction," *Internet Reference Services Quarterly* 18, no. 1 (2013): 15–41, doi:10.1080/10875301.2013.777010.

120. Mardis and Ury, "Innovation."

THREE

Implications of Change

Competencies and Philosophies

The core of reference has remained virtually unchanged in more than one hundred years of service, but as technology offers us new tools for content and service delivery and user expectations shift, reference librarians and information professionals are both adapting delivery models and overlaying additional services and responsibilities onto the basic reference model. However, adaptation of current services is not enough—"we are charged to push beyond incremental changes, abandon current outdated and dying practices and assume new critical roles."[1] It stands to reason that a paradigm shift of this nature will impact the nature of the reference position and that new responsibilities and service areas will entail new skills and competencies for librarians. Some of these changes are reflected in job titles and position descriptions. The *Library Journal* salary and placement survey finds that, while reference librarian remains one of the top five job titles for now, the overall number of job openings with that title has dropped.[2] Still, the report suggests the decreasing numbers can be "deceiving," as the position often includes additional responsibilities, such as instruction, collection development, and administrative work. In addition, other jobs, such as electronic resource management, data librarianship, and scholarly communications/repository management, often include reference responsibilities.

On the other hand, the report identifies several "new and unusual" titles, such as digital assets manager, emerging technology specialist, health/science informatics analyst/administrator, technology development librarian, and user experience designer. Employees in these positions indicate a focus on "developing the agency's online presence through mobile and social media and web accessibility, managing digitization initiatives and workflow, and gathering data and analytics," suggesting some new directions for librarianship.[3] These new job descriptions suggest that librarians' responsibilities are no longer isolated by a specific function. Rather, most reference jobs are "multifunctional, meaning that they require additional responsibilities and duties beyond the traditional question-answering services" and as such entail new and additional competency areas.[4]

The question of emerging roles and competencies is an intriguing one, and various authors, researchers, and professional organizations are tracking these changes and offering insights into the skills and qualifications reference librarians and information professionals will need as the profession continues to change and adapt. As librarians and information professionals develop these new roles and practices, they will likely also need to develop new competencies to support those roles. In general, these skills tend to fall into a number of broad areas, including technology, soft skills, and professional and subject knowledge. Further, some of the changes in service delivery and practice may entail a fundamental shift in some of the philosophies that have traditionally guided reference services. Reference librarians may need to rethink not only what types of services they deliver and how but also why—in other words, what values, goals, and purposes underlie the provision of services and ultimately define the role of the reference librarian. Chapter 1 examines the range of competencies currently expected of reference librarians, demonstrating the need for librarians to be at least familiar with if not proficient in a wide variety of hard and soft skills, and chapter 2 outlines some of the competitive pressures impacting libraries and information settings, specifically reference services. The rest of this chapter examines the shifting expectations of competencies in terms of skills, knowledge, and philosophies and touches on the implications for library and information sciences (LIS) curricula in these areas.

TECHNOLOGY

Not surprisingly, many of the new competence areas are related to changes in technology and include everything from basic familiarity and comfort with a range of hardware and software applications to in-depth design and analysis abilities. While there are some differences across position types, with public services requiring computer skills marginally more often than technical services positions (62.8 percent to 59.3 percent, respectively), a review of job postings at the beginning of the millennium confirmed the increasing focus on computer skills.[5] Further, the study identified an emerging category of electronic services librarian, which required computer skills in 96 percent of the postings. By 2006, researchers analyzing technical services job descriptions concluded that "computer skills should be considered a 'given' for any technical services job."[6] Nine years later, Mathews and Pardue found a "significant intersection between the skill sets of librarians and the skill sets of IT professionals."[7] These researchers found that 72 percent of librarian job ads listed at least one IT competency and identified web development skills as the most highly sought competence, along with project management, systems development, and systems applications.

Using content analysis to examine the kinds of questions and assistance being asked through virtual reference services, Resnick compiled a list of twelve core competencies for reference librarians in the digital age. These include abilities related to selecting, managing, and facilitating access to electronic collections, which includes an ability to recognize and correct problems with link resolvers; familiarity with the various systems employed within an institution (such as cataloging, acquisitions, SFX, and MetaLib) and how they interact with each other; the ability to deal with proxy servers and other systems related to remote authentication; and an ability to communicate with vendors and negotiate contracts and license agreements.[8] These competencies clearly show the merging of responsibilities associated with collections and those associated with reference.

While not limited to reference, a survey of one hundred librarians found the most frequently used keywords to describe competencies included *Internet competent, interactive, Internet minded*, and *virtual*. The researchers note that librarians need to have current technical skills and need to keep those skills up to date through continuous learning, leading to what the researchers describe as a dual profile in which librarians are "experts on one hand (IT skilled guide, expert, teacher, and Internet minded), and learners on the other hand (adaptive, learner, curious, open, and interested)."[9] Pussadee Nonthacumjane used content analysis to develop a list of competencies that includes knowledge of metadata; database management and development; knowledge of languages and protocols, such as Functional Requirements for Bibliographic Records (FRBR), the Semantic Web, Resource Description Framework, and SPARQL; as well as an ability to analyze user needs with regards to resources and services.[10] A fundamental understanding of databases and search engines, including how they execute search strategies and rank results, will allow the librarian to add value to their patron's search and assist them in evaluating and selecting from the abundance of information.[11]

Much attention has been given to Web 2.0 and social media applications as well. David Lee King offers a list of specific skills he believes should be mastered by librarians working in a 2.0 environment. He includes the ability to: write blog posts; create and edit screencasts, podcasts, photos, and so on; embed widgets in personal pages; use instant messaging and SMS tools; use and explain how to use RSS feeds; and do basic HTML editing, including some knowledge of (X)HTML and CSS.[12] Stephen Abram offers a list of more than a dozen skill and knowledge areas, including an ability to use many different devices, communicate with patrons in their preferred formats, and recognize the power and potential of both open-access and user-driven content.[13] Similarly, Danielle De Jager-Loftus identifies RSS feeds, widgets to embed library services in patron's web space, blogs to promote research and faculty publications, and LibraryThing to promote collections as tools medical librarians can use to add value to their services.[14]

In the past, users mostly relied on libraries to access information, but as access has become ubiquitous, they are spending more time creating their own content. As a result, librarians and information professionals must gain proficiency in a range of productivity tools, from basic word processing and spreadsheet software to multimedia and web design tools, in order to assist and instruct users in the use of these tools. Likewise, many librarians and information professionals are creating their own content, prompting Julie Lefevre and Terence K. Huwe to argue that digital publishing is now a core competency for librarians and information professionals.[15] Included within their umbrella of digital publishing is administering a content management system, applying metadata standards, understanding and adhering to copyright laws, and engaging in editorial processes. Also related to the development of online content, Randolph G. Bias, Paul F. Marty, and Ian Douglas argue that knowledge of usability trends and user-centered design is important and relevant for all librarians and information professionals.[16]

In addition to using technology, librarians and information professionals must also be able to develop policies around it and plan and manage the implementation of technology within their institutions.[17] Finally, they must be able to evaluate new tools and technologies as they emerge in order to make informed decisions about whether to incorporate those tools into the service and/or recommend them to users.[18] User privacy has also been important to libraries and information settings, and technology adds a new layer of complexity to the issue. As social media sites and cloud computing become increasingly popular and both users and librarians and information professionals store and share more information through these sites and systems, librarians and information professionals need to consider the challenges and implications for privacy. Karen Sorensen and Nancy R. Glassman point to such issues as data security and the fact that privacy laws can vary depending on provider locations and vendor agreements.[19] Librarians will need to keep abreast of these issues in order to make good decisions about their own technologies, set local policies, and help users stay informed.[20]

While the list of technical skills expected of librarians seems staggering, it is important to note that the specific requirements can vary widely by type of library and position and from institution to institution. In fact, general attitudes toward and interest and curiosity about technology might be more important than any single set of skills. Participants in a series of Australian focus groups contended that "while technology is important within the context of Library 2.0 and librarian 2.0, it is not the dominant or main aspect."[21] These librarians and information professionals distinguished between being an IT professional and having an understanding and appreciation of IT. They believe librarians and information professionals should be comfortable with technology, able to talk with IT professionals, translate technology for users, and have a web presence. Essentially, librarians and information professionals need to "be aware of, and have some fundamental understanding of, the emerging technology—what is available and what it can do and how to make it do what is needed—but they do not need to be IT professionals per se."[22] It is important to note, however, that the depth and scope of specific IT knowledge also varies widely by type of library. Focus groups of library employers in the United States found substantial differences in the technology competency expectations among public, academic, and special/corporate libraries, with corporate libraries generally expected to have the most technical knowledge.[23]

In fact, much of the discussion about technology competencies over the past several years seems to focus on flexibility, comfort with change, and learning how to learn. Meredith Farkas sums it up thus: "More important than knowing specific tools is a general comfort in the online environment."[24] She lists comfort with change, ability to learn new technologies quickly, and keeping abreast of new and changing technologies as essential abilities for twenty-first-century librarians and information professionals. Similarly, Cheryl Peltier-Davis contends that librarians must "have the capacity to learn constantly and quickly," "monitor trends in technology," and "be skillful at enabling and fostering change."[25] It is also important for librarians and information professionals to recognize technology as a tool and to critically evaluate it prior to adoption. In other words, librarians should be selective in their use of technology and not necessarily implement technology for technology's sake but be driven by organization and user needs.[26]

SOFT SKILLS

The discussion around flexibility and learning to learn with regard to technology actually coincides with the soft skills, such as communication and interpersonal skills, that many contend are at least as important—if not more so—than specific technical skills.[27] As with technology, the list of soft skills required of librarians is extensive. The importance of soft skills is underscored by the fact that ALA's Reference and User Services Association (RUSA) offers a separate set of behavioral competencies for reference librarians to supplement their list of professional competencies. According to the RUSA guidelines, reference librarians should be approachable, show interest in their patrons while reserving judgment about their information pursuits, and be able to communicate effectively with a diverse patron base across a variety of formats.[28] Michael Stephens highlights communication, initiative, empathy, and a commitment to continuous learning as essential soft skills but also includes intuition and an awareness and understanding of organizational politics.[29] In general, librarians and information professionals need an array of competencies related to communication and other interpersonal skills, such as adaptability or flexibility, problem solving, and commitment to continuous learning.

While communication and interpersonal skills and a customer service focus have always been important for reference librarians, the same changes in technology and user expectations discussed earlier have impacted the emphasis of these soft skills as well. Indeed, explicit requirements for interpersonal skills in job ads increased from 22.6 percent in 1974 to 68.4 percent in 2004, while job postings requiring behavioral skills increased from 16.1 percent to 63.2 percent over the same time period.[30] Further, some employers maintain that, when hiring, they prioritize soft skills over technology, contending that the technology can be learned on the job or through training but communication and interpersonal skills cannot be easily taught.[31] While these skills continue to be important, in some cases changes in the field impact how these soft skills are expressed.

Communication

It has always been important for reference librarians to have good communication skills in order to conduct effective reference interviews and interact with diverse users, but the formats for such communication were primarily in-person and phone conversations. More recently, librarians and information professionals have added such formats as chat, texting, and videoconferencing platforms, such as Skype, to their suites of services. As new formats and technologies evolve and are adopted, reference librarians and information professionals will need to continuously adapt their skills to fit the new service models. They need to understand and apply online communication conventions, including an understanding of chat etiquette, while still maintaining a professional presence. Librarians and information professionals providing virtual reference must be able to multitask in order to maintain word contact with a remote patron while searching for information. An ability to type quickly and accurately is important to such communications.[32] Finally, in many virtual environments, librarians and information professionals must both be able to understand their users and learn to convey interest, enthusiasm, and empathy without the use of visual cues and body language that are present in face-to-face transactions.[33] When offering reference support by texting or tweeting, librarians and information professionals need to communicate information that fully addresses their users' questions using very limited numbers of characters. Once again, each new format or platform entails different competencies and skills.

Not only do librarians and information professionals need to be able to communicate across various platforms, but they also need to be able to communicate with a widely varied and diverse user base. While the specific makeup of the community will vary, all libraries and information settings have patrons from different backgrounds, including different ethnic, religious, language, literacy, and socioeconomic backgrounds. Further, with increasing globalization evidenced by growing numbers of immigrants and international students as well as increased cross-country collaborations, librarians also need to be culturally sensitive. Patricia Montiel Overall argues that librarians must develop cultural competence, which she defines as the

> ability to recognize the significance of culture in one's own life and the lives of others; and to come to know and respect diverse cultural backgrounds and characteristics through interaction with individuals from diverse linguistic, cultural, and socioeconomic groups; and to fully integrate the culture of diverse groups into services, work, and institutions in order to enhance the lives of both those being served and those engaged in service.[34]

Similarly, Paul T. Jaeger, John Carlo Bertot, and Mega Subramaniam emphasize the importance of librarians and information professionals reaching out to diverse and underserved populations.[35]

Outreach and Marketing

Also related to communication, there is some emphasis in the LIS literature on the need for reference librarians—and really all information professionals—to be able to market their services and resources. Library usage statistics, including the number of reference questions, have been declining dramatically,[36] prompting some librarians and information professionals to focus efforts on finding creative ways to promote their services to patrons. Meredith Farkas argues that an ability to sell the library and its services is a core skill for librarians and information professionals of the twenty-first century. She contends that in her job she needs "serious marketing skills and salesmanship to be a librarian" and laments that the topic is not often covered in LIS curricula.[37] A content analysis of job postings between 2000 and 2010 found that promotional activities of some sort were included in 45.6 percent of ads. The activities listed include general marketing and promotion, creating web content or other communication materials, and creating a marketing communications plan.[38] The study also found that promotional activities were most often assigned to librarians rather than library managers or administrators. Another content analysis of job postings found that client services that included marketing and promotional activities increased three ranks from 2000 to 2010.[39]

Flexibility and Adaptability

Among the most frequently discussed and desired soft skills for librarians and information professionals is flexibility and adaptability, or comfort with change. As noted in the previous section, the extremely rapid changes in technology have encouraged employers to look beyond the specific set of skills and knowledge that job applicants have to their personality and behavioral characteristics. In particular, employers are interested in applicants' comfort with the rapid pace of change and ability to keep up with new trends and learn new resources. Myung Gi Sung includes adaptability as one of the ten essential qualities for success and suggests that librarians not only need to adapt to new technologies but also to understand and be able to work with the different expectations across different settings or organizations.[40] A national survey found that flexibility/adaptability were among the top five interpersonal skills selected as important by both public and academic reference librarians.[41] The importance of this trait is underscored by Betha Gutsche, who writes that "there is one skill that might be considered an 'ubercompetency'— the ability to adapt to change, to be flexible and fluid. This overarching competency helps to unlock the achievement of all other skills and knowledge."[42] While flexibility might be important, it is perhaps important to note that it does not mean simply being unflustered by change but implies someone who is willing to continuously learn, who is unafraid to try new things, and who can seek out their own educational opportunities.

ADDITIONAL KNOWLEDGE AND ABILITIES

In addition to the specific skills, there are certain areas of knowledge and abilities librarians and information professionals are expected to have. These areas span everything from broad content, such as instruction or evaluation, to more narrow domains, such as data or project management. While the emphasis and depth will vary, many of these knowledge and ability areas cut across different types of libraries and intersect with the technical and soft skills described earlier.

Instruction

As noted in chapter 1, instruction has always been integrated into reference services, as librarians and information professionals have usually tried to incorporate some guidance in the location and use of resources as they assisted users in answering their information needs. In the past few decades, however, many librarians and information professionals across different types of information settings have taken on an increased, and often more formal, instructional role. The number of job postings specifying instruction skills for academic librarians has increased to the extent that Hanrong Wang, Yingqi Tang, and Carley Knight conclude that it has been a core competency since the 1960s[43] and might be considered an integral part of any public services position.[44] According to a content analysis, job ads requiring instruction tripled between 1982 and 2002.[45] Not only is demand for instructional skills increasing, but those skills are also "in demand across a range of [information professional] roles, whether in libraries, corporate information management, or records management roles."[46]

In order to be effective instructors, reference librarians and information professionals need to have excellent oral communication and presentation skills. However, instruction involves more than public speaking. As librarians' formal instructional roles expand, they will need to develop deeper understanding of theories and practices related to pedagogy, learning, and teaching.[47] Philip Russell, Gerard Ryder, Gillian Kerins, and Margaret Phelan offer a solid review of the knowledge areas and abilities instruction librarians must possess, including understanding pedagogical theories, such as constructivism and active learning; being familiar with and able to teach to various learning styles; aligning curricula with learning outcomes; being able to assess for learning; and planning instruction sessions.[48] The Association of College and Research Libraries (ACRL) outlines twelve competency areas for instruction librarians:

1. Administrative skills
2. Assessment and evaluation skills
3. Communication skills
4. Curriculum knowledge
5. Information literacy integration skills
6. Instructional design skills
7. Leadership skills
8. Planning skills
9. Presentation skills
10. Promotion skills
11. Subject expertise
12. Teaching skills

Each of these is further defined by examples of duties or responsibilities.[49] For instance, the frameworks indicate that instruction librarians and information professionals should be able to adapt to different learning styles and develop active and collaborative learning activities, and they should be able to design effective tools to assess student learning. Further, ACRL offers an immersion program, a week-long intensive education program to help instruction librarians and information professionals develop their abilities in these areas.

As librarians and information professionals engage in more online instructional opportunities, they will need to become familiar with best practices in instructional design and adept at selecting among and using the various technologies to deliver this online instruction. Amy C. York and Jason M. Vance underscore the importance of becoming proficient in the specific technologies and course management systems in use in a given institution and building a relationship with IT administrators.[50] As librarians and information professionals create online tutorials or other digital learning objects, they must become familiar with multimedia teaching and learning theories, learn the relevant technologies, and know how to use these technologies effectively to engage students in learning.[51] The shift to online and technology-enhanced education is reflected in such job titles as instructional design librarian and distance learning librarian. These positions may replace reference librarians or supplement them.

In examining reference librarians' constructions of identity, Amy Van-Scoy notes that historically there has been some tension between adherence to information provision and to instruction.[52] Some reference librarians believe the focus of their job should be to use their expertise to locate and communicate answers and information to users, while others emphasize the librarian's role in educating the user in search strategies and use and evaluation of resources. The job analyses cited earlier suggest that currently the focus is shifting more toward instruction, and indeed research reveals that many librarians and information professionals, especially in academic libraries, are beginning to identify themselves as teachers or educators.[53]

Data Management

Increased storage capacities and computational possibilities, a focus on collaboration, and new requirements of grant-funded projects have all impacted the world of data, which in turn has implications for librarians and information professionals.[54] In fact, data curation was included in ACRL's list of the top ten trends facing academic libraries in 2012.[55] Scientists and researchers have a host of needs related to managing and using their data, creating the opportunity for new roles and responsibilities within academic libraries. Here again, the emerging roles are reflected in new job titles and requirements, such as data services librarian, data management specialist, and e-science librarian.[56] Carol Tenopir, Ben Birch, and Suzie Allard found that, while only a small number of academic libraries are currently offering data management services, about one-quarter to one-third have plans to develop some of these services.[57] Right now, online guides are the most common service, but libraries and information settings are also involved in consulting with faculty and staff on data management and metadata plans and policies; assisting researchers in finding and citing data sets; and supporting research data services, such as institutional repositories and discovery systems.

In order for librarians and information professionals to offer such a range of services, however, they will need to have the requisite skills and competencies. Interestingly, an analysis of job postings found many of the same interpersonal and communication skills discussed earlier were the most frequently mentioned skills and competencies for data services jobs as well. However, these soft skills still need to be underpinned by skills specific to the domain, including extensive knowledge of data curation tools and technologies as well as data sources, an understanding of quantitative research methods, and familiarity with metadata standards and trends.[58]

These data management and research support services have further implications for librarians and information professionals. Kristin Partlo notes that reference librarians will need to employ different strategies in the reference interview when discussing data, especially when dealing with undergraduate students who do not have the background knowledge of specialized researchers.[59] She suggests some strategies for supporting both discovery and instruction when assisting undergraduates with data-related questions. Similarly, Javier Calzada Prado and Miguel Angel Marzal argue that the definition of *information literacy* should be adapted to include components of data literacy. They offer suggestions for incorporating information about finding and using data into library instruction sessions.[60] Other authors note that, because most data services are relatively new areas, librarians need to actively market and promote the services in order to generate use.[61]

Assessment and Evaluation

Assessment of resources, services, and even student learning is incorporated into the RUSA professional competencies for reference librarians,[62] as well as ACRL's competencies for instruction librarians.[63] In addition, assessment and evaluation are included as a core competency in ALA's "Core Competences of Librarianship,"[64] ACRL's "Guidelines: Competencies for Special Collections Professionals,"[65] and the Special Library Association's "Competencies."[66] Megan Oakleaf emphasizes the need for librarians and information professionals to develop a research agenda to collect and disseminate data that will demonstrate their value to their constituencies.[67] With regard to technology, librarians and information professionals must be able to evaluate new tools and technologies as they emerge in order to make informed decisions about whether to incorporate those tools into the service and/or recommend them to users.[68] Meredith Farkas underscores the need for librarians to carry out assessment for several purposes, including assessing services, evaluating needs of various stakeholders, and assessing technology.[69] In order to engage in such assessment, however, librarians will need to understand evaluation research, including creating a research proposal, understanding various methodologies, developing data collection instruments, and perhaps developing some knowledge of basic statistical analysis.

Project and Change Management

Chapter 1 notes that management is considered an important competence for many librarians. In addition to general personnel and budget management and supervisory skills, however, there seems to be some increased demand for specific management skills. For instance, Jane Kinkus reviewed more than one thousand job postings from 1993, 2003, and 2004 and found that the number of positions requiring project management skills increased sharply from 1993 to 2003.[70] Although the numbers fell again in 2004, the use of the phrase *project management* and variations or related terms continued to increase, leading her to conclude that project management will continue to be important to library positions. She notes that the term *project management* encompasses a number of skills and abilities, including interpersonal skills, such as the ability to motivate, understand, and persuade others; conceptual organizational skills, or an ability to frame the project within the larger work; and technical skills relevant to the project at hand. Similarly, Jennifer Swanson notes that managing projects is becoming more common and urges librarians and information professionals to develop project management skills.[71]

Elan Harison and Albert Boonstra contend that project management is essential for effective change management, which is another area of knowledge or ability that seems to be on the horizon for librarians and information professionals.[72] The constant and rapid rate of change in the field is a frequent discussion, as evidenced by the consistent emphasis on adaptability and flexibility as core competencies. As librarians and information professionals strive to adapt to these changes, they are expected to continuously renew their skills and abilities, learn new technologies, and create new services. For organizations and individuals to be successful in the face of such disruption requires the leadership of people who can effectively manage and facilitate change. The pressure of keeping pace with change can be stressful and disruptive for many employees and may engender resistance in some. The concepts of change manage-ment and change leadership are expanded upon in chapter 6, but for now it is worth noting that good change managers will have to combat these negative feelings and overcome instances of opposition. They must have a strong understanding of economic factors impacting change, including how to deal with both cuts and deficits in budgets as well as how to harness economic opportunities.[73] Meredith Gorran Farkas elaborates on Kotter's eight-step model for change leadership, which includes estab-lishing a sense of urgency to motivate action, creating and communicat-ing a vision, empowering others to act, and building on improvements.[74] While she views this model as one that could be adapted to help librar-ians and information professionals effect change in their organizations by changing behaviors, she also notes that there are no one-size-fits-all solu-tions. She goes on to conclude that a true leader needs to be creative and flexible in responding to change rather than trying to follow a formula, a sentiment that seems to fit well with the consistent message emphasizing the importance of flexibility and comfort with change throughout the literature related to competencies.

PHILOSOPHIES

As important as these new competencies might be, they are in many ways just natural extensions of changes in technology and formats. For instance, reference librarians and information professionals have always had to understand cataloging and classification systems to be effective searchers. As more information moves online and new tools and stan-dards are developed to handle that information, it stands to reason that reference librarians and information professionals will need to keep abreast of those changes, as reflected in new expectations for understand-ing metadata and databases. What might be more of a challenge is the change of philosophy that might need to accompany new service models and changes in user expectations. Nevertheless, such changes might be necessary to remain relevant.

Much of the discussion around reference focuses on defining the refer-ence librarian as a professional and an expert, but some authors argue that perspective is limiting and less user centered.[75] To that end, Ronald Martin Solorzano argues that reference services should "shift the focus away from information provision in its simplest form and toward an emphasis on services that add value to the interaction between librarian and user."[76] He builds on Amy VanScoy's work on the professional iden-tities of reference librarians, which centers on six dimensions of reference work: information provision, instruction, interpersonal dimensions, guidance, counseling, and partnerships.[77] While the first four dimensions reflect traditional areas of interaction with patrons to either provide an-

swers or facilitate information seeking, the areas of counseling and partnerships seem to take the librarian–user relationship further.

As Amy VanScoy describes it, counseling moves beyond basic provision of information or guidance toward guiding the patron to a deeper
understanding of their information need and of the research process in
general. With counseling librarianship, the emphasis is "not upon any
information that is to be imparted, but upon aiding of the individual
toward self-motivation and self-decision."[78] She argues that this perspective on reference librarianship is at odds with the more traditional approach of information provision.[79] Similarly, more traditional approaches to reference service assume a certain power relationship in
which the librarian is the expert imparting knowledge to the unsophisti-
cated user.[80] In the partnership perspective described by Amy VanScoy
and advocated by Mark Stover and Ronald Martin Solorzano, the patron
is recognized as an expert in his or her own right, and the focus is on a
balance of power in which the two parties share expertise to collabora-
tively build knowledge. In this model, the librarian is continuously learning, and her perspective on the information might change with the needs
of different users. As such, the counseling and partnership models are
more user or human centered and entail emotional competence as well as
high-level interpersonal skills, such as responsiveness, assurance, and
empathy. In these approaches, the librarian does not impose answers or
information but allows the user to determine success.[81] Both the counseling and partnership models signal a departure from the more traditional
model of reference services. As Solorzano notes, "abandoning the as-
sumption that the user will automatically view the librarian as a figure of
authority represents a true shift in the expectations of librarians when
interacting with users."[82]

Being responsive to current user needs and expectations might also
impact traditional notions of the role of the librarian in providing information or answers to direct reference questions. In an analysis of unanswered questions at the Internet Public Library, Lynn Westbrook found a
disconnect between user and librarian expectations about what constitutes a legitimate reference question.[83] Traditionally, librarians have
avoided certain categories of questions. As Mark Stover notes, librarians
"do not take part in (indeed are proscribed from engaging in) inference,
synthesis, interpretation, or other kinds of evaluative activities."[84] Similarly, Kay Ann Cassell and Uma Hiremath caution librarians to treat
medical, financial, and legal questions carefully because of both the criti-
cality of the information and the vast difference between expert and non-
expert understanding of such information.[85] However, Lynn Westbrook's research indicates that users do not generally make distinctions
between question types, such as fact finding, synthesis, or even advice/
opinion, and often have trouble when asked to categorize their questions
as such. Instead, they expect librarians and information professionals to

provide answers to a wide range of queries, many of which include requests for advice, assistance in applying information in context, and evaluating or analyzing information. These expectations seem to be driven in part by the proliferation of such ask-an-expert sites as Yahoo! Answers and Answerbag, in which such questions are regularly asked and answered by community members.[86]

If reference librarians and information professionals really do intend to be user centered and responsive to changing user needs and expectations, they may need to revisit core values regarding the handling of such questions. Indeed, Thomas A. Peters argues that, if users need advice and opinions, librarians should not ignore those questions but should "provide opinions and advice in a professional, disinterested manner."[87] He does not advocate librarians and information professionals offering personal opinions but rather using their extensive resources and knowledge to help users locate the needed information or by connecting them with experts or guiding them to websites for such advice, such as restaurant or book reviews. Likewise, Lynn Westbrook suggests that librarians and information professionals might need to reconsider their reluctance to answer certain questions that fall into what has historically been considered out of scope. She contends that if the librarian and information professional contextualizes questions and answers properly "as judgment, rather than fact, advice on how to problem-solve, understand, analyze, and learn about information tools, strategies, and resources should be taken as the professional norm."[88] Librarians and information professionals may also need to gather and synthesize information from disparate sources when a complete answer is not available in one place. Indeed, within its "Guidelines for Information Services," RUSA indicates that, "when information is not immediately useful as presented in its source, the information professional should add value to that information. This process of adding value can range from simply sorting and packaging the information to reviewing and analyzing it for library users as appropriate."[89]

IMPLICATIONS FOR LIS EDUCATION

The previous discussion focused on a wide range of new competencies for librarians. Table 3.1 summarizes these competencies. These new competencies need to be reflected in library and information science curricula and in continuing education programs in order to prepare librarians and information professionals for the future.

While a comprehensive analysis of LIS curriculum is needed to determine the gaps and to develop a plan for revisions, several authors have indicated that LIS curricula is lagging behind the emergence of new com-

Table 3.1.   New Competencies for Reference Librarians

Area	New Competencies
Technology	Comfort with hardware and software applications Ability to learn new technologies quickly Knowledge of web and system development, system applications, database management and development, software languages and protocols, metadata, search engines, social media applications, blog platforms, multimedia and web design, and digital publishing Ability to create and edit podcasts Ability to embed widgets In-depth design and analysis abilities Ability to develop policies and plan and manage the implementation of technology within institutions Ability to evaluate new tools and determine whether to incorporate and/or recommend them Ability to converse in the language of IT
Soft Skills	Flexibility Adaptability Interpersonal skills RUSA behavioral competencies: approachable, show interest in patrons while reserving judgment about their information pursuits, and communicate effectively across a variety of formats Initiative Empathy Commitment to continuous learning Intuition Awareness and understanding of organizational politics Problem-solving abilities Ability to communicate in different channels Ability to apply online communication conventions Ability to multitask Ability to communicate with a widely varied and diverse patron base Ability to keep up with trends
Professional and Subject Knowledge	
Outreach and Marketing	Marketing services and resources Promoting the value of the library and library services Creating web content or other communication materials Creating a marketing communications plan Handling promotional activities

Instruction	Administrative skills
	Assessment and evaluation skills
	Communication skills
	Curriculum knowledge
	Information literacy integration skills
	Instructional design skills
	Leadership skills
	Planning skills
	Presentation skills
	Promotion skills
	Subject expertise
	Teaching skills
	Ability to provide guidance on the location and use of resources
	Public speaking skills
	Formal instructional knowledge of theories and pedagogy, learning, and teaching practices
	Familiarity and ability to teach to various learning styles
	Ability to align curricula with learning outcomes
	Ability to assess for learning
	Ability to plan instructional sessions
	Knowledge of course management systems
Data Management	Data Curation
	Management and use of data
	Metadata plans and policies and familiarity with metadata standards and trends
	Ability to assist researchers in finding and citing data sets
	Ability to support research data services, such as institutional repositories and discovery systems
	Quantitative and qualitative research methods
	Data literacy
Assessment and Evaluation	Assessment of resources, services, and student learning
	Data-informed decision making and business intelligence
	Evaluation research, including creating research proposals
	Ability to develop data collection instruments
	Basic statistical analysis
Project and Change Management	Personnel and budget management and supervisory skills
	Project management skills
	Change management and change leadership, such as motivating action, creating and communicating a vision, and empowering others to act

petencies. Three competencies identified are technology, instruction, and assessment and evaluation.

Technology

Many librarians and information professionals report feeling less than proficient with regard to some of the more complex technological applications, especially tools to support web design and multimedia, and they express a desire to increase their knowledge and abilities in these areas.[90] A content analysis of LIS curricula suggests that, while LIS schools offer a wide range of technology courses, there are gaps in the areas of electronic resource management, operating systems, and hardware.[91] Based on an analysis of LIS curricula, the study authors recommend that LIS programs offer courses to support the development of these competencies, including courses in XML, research methods, and data and statistical analysis.

Instruction

As librarians are being asked to take on increasing instructional roles and are beginning to see themselves as educators, many report feeling unprepared or underprepared to take on teaching roles.[92] Formal training in instruction is correlated with greater feelings of competence and confidence, suggesting that libraries and LIS schools should provide librarians with opportunities to engage in such training.[93] Unfortunately, while a majority of LIS schools (85.2 percent) offer courses on instruction, they are not generally required courses.[94] In fact, more than 90 percent of instruction librarians report that on-the-job training and observation of other instructors are the most common way for them to learn how to teach, far outweighing library school programs or workshops.[95]

Assessment and Evaluation

LIS education is also lacking in attention to assessment and evaluation, which is especially troubling, given the pressure on libraries of all kinds to be accountable to their stakeholders by producing evidence of their contributions to and impacts on their communities. Closely related to assessment and evaluation is research methods. While 61 percent of ALA-accredited library schools have a required research methods course, Marie R. Kennedy and Kristine R. Brancolini note that these are often geared toward doctoral students and may not transfer readily to the kind of action research practitioners will likely need to undertake.[96] Indeed, after conducting a survey of academic librarians, the authors found that, while the majority of practitioners felt confident in their abilities to find and understand research literature, "only 26 percent (n = 815) believe that their LIS master's degree adequately prepared them to conduct original research."[97]

TIME FOR A PARADIGM SHIFT

For more than one hundred years, reference services have been linked to a physical location symbolized by the reference desk. While this model of service may have been effective at one time, as reference services expand, the desk model has increasingly been criticized as limiting and inefficient. Indeed, by strict definition, many of the questions fielded at the reference desk would not be considered reference transactions, while much reference work—such as formal instruction and creation of resources—takes place away from the desk. As such, more and more librarians are moving away from the desk in favor of more dynamic and proactive services. However, these are incremental changes to reference. In order to make the paradigm shift and to become truly user centered, librarians and information professionals will need to develop new competencies and engage or nurture new philosophies that are more responsive to user needs and expectations in the twenty-first century. The next chapter offers some examples of libraries and information settings that have initiated such innovative services.

NOTES

1. Julie Garrison, "What Do We Do Now? A Case for Abandoning Yesterday and Making the Future," *Reference and User Services Quarterly* 51, no. 1 (2011): 12, accessed December 16, 2013, http://web.ebscohost.com/ehost/pdfviewer/pdfviewer?vid=15& sid=5f253605-c7db-40ac-9908-cdc2ee3d4668%40sessionmgr111&hid=120.

2. Stephanie L. Maatta, "A Job by Any Other Name: A Few Bright Spots Shine for the Class of 2011," *Library Journal* 137, no. 17 (2012): 18–25, accessed January 8, 2014, http://web.ebscohost.com/ehost/pdfviewer/pdfviewer?sid=f5039f97-67a1-45ac-b70f-317ae12ae9b9%40sessionmgr198&vid=5&hid=120.

3. Ibid., 23.

4. Laura Saunders and Mary Wilkins Jordan, "Significantly Different? Reference Services Competencies in Public and Academic Libraries," *Reference and User Services Quarterly* 52, no. 3 (2013): 216–23, accessed February 11, 2014, http:// web.a.ebscohost.com/ehost/pdfviewer/pdfviewer?vid=4&sid=526aa9b0-c2d3-40d6-bedb-59395785da78%40sessionmgr4003&hid=4107.

5. Penny M. Beile and Megan M. Adams, "Other Duties as Assigned: Emerging Trends in the Academic Library Job Market," *College and Research Libraries* 61, no. 4 (2000): 336–47, accessed January 10, 2014, http://web.ebscohost.com/ehost/detail?vid=9&sid=ec30ebe1-d7c9-4759-b7af-06acd1905c54%40sessionmgr111&hid=120& bdata=JnNpdGU9ZWhvc3QtbGl2ZSZzY29wZT1zaXRl#db=lls&AN=502850612.

6. JoAnne Deeken and Deborah Thomas, "Technical Services Job Ads: Changes since 1995," *College and Research Libraries* 67, no. 2 (2006): 143, accessed July 12, 2014, http://crl.acrl.org/content/67/2/136.full.pdf+html.

7. Janie M. Mathews and Harold Pardue, "The Presence of IT Skill Sets in Librarian Position Announcements," *College and Research Libraries* 70, no. 3 (2009): 255, accessed January 10, 2014, http://web.ebscohost.com/ehost/pdfviewer/pdfviewer?sid=6af7ca73-d76d-4fe3-87f9-b594cf4dae0f%40sessionmgr113&vid=2&hid=120.

8. Taryn Resnick, "Core Competencies for Electronic Resources Access Services," *Journal of Electronic Resources in Medical Libraries* 6, no. 2 (2009): 101–22, doi:10.1080/15424060902932185.

9. Isto Huvila, Kim Holmberg, Maria Kronqvist-Berg, Outi Nivakoski, and Gunilla Widen, "What Is Librarian 2.0—New Competencies or Interactive Relations? A Library Professional Viewpoint," *Journal of Librarianship and Information Science* 45, no. 3 (2013): 203, doi:10.1177/0961000613477122.

10. Pussadee Nonthacumjane, "Key Skills and Competencies of a New Generation of LIS Professionals," *IFLA Journal* 37, no. 4 (2011): 280–88, doi:10.1177/0340035211430475.

11. Ronald Martin Solorzano, "Adding Value at the Desk: How Technology and User Expectations Are Changing Reference Work," *The Reference Librarian* 54, no. 2 (2013): 89–102, doi:10.1080/02763877.2013.755398.

12. David Lee King, "Basic Competencies of a 2.0 Librarian, Take 2," *davidleeking.com*, accessed January 9, 2014, http://www.davidleeking.com/2007/07/11/basic-competencies-of-a-20-librarian-take-2/#.U_FJvfldWSp.

13. Stephen Abram, "Social Libraries: The Librarian 2.0 Phenomenon," *Library Resources and Technical Services* 52, no. 2 (2008): 19–22, accessed January 11, 2014, http://web.ebscohost.com/ehost/pdfviewer/pdfviewer?vid=22&sid=751831c1-1cab-4318-b014-72829bb5b8f2%40sessionmgr4004&hid=4112.

14. Danielle De Jager-Loftus, "Value-Added Technologies for Liaison and Outreach," *Journal of Electronic Resources in Medical Libraries* 6, no. 4 (2009): 307–15, doi:10.1080/15424060903364800.

15. Julie Lefevre and Terence K. Huwe, "Digital Publishing from the Library: A New Core Competency," *Journal of Web Librarianship* 7, no. 2 (2013): 190–214, doi:10.1080/19322909.2013.780519.

16. Randolph G. Bias, Paul F. Marty, and Ian Douglas, "Usability/User-Centered Design in the iSchools: Justifying a Teaching Philosophy," *Journal of Education for Library and Information Science* 53, no. 4 (2012): 274–89, accessed January 11, 2014, http://0-search.ebscohost.com.library.simmons.edu/login.aspx?direct=true&db=lls&AN=82056640&site=ehost-live&scope=site.

17. Nonthacumjane, "Key Skills and Competencies."

18. Emily F. Blankenship, "Who Holds the Keys to the Web for Libraries?" *Journal of Library Administration* 47, nos. 1–2 (2008): 55–66, doi:10.1080/01930820802110670.

19. Karen Sorensen and Nancy R. Glassman, "From Desktop to Cloud: A Primer on Internet-Based Computing for Librarians," *Journal of Electronic Resources in Medical Libraries* 8, no. 3 (2011): 243–55, doi:10.1080/15424065.2011.601991.

20. John W. W. Cyrus and Mark P. Baggett, "Mobile Technology: Implications for Privacy and Librarianship," *The Reference Librarian* 53, no. 3 (2012): 284–96, doi:10.1080/02763877.2012.678765.

21. Helen Partridge, Julie Lee, and Carrie Munro, "Becoming 'Librarian 2.0': The Skills, Knowledge, and Attributes Required by Library and Information Science Professionals in a Web 2.0 World (and Beyond)," *Library Trends* 59, nos. 1–2 (2010): 325, accessed January 11, 2014, http://0-muse.jhu.edu.library.simmons.edu/journals/library_trends/v059/59.1-2.partridge.html.

22. Ibid., 326.

23. Laura Saunders, "Professional Perspectives on Library and Information Science Education," *Library Quarterly* (forthcoming).

24. Meredith Farkas, "Skills for the 21st Century Librarian," *One-Person Library* 24, no. 10 (2008): 6, accessed January 11, 2014, http://web.ebscohost.com/ehost/pdfviewer/pdfviewer?vid=14&sid=751831c1-1cab-4318-b014-72829bb5b8f2%40sessionmgr4004&hid=4112 .

25. Cheryl Peltier-Davis, "Web 2.0, Library 2.0, Library User 2.0, Librarian 2.0: Innovative Services for Sustainable Libraries," *Computers in Libraries* 29, no. 10 (2009): 20, accessed January 11, 2014, http://web.ebscohost.com/ehost/pdfviewer/pdfviewer?vid=16&sid=751831c1-1cab-4318-b014-72829bb5b8f2%40sessionmgr4004&hid=4112.

26. Michael Stephens, "Into a New World of Librarianship: Sharpen These Skills for Librarian 2.0," *Next Space*, no. 2 (2006): 8, accessed January 11, 2014, http://

www.oclc.org/content/dam/oclc/publications/newsletters/nextspace/next-space_002.pdf.

27. Anthony S. Chow, Theresa L. Shaw, David Gwynn, Dan Martensen, and Margaret Howard, "Changing Times and Requirements: Implications for LIS Education," *LIBRES: Library and Information Science Research Electronic Journal* 21, no. 1 (2011): B1–B23, accessed January 12, 2014, http://web.ebscohost.com/ehost/pdfviewer/pdfviewer?vid=16&sid=beaa0ccd-9c64-4864-a232-d37df41f7e4e%40sessionmgr198&hid=123.

28. RASD Ad Hoc Committee on Behavioral Guidelines for Reference and Information Services, "Guidelines for Behavioral Performance of Reference and Information Service Providers," *Reference and User Services Association*, last updated May 28, 2013, accessed January 13, 2014, http://www.ala.org/rusa/resources/guidelines/guidelines-behavioral.

29. Michael Stephens, "Essential Soft Skills: Office Hours," *Library Journal* 138, no. 3 (2013): 39, accessed January 13, 2014, http://lj.libraryjournal.com/2013/02/opinion/michael-stephens/essential-soft-skills.

30. Mary Anne Kennan, Patricia Williard, and Concepcion Wilson, "What Do They Want? A Study of Changing Employer Expectations of Information Professionals," *Australian Academic and Research Libraries* 37, no. 1 (2006): 17–37, accessed January 12, 2014, http://web.ebscohost.com/ehost/pdfviewer/pdfviewer?vid=7&sid=beaa0ccd-9c64-4864-a232-d37df41f7e4e%40sessionmgr198&hid=123.

31. Megan Hodge and Nicole Spoor, "Congratulations! You've Landed an Interview: What Do Hiring Committees Really Want?" *New Library World* 113, nos. 3/4 (2012): 139–61, doi:10.1108/03074801211218534.

32. Lili Luo, "Toward Sustaining Professional Development: Identifying Essential Competencies for Chat Reference Service," *Library and Information Science Research* 30, no. 4 (2008): 298–311, doi:10.1016/j.lisr.2008.02.009.

33. Jody Condit Fagan and Christina M. Desai, "Communication Strategies for Instant Messaging and Chat Reference Services," *Reference Librarian*, nos. 79/80 (2003): 121–55, doi:10.1300/J120v38n79_09.

34. Patricia Montiel Overall, "Cultural Competence: A Conceptual Framework for Library and Information Science Professionals," *Library Quarterly* 79, no. 2 (2009): 189–90, accessed January 14, 2014, http://web.ebscohost.com/ehost/pdfviewer/pdfviewer?sid=6ec624b3-0635-4c03-a239-52ea956a0924%40sessionmgr110&vid=2&hid=123.

35. Paul T. Jaeger, John Carlo Bertot, and Mega Subramaniam, "Preparing Future Librarians to Effectively Serve Their Communities," *Library Quarterly* 83, no. 3 (2013): 243–48, accessed January 14, 2014, http://web.ebscohost.com/ehost/pdfviewer/pdfviewer?sid=6ec624b3-0635-4c03-a239-52ea956a0924%40sessionmgr110&vid=2&hid=123.

36. Charles Martell, "The Absent User: Physical Use of Academic Library Collections and Services Continues to Decline 1995–2006," *The Journal of Academic Librarianship* 34, no. 5 (2008): 400–407, doi:10.1016/j.acalib.2008.06.003.

37. Farkas, "Skills," 7.

38. Karen Okamoto and Mark Aaron Polger, "Off to Market We Go," *Library Leadership and Management* 26, no. 2 (2012): 1–20, accessed January 14, 2014, http://web.ebscohost.com/ehost/pdfviewer/pdfviewer?vid=5&sid=9b6e3b68-412e-4d15-b54f-765d1c335051%40sessionmgr112&hid=123.

39. Sharyn Wise, Maureen Henninger, and Mary Anne Kennan, "Changing Trends in LIS Job Advertisements," *Australian Academic and Research Libraries* 42, no. 4 (2011): 268–95, accessed January 14, 2014, http://web.ebscohost.com/ehost/pdfviewer/pdfviewer?vid=5&sid=9b6e3b68-412e-4d15-b54f-765d1c335051%40sessionmgr112&hid=123.

40. Myung Gi Sung, "Ten Essential Qualities for Success: A New Cataloging Librarian's Guide from a Supervisor's Perspective," *Public Libraries* 52, no. 3 (2013): 32–35,

accessed   January   17,   2014,   http://web.ebscohost.com/ehost/pdfviewer/pdfview-
er?vid=8&sid=ee6a7fb5-9495-491f-b2dd-a01a1b4a9bcc%40sessionmgr198&hid=124.

41. Saunders and Jordan, "Significantly Different?"

42. Betha Gutsche, "Coping with Continual Motion," *Library Journal* 135, no. 4
(2010):   28–31,   http://web.ebscohost.com/ehost/pdfviewer/pdfviewer?vid=9&
sid=ee6a7fb5-9495-491f-b2dd-a01a1b4a9bcc%40sessionmgr198&hid=4214.

43. Hanrong Wang, Yingqi Tang, and Carley Knight, "Contemporary Development
of Academic Librarianship in the United States: A 44-Year Content Analysis," *The
Journal of Academic Librarianship* 36, no. 6 (2010): 489–94, doi:10.1016/
j.acalib.2010.08.004.

44. Russell A. Hall, "Beyond the Job Ad: Employers and Library Instruction," *College and Research Libraries* 74, no. 1 (2013): 24–38, http://crl.acrl.org/content/74/1/
24.full.pdf+html.

45. Claudene Sproles and David Ratledge, "An Analysis of Entry-Level Job Ads
Published in *American Libraries*, 1982–2002," *Electronic Journal of Academic and Special
Librarianship* 5, nos. 2/3 (2004): 1, accessed July 12, 2014, http://southernlibrarian-
ship.icaap.org/content/v05n02/sproles_c01.htm.

46. Wise, Henninger, and Kennan, "Changing Trends," 281–82.

47. Kimberly Davies-Hoffman, Michelle Costello, and Debby Emerson, "Keeping
Pace with Information Literacy Instruction for the Real World," *Communications in
Information Literacy* 7, no. 1 (2013): 9–23, accessed January 15, 2014, http://
web.ebscohost.com/ehost/pdfviewer/pdfviewer?vid=11&sid=d01df386-d836-4d8d-
afcf-763453c87761%40sessionmgr111&hid=120.

48. Philip Russell, Gerard Ryder, Gillian Kerins, and Margaret Phelan, "Creating,
Sharing, and Re-Using Learning Objects to Enhance Information Literacy," *Journal of
Information Literacy* 7, no. 2 (2013): 60–79, doi:10.11645/7.2.1744.

49. "Association of College and Research Libraries Standards for Proficiencies for
Instruction Librarians and Coordinators," *Association of College and Research Libraries*,
June 24, 2007, accessed December 17, 2013, http://www.ala.org/acrl/standards/prof-
standards.

50. Amy C. York and Jason M. Vance, "Taking Library Instruction into the Online
Classroom: Best Practices for Embedded Librarians," *The Journal of Library Administration* 49, nos. 1/2 (2009): 197–209, doi:10.1080/01930820802312995.

51. Barbara A. Blummer and Olga Kristkaya, "Best Practices for Creating an Online
Tutorial: A Literature Review," *The Journal of Web Librarianship* 3, no. 3 (2009): 199–216,
doi:10.1080/19322900903050799.

52. Amy Dianne VanScoy, "Practitioner Experiences in Academic Research Libraries: An Interpretive Phenomenological Analysis of Reference Work" (PhD diss., University of North Carolina, Chapel Hill, 2010).

53. See, for example, Scott Walter, "Librarians as Teachers: A Qualitative Inquiry
into Professional Identity," *College and Research Libraries* 69, no. 1 (2008): 51–71, accessed   December   17,   2013,   http://web.ebscohost.com/ehost/pdfviewer/pdfview-
er?vid=5&sid=946b0586-841d-436f-8951-73dada676b44%40sessionmgr114&hid=128;
and Heidi Julien and Shelagh K. Genuis, "Librarians' Experience of the Teaching Role:
A National Survey of Librarians," *Library and Information Science Research* 33, no. 2
(2011): 103–11, doi:10.1016/j.lisr.2010.09.005.

54. Carol Tenopir, Ben Birch, and Suzie Allard, "Academic Libraries and Research
Data Services: Current Practices and Plans for the Future: An ACRL White Paper,"
Association of College and Research Libraries, June 2012, accessed January 16, 2014, http://
www.ala.org/acrl/sites/ala.org.acrl/files/content/publications/whitepapers/Teno-
pir_Birch_Allard.pdf.

55. ACRL Research Planning and Review Committee, "2012 Top Ten Trends in
Academic Libraries: A Review of the Trends and Issues Affecting Academic Libraries
in Higher Education," *College and Research Libraries News* 73, no. 6 (2012): 311–20,
accessed January 16, 2014, http://crln.acrl.org/content/73/6/311.full.

56. Li Si, Xiaozhe Zhuang, Wenming Xing, and Weining Guo, "The Cultivation of Scientific Data Specialists: Development of LIS Education Oriented to e-Science Service Requirements," *Library Hi Tech* 31, no. 4 (2013): 700–724, doi:10.1108/LHT-06-2013-0070.

57. Tenopir, Birch, and Allard, "Academic Libraries."

58. Si et. al., "Cultivation of Scientific Data Specialists."

59. Kristin Partlo, "The Pedagogical Data Reference Interview," *IASSIST Quarterly* 33/34, nos. 4/1 (Winter 2009/Spring 2010): 6–10, accessed January 17, 2014, http://web.ebscohost.com/ehost/pdfviewer/pdfviewer?sid=cbbdceb1-0116-4f9f-ae05-6544366636fc%40sessionmgr114&vid=2&hid=120.

60. Javier Calzada Prado and Miguel Angel Marzal, "Incorporating Data Literacy into Information Literacy Programs: Core Competencies and Content," *LIBRI: International Journal of Libraries and Information Science* 63, no. 2 (2013): 123–34, doi:10.1515/libri-2013-0010.

61. Eleanor J. Read, "Data Services in Academic Libraries: Assessing Needs and Promoting Services," *Reference and User Services Quarterly* 46, no. 3 (2007): 61–75, accessed January 17, 2014, http://0-search.ebscohost.com.library.simmons.edu/login.aspx?direct=true&db=lls&AN=502914035&site=ehost-live&scope=site; and Hailey Mooney and Breezy Silver, "Spread the News: Promoting Data Services," *College and Research Libraries News* 71, no. 9 (2010): 480–83, accessed January 17, 2014, http://web.ebscohost.com/ehost/pdfviewer/pdfviewer?sid=542a7287-a079-4fe1-a940-46c80ccc2573%40sessionmgr114&vid=2&hid=120.

62. RUSA Task Force on Professional Competencies, "Professional Competencies for Reference and User Services Librarians," *Reference and User Services Association*, January 26, 2003, accessed January 15, 2014, http://www.ala.org/rusa/resources/guidelines/professional.

63. "Association of College and Research Libraries Standards."

64. "ALA's Core Competences of Librarianship," *American Library Association*, January 27, 2009, accessed December 17, 2013, http://www.ala.org/educationcareers/sites/ala.org.educationcareers/files/content/careers/corecomp/corecompetences/finalcorecompstat09.pdf.

65. "Guidelines: Competencies for Special Collections Professionals," *Association of College and Research Libraries*, July 1, 2008, accessed December 17, 2013, http://www.ala.org/acrl/standards/comp4specollect#msa.

66. "Competencies for Information Professionals of the 21st Century," *Special Library Association*, last updated June 2003, accessed December 17, 2013, http://www.sla.org/about-sla/competencies.

67. Megan Oakleaf, *The Value of Academic Libraries: A Comprehensive Research Review and Report* (Chicago: ACRL, 2010), accessed December 18, 2013, http://www.ala.org/acrl/sites/ala.org.acrl/files/content/issues/value/val_report.pdf.

68. Blankenship, "Who Holds the Keys."

69. Farkas, "Skills."

70. Jane Kinkus, "Project Management Skills: A Literature Review and Content Analysis of Librarian Position Announcements," *College and Research Libraries* 68, no. 4 (2007): 352–63, accessed January 15, 2014, http://web.ebscohost.com/ehost/pdfviewer/pdfviewer?vid=3&sid=2cbb45fd-4292-4a2d-ba69-bac38a3faeda%40sessionmgr112&hid=123.

71. Jennifer Swanson, "Start Learning Project Management Skills," *Information Outlook* 17, no. 4 (2013): 18, accessed January 15, 2014, http://0-go.galegroup.com.library.simmons.edu/ps/retrieve.do?sgHitCountType=None&sort=RELEVANCE&inPS=true&prodId=AONE&userGroupName=mlin_b_simmcol&tabID=T002&searchId=R1&resultListType=RESULT_LIST&contentSegment=&searchType=AdvancedSearchForm&currentPosition=1&contentSet=GALE%7CA348998040&&docId=GALE|A348998040&docType=GALE&role=&docLevel=FULLTEXT.

72. Elan Harison and Albert Boonstra, "Essential Competencies for Technochange Management: Towards an Assessment Model," *International Journal of Information Management* 29, no. 4 (2009): 283–94, doi:10.1016/j.ijinfomgt.2008.11.003.

73. Cheryl Cuillier, "Choosing Our Futures . . . Still," *The Journal of Library Administration* 52, no. 5 (2012): 436–51, doi:10.1080/01930826.2012.700806.

74. Meredith Gorran Farkas, "Building and Sustaining a Culture of Assessment: Best Practices for Change Leadership," *Reference Services Review* 41, no. 1 (2013): 13–31, doi:10.1108/00907321311300857.

75. Mark Stover, "The Reference Librarian as Non-Expert: A Post-Modern Approach to Expertise," *The Reference Librarian*, nos. 87/88 (2004): 273–300, doi:10.1300/J120v42n87_10.

76. Solorzano, "Adding Value," 90.

77. VanScoy, "Practitioner Experiences."

78. David Kemp Maxfield, *Counselor Librarianship: A New Departure* (Chicago: University of Illinois, Occasional Papers, 1954), 19.

79. VanScoy, "Practitioner Experiences," 43.

80. Stover, "Reference Librarian."

81. Ibid.

82. Solorzano, "Adding Value," 97.

83. Lynn Westbrook, "Unanswerable Questions at the IPL: User Expectations of E-mail Reference," *Journal of Documentation* 65, no. 3 (2009): 367–95, doi:10.1108/00220410910952393.

84. Stover, "Reference Librarian," 281.

85. Kay Ann Cassell and Uma Hiremath, *Reference and Information Services in the 21st Century: An Introduction* (New York: Neal-Schuman, 2009).

86. Westbrook, "Unanswerable Questions."

87. Thomas A. Peters, "Left to Their Own Devices: The Future of Reference Services on Persona, Portable Information, Communication, and Entertainment Devices," *The Reference Librarian* 52, nos. 1/2 (2011): 95.

88. Westbrook, "Unanswerable Questions," 386.

89. Standards and Guidelines Committee, Reference and User Services Association, "Guidelines for Information Services," *Reference and User Services Association*, last updated July 2000, accessed December 18, 2013, http://www.ala.org/rusa/resources/guidelines/guidelinesinformation.

90. John H. Heinrichs and Jeen-Su Lim, "Emerging Requirements of Computer Related Competencies for Librarians," *Library and Information Science Research* 31, no. 2 (2009): 101–6, doi:10.1016/j.lisr.2008.11.001.

91. Vandana Singh and Bharat Mehra, "Strengths and Weaknesses of the Information Technology Curriculum in Library and Information Science Graduate Programs," *Journal of Librarianship and Information Science* 45, no. 3 (2012): 219–31, doi:10.1177/0961000612448206.

92. Julien and Genuis, "Librarians' Experience."

93. Ibid.

94. Claudene Sproles, Anna Marie Johnson, and Leslie Farison, "What the Teachers Are Teaching: How MLIS Programs Are Preparing Academic Librarians for Instructional Roles," *Journal of Education for Library and Information Science* 49, no. 3 (2008): 195–209, accessed December 17, 2013, http://web.ebscohost.com/ehost/pdfviewer/pdfviewer?vid=11&sid=946b0586-841d-436f-8951-73dada676b44%40sessionmgr114&hid=128.

95. Hall, "Beyond the Job Ad."

96. Marie R. Kennedy and Kristine R. Brancolini, "Academic Librarian Research: A Survey of Attitudes, Involvement and Perceived Capabilities," *College and Research Libraries* 73, no. 5 (2012): 431–48, accessed January 16, 2014, http://crl.acrl.org/content/73/5/431.full.pdf+html.

97. Ibid., 437.

FOUR

Thinking outside the Box

Entrepreneurship in Reference Service Provision

The future of libraries is a topic of continuing concern for practitioners, researchers, educators, and other community stakeholders. Librarians and information professionals have recognized that action is needed to reinvigorate libraries and librarian functions so that they are better utilized within their communities. Ingenuity and experimentation are crucial for ensuring that libraries and information organizations remain a priority within their cultural or institutional contexts, particularly when complexities in parent organizations, shifting strategic objectives, and competition for resources are the norm.

In May 2014 the invited participants at the American Library Association's Summit on the Future of Libraries discussed important issues and questions around reenvisioning the library and the values expressed in library services and accelerating library innovation.[1] Similarly, since August 2013 an ongoing conversation has been taking place for members of the Aspen Institute's Dialogue on Public Libraries Working Group, supported by the Bill and Melinda Gates Foundation, with the goal of "fostering concrete actions to support and transform public libraries for a more diverse, mobile and connected society."[2] Turning to efforts within academic and research libraries, the 2012 symposium of the greater New York metropolitan chapter of the Association for College and Research Libraries focused on cultivating entrepreneurship and ways for librarians to seek out "new opportunities for collaboration, innovation, and creative service offerings."[3] The aforementioned meetings (among others) were convened to catalyze library transformation broadly, which includes inspiring changes to reference services, and meetings to discuss innovating reference librarianship specifically have also taken place. For instance,

Reference Renaissance 2010, with the theme "Inventing Our Future," explored the evolving nature of reference and future possibilities.[4]

Parallel to these discussions, there is evidence of risk taking and an entrepreneurial spirit within libraries and information organizations, with notable innovations in libraries in general and in reference explicitly that have transformed library services and departments and librarian roles. This chapter investigates both innovation in libraries and innovation specific to reference service provision. To begin, descriptions of entrepreneurial reference services are presented alongside a discussion of the success factors that influenced the reference innovations, followed by an overview of innovation in libraries. Next, this chapter examines the concept of innovation as part of the curriculum in library and information science (LIS) graduate education as well as potential next steps for reference innovation.

DESCRIPTIONS OF INNOVATION IN REFERENCE SERVICES

For many libraries and information organizations, changes to transform library reference services—to make them current or relevant to the institution or stakeholders or to extend the librarians' reach—have primarily been small changes, such as consolidating service points, removing the physical reference desk from the library altogether, and capturing reference statistics using the latest software tools, like LibAnalytics.[5] Other libraries and information organizations are reconceptualizing what constitutes reference for the library and its users and the librarians' role in service provision and are offering something entirely novel.

The concept of entrepreneurship has a rich history and a wide range of meanings that are not visited here. Howard H. Stevenson of Harvard Business School provided one regularly referenced definition: "Entrepreneurship is the pursuit of opportunity without regard to resources currently controlled."[6] From this perspective, entrepreneurship is a process, and opportunity is the only real resource that either an organization or an individual has. An entrepreneur, according to management expert Peter F. Drucker, "sees change as the norm and as healthy [and] always searches for change, responds to it, and exploits it as an opportunity."[7] Following, descriptions of entrepreneurship in reference services are provided, with several examples of transformations to reference services organized in five groupings. These examples demonstrate libraries and information organizations that have developed an innovative service, devised a fresh method or solution, created a change of direction, or introduced a new technology or process to alter reference service provision.

Tackling False Claims

In today's information- and media-rich environment, using information resources to verify the accuracy of assertions of factual information—fact-checking—is a necessity. There are organizations and services dedicated to determining the correctness of information, such as Fact-Check.org of the Annenberg School for Communication at the University of Pennsylvania, PolitiFact.com of the *Tampa Bay Times*, and Snopes.com for "rumor research" on American popular culture. Librarians perform fact-checking in a variety of settings. For example, Katie Daugert, a librarian at National Public Radio (NPR), provided an overview of fact-checking practices in the context of NPR's reporting segments or talk shows, in which she explained that NPR librarians are embedded with different NPR programs to verify information (e.g., *All Things Considered*).[8] Also, the nonprofit membership organization Catalyst, a leading organization focused on expanding opportunities for women and business, employs a fact-checking specialist in its information center who helps to ensure that the organization is a trusted resource for research, information, and advice about women at work.[9]

One noteworthy, public library–initiated fact-checking program occurred around the U.S. presidential election in 2012. The Oak Park Library in Johnson County (Kansas) hosted a live watch party for the final presidential debate on October 22, 2012, and invited the library's community members to attend and actively participate by asking their questions about the accuracy of the presidential candidates' statements made during the debate.[10] During the live viewing, three reference librarians fact-checked more than ten questions posed by over sixty program attendees, using print and online information sources, Twitter streams, and bookmarked websites. The results of the librarians' fact-checking were projected on the library wall during the watch party.[11] When discussing the motivation for the program, Oak Park Library's reference librarian Louisa Whitfield-Smith explained that the public library is "uniquely positioned [to provide nonpartisan information] because [of librarians'] commitment to neutrality."[12] This example shows the slight twist on reference librarians' traditional question-and-answer service in that the reference activity was conducted in an open format for all participants to view the answers to the questions and because of the timeliness of the activity around a distinct topic and occurrence. More importantly, this example is distinctive because, while the librarians still had to wait for questions from information seekers, the library conceived and created an environment that facilitated the asking of questions.

Also in 2012, librarians from the Seattle Public Library's Business, Science, and Technology Department began serving as the official on-call fact-checking resource for the Living Voters Guide, an online, nonpartisan discussion forum of Washington State ballot measures. The forum was conceived as a place for Washingtonians to learn about ballot choices, express their values and concerns about political issues that affect their daily lives, explore common ground, and reach informed decisions. The Living Voters Guide[13] was created in 2010 as a partnership between the Seattle CityClub, a nonprofit organization committed to strengthening civic health, and computer science, communication, human-centered design, and political science researchers at the University of Washington, including one researcher who created the technical platform (ConsiderIt) to power the forum. The decision was made to incorporate the Seattle Public Library: "[Librarians] are a trusted nonpartisan resource, just like us. We wanted to create a space where people could have their voices heard as a community." In summary, the existing community partners welcomed librarian involvement to support the goals of the initiative.

Facilitated by the ConsiderIt technical platform, the Living Voters Guide encourages voters to think through the tradeoffs of a proposed ballot measure by allowing them to create a pro/con list that captures the important factors in their decision around a referendum topic (e.g., charter schools, same-sex marriage, university investments). Forum participants can also include into their own pro/con lists the points others have already contributed, thereby encouraging people to use the considerations of others to help them reach their own conclusions on crucial election issues.

As experts in finding information, reference librarians from the Seattle Public Library joined the Living Voters Guide to help people understand which statements are trustworthy. Any registered participant of the Liv-

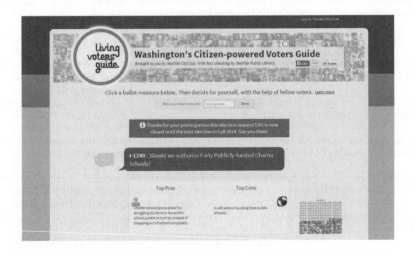

Figure 4.1.   Living Voters Guide. *Source: Living Voters Guide, accessed at https://livingvotersguide.org on June 22, 2014*

ing Voters Guide can use the "Request a fact check of this point" feature of the ConsiderIt technical platform to ask a librarian to do further research on claims made on any pro or con point contributed by others. In response, a librarian will post a fair, balanced, and complete description of the fact-checking results based on the information they locate and will include in the response relevant information and citations to the sources used to evaluate and/or substantiate the claim. Within forty-eight hours of the flagged claim, a librarian also assigns to each claim a status of either "Consistent with sources found," "Inconsistent with sources found, "Inconclusive given sources found," or "Outside the scope of the service."

Importantly, the librarians' fact-checks are accessible and visible to all users of the Living Voters Guide website and, as a result, demonstrate librarians' research skills to the public and widen the benefit of library services beyond the traditional one-to-one reference interaction. This partnership shows the Seattle Public Library's capacity to embed online reference successfully, support civic engagement, and help the library to connect with the community. An assessment of the reference component of the Living Voters Guide has demonstrated that there was significant demand for fact-checks, and at times librarians were challenged to respond to the requests.[14] Further, surveyed participants agreed with the librarians' analyses provided in the fact-checks and found value in them (74.3 percent strongly agreed or agreed). Participants also reported that they believed the librarians' fact-checks increased their understanding of the pro/con points and helped them become more generally informed about the ballot measure itself (80 percent strongly agreed or agreed). The same held true for users who were fact-checked (68.8 percent said fact-checks were "informative"). Lastly, and notably, the librarians' fact-checking service improved users' perceptions of the overall credibility of the Living Voters Guide (91.4 percent strongly agreed or agreed).

There may be other opportunities for librarians to employ fact-checking to extend the reach of their expertise in a similar way. However, it is worth noting that the success of the two services described here depended on several factors, including but not limited to:

- Librarians' Competencies: Librarians used their skills in finding, assessing, synthesizing, and communicating about authoritative and useful information sources and adhered to parameters for handling informational requests that have in-depth legal and/or financial aspects to them. For their work on the Living Voters Guide, the Seattle Public Library's reference librarians pointed the users to the research already conducted and only evaluated the factual components.[15]
- Technical Assessment: Librarians examined the role of technology involved in providing the service. In the case of the Living Voters

Guide, a predeveloped, sound technical infrastructure was built by technologists unaffiliated with the Seattle Public Library, though the reference librarians provided their insights and recommendations on the functionality of the ConsiderIt technical platform.[16]

* Collaboration: Librarians developed cooperative and mutually beneficial relationships with external community organizations or worked closely with internal departments (e.g., marketing) to implement the service.

Proactive Chat Reference

Traditionally, chat reference services in libraries are reactive to a user's request for assistance, requiring that the user seek out the librarian and initiate the interaction in a chat widget or comparable instant-messaging portal that is usually positioned on the library's website. In contrast, e-commerce services in a variety of industries outside of libraries and information organizations rely on trigger-initiated chat to proactively start conversations with customers, noting that such engagement leads to increased sale conversions. Trigger-initiated chat relies on predetermined conditions to commence proactive interaction with a website visitor, such as the amount of time spent on the website or the number of pages viewed, specific areas of the website viewed, the search terms or search channels used that led to the visit, or the location of the website visitor.

A few academic libraries are beginning to apply this business-oriented practice for their communities and report positive outcomes from implementing trigger-initiated chat. Jie Zhang and Nevin Mayer described the implementation of trigger-initiated chat for the Grasselli Library at John Carroll University, which serves approximately 4,000 FTE students and 380 faculty members.[17] Using the Zopim trigger-initiated chat software beginning in October 2012, librarians at the Grasselli Library saw a sizeable increase in the number of chat reference interactions. Of the library's 1,050 chat reference interactions that took place between October 2012 and March 2013, 70 percent were initiated by trigger, compared to the 30 percent that were initiated by information seekers, and an analysis of the users' questions found that the trigger-initiated chat reference interactions were more "reference and research related" than the user-initiated chats.[18] Zhang and Mayer noted that switching from reactive to proactive chat reference has had a positive impact in making the library's intended user communities aware of the availability of research consultation in the virtual domain.

At the Mamye Jarrett Library of East Texas Baptist University, trigger-initiated chat reference has similarly resulted in a dramatic increase in the number of chat reference interactions, according to information shared as part of the RSS/RUSA Management of Reference "New Models of Reference" e-forum held virtually on May 6 and 7, 2014.[19] Elizabeth Ponder, manager of instruction and information services at East Texas Baptist University, explained to e-forum participants that the library uses the SnapEngage software to proactively initiate an interaction with library users who have lingered on one of the library pages for more than forty-five seconds. The trigger-initiated chat engages the user with the statement "Hi, I'm an ETBU librarian. Can I help you find something?" Ponder also reported that the types of questions that librarians are handling during their chat reference interactions are more research oriented.

Overall, proactive chat reference accomplished through trigger-initiated software is akin to roving reference in an online environment and provides librarians the opportunity to reach digital information seekers in a modern way. While proactive chat reference does not change the medium or the substance of the user–librarian interaction, the novelty lies in connecting librarians with information seekers who may not have consulted the librarian using the traditional method of chat reference, either because the information seeker wasn't aware of the chat reference service offering, the information seeker was hesitant to consult the librarian for his or her information need, or for any other reason.

The initial success reported from the academic libraries that have adopted proactive chat reference service depended on four important and related factors:

1. Environmental Scanning: Librarians learned of trigger-initiated chat used in industries outside of libraries and information organizations and envisioned its potential for library-based reference.
2. Needs Assessment: Librarians evaluated the software and purpose for their respective organizational contexts, including user communities.
3. Technical Assessment: Librarians examined the software's technical features and devised and executed an implementation strategy to incorporate the software at their library.
4. Policy Development: Librarians devised protocols for handling and managing trigger-initiated chat reference interactions with library users.

As a result, the academic libraries identified in this section are seeing positive outcomes and replicating the success of the trigger-initiated chat software adopted from e-commerce in libraries and information organizations.

Personal Reference Services

Increasingly, public libraries are offering individual and personalized reference services, which in academic libraries are commonly referred to as research consultations or My Personal Librarian programming. For instance, the Arapahoe Library District, consisting of eight library branches and a mobile library service serving the south Denver metropolitan area in Colorado, provides library users with free, individualized thirty-minute sessions through their Book a Librarian service, and appointments can even be secured for library users whose language preference is Spanish or Russian.[20] In addition, the Arapahoe Library District's Book a Studio Librarian service is available for library users who have specific technical questions or require instructional support using GarageBand, podcasting tools, iMovie, and similar technologies for gaming or web design, music or video creation, and art and design.

A similar personalized reference service at the Sno-Isle Libraries in Washington, known as Book-A-Librarian, has been expanded to all twenty-one community public libraries to offer library users individualized assistance addressing their information needs, ranging from how to use the library's downloadable media to research fundamentals. The service was implemented as a response to customer input for increased library instruction, despite low turnout when classes were offered at the library on various days and times. The Sno-Isle Libraries have reported strong customer interest with the Book-A-Librarian service, with nearly three hundred sessions at the libraries in the first three months of 2012, and that the libraries have learned that customers value librarians' time, patience, and professionalism.[21] In general, personalized reference services are convenient for library users, as they can be arranged at a time that suits their needs, and ensure that the users receive the librarian's full attention. Another benefit of personalization is that the information seeker can be matched more closely to a librarian with expertise relevant to the information seeker's questions or interests.

The Multnomah County Library (Oregon) is taking this concept further in public libraries by making the virtual experience more personalized around a specific type of reference interaction—readers' advisory. The public library system launched My Librarian, a service that allows library users to build a relationship with one of thirteen librarians through video chats, blogs, and phone calls to discuss their favorite books and receive tailored reading suggestions. The librarians are not anonymous; every librarian maintains a blog to share what they have been reading, to curate reading lists, and to describe personal and professional interests. One goal of the service is to humanize the online interaction, as expressed by Library Director Vailey Oehlke, who distinguished the My Librarian service with readers' transactional experience through websites like Amazon.[22]

There are additional opportunities for developing novel personalized in-person or online reference services for librarians to handle general or very specialized topics and information seekers' questions. As is clear from the services explained here, two prominent success factors associated with offering personalized reference are:

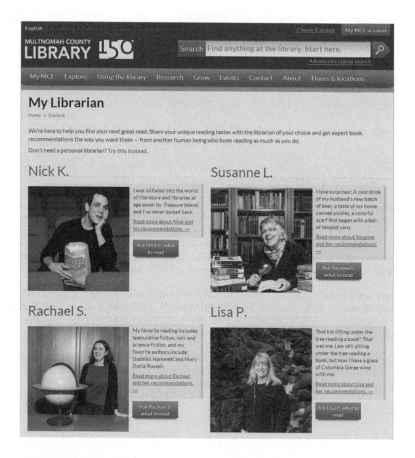

Figure 4.2. Multnomah County Library's My Librarian Service. *Source: Multnomah County Library*

1. Organizational Commitment: Librarians embraced the mission and purpose of the library as a service institution, dedicating a number of resources to build personal relationships with individual library users.
2. Knowledge of Community Needs: Librarians used their deep knowledge of library users to design and deliver targeted services that meet the informational and recreational needs of their communities.

Getting Out from Behind the Desk

Technologies afford librarians the ability to move out from behind the physical reference desk and interact with information seekers wherever they are, which may be inside or outside the walls of the library. Roving reference in public libraries have used Vocera badges and walkie-talkies for voice communication[23] and iPods to connect reference librarians and information seekers[24] while inside the library. Public and academic libraries who have embraced roving reference as a model of service provision have updated to tablets, such as iPads.[25] Further, academic librarians are setting up reference services in campus residence halls or dormitories (e.g., Purdue University)[26] and embedding chat widgets in course learning management systems to meet users where they are.[27] This mobility and flexibility on the part of the librarian helps library users realize that the library is relevant and current in meeting the technological advances of the twenty-first century.

In 2013, the Seattle Public Library launched a pilot program known as Books on Bikes, bringing library services to popular community events around the city of Seattle.[28] Along with their bikes, a team of librarians was equipped with a trailer holding print materials, a display rack, an umbrella, and an iPad. The librarians for the Books on Bikes program use the iPad for library card sign-ups in addition to answering users' reference questions and in particular questions about the library's electronic resources and ways to use the library's downloadable media. One benefit of the Books on Bikes offering is that it can be made available in places where bookmobiles would never fit. Further, the bikes provide librarians with the freedom to be outside mingling with existing and potential library users, allowing for more opportunities for interaction.

A final example of altering reference services in an effort to meet information seekers where they are is evident from a collaboration between WikiProject Australia and reference librarians at the National Library of Australia that has resulted in the placement of a link to the national Ask a Librarian service in Australian-specific Wikipedia articles.[29] The purpose of embedding a link to the asynchronous reference service is to more easily connect Wikipedia editors with librarians' information expertise and library collections as editors seek authoritative information sources to improve Wikipedia articles about Australia's cultural record. This collaboration between WikiProject and the National Library of Australia's Ask a Librarian service is distinguished because of its scale. According to Wikimedian Liam Wyatt, "it's a great precedent for the library community here (and also internationally) to see Wikimedians as a potential user group of their services that they *really* want to engage with. After all—answering a reference enquiry from one person helps that person, but answering a Wikipedian helps thousands!"[30]

The factors that appear to influence the success of librarians getting out from behind the desk depended on:

- Self-Assessment and Introspection: Librarians recognized that information seekers may not visit the library even though they could use the help of a librarian, and the librarians asked the difficult question, Where are we if not in the library?

- Willingness to Roam: Librarians demonstrated their readiness to work outside their comfort zone and be identified rather than seek refuge and remain anonymous behind a reference desk.
- Librarian's Competencies: Librarians used their interpersonal and communication skills, including active listening, assertiveness, friendliness, and sensitivity.

Self-Help Reference Tools

As was discussed in chapter 2, today's information seekers show a preference for self-help during information search with a proclivity for easy-to-use and accessible information sources. Four examples are presented in this section to demonstrate ways that libraries and information organizations have collected and disseminated information and knowledge via web interfaces to allow information seekers to self-help.

Answerland[31] is a 24/7 chat, e-mail, and text messaging reference service consortium consisting of thirty-seven Oregon libraries serving people who live, work, or attend school in Oregon (though they will answer questions about Oregon and local history for people who live outside of the state). As is standard for most reference services, users' questions and librarians' answers are not publicly available on Answerland. However, Answerland developed a Favorite Sites online portal[32] consisting of a search box allowing individuals to search the more than nine thousand freely available online information sources that Answerland librarians have shared with library users in their response to their reference questions received via chat, e-mail, and text messaging. Answerland's Favorite Sites only includes information resources that its librarians have shared with users at least two times, and with consideration of the volatility of the resources on the web, the portal's search function only searches sites shared in recent years. Making available librarians' recommended sources is a novel way to curate trustworthy information, as well as discern patterns about users' information needs, without affecting the privacy of individual user–librarian interactions.

Library Extension[33] is a uniquely different reference tool and serves as an example of librarians building tools to extend their reach and allow users to help themselves. As an information seeker browses book and e-book titles on Amazon, the Library Extension tool checks the person's library's online catalog and displays the availability of that title. If the book is available, the details will appear right on the page instantly with a quick link to the library. Library Extension promotes its service as easy and convenient to use, in particular when librarians aren't available or when a user prefers to locate materials independently.

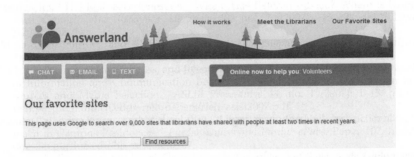

Figure 4.3. **Answerland's Favorite Sites** *Source: Answerland is supported in whole or part by the Institute of Museum and Library Services through the Library Services and Technology Act, administered by the Oregon State Library*

Another example in this grouping of self-help reference tools, the Orange County (Florida) Public Library System developed Right Service at the Right Time,[34] a virtual reference service in the form of a database-driven web application that connects people in need of government and nonprofit public services with the appropriate public services.[35]

As a final example, the Smithsonian is known for iconic objects in collections and exhibits but is also a place of scientific discovery, cultural exploration, and collaborative learning. The Smithsonian launched Questions Alive, part of the Seriously Amazing[36] portal, to showcase the deep research and resources in the Smithsonian Institution Libraries and museum collections across seven subject domains: world and universe, about America and storytelling, technology and creativity, animal kingdom, natural landscapes, artistic expression, and sharing culture. While the driver for this effort was an advertising campaign about the institution's identity, the portal provided by the Smithsonian evokes important scholarship and presents an open resource for information discovery, exploration, and learning.

Finding answers to thought-provoking questions is at the heart of the Smithsonian, questions including "What kind of 'fruit' was recently found on Mars?" and "How did learning French help the first African American pilot?" Some of the questions on Questions Alive have been asked by visitors of the Smithsonian. The answers to questions include links to longer articles and multimedia from the Smithsonian Libraries and archives and curatorial collections but do not contain any instructional component about how the answer was located. What makes Questions Alive unique is that it uses the organization's vast collections to enrich the question-asking and -answering process. By providing a dashboard of questions and answers, the Smithsonian is helping users to make "unexpected intellectual connections,"[37] even for users who didn't ask the question in the first place. Although the role of librarians in Ques-

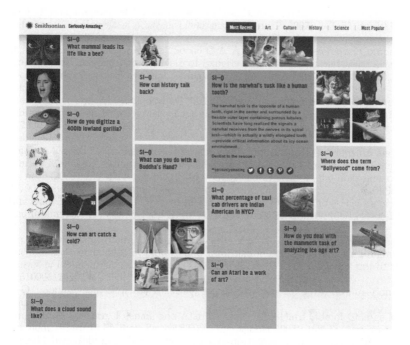

Figure 4.4.   Smithsonian Institution's *Seriously Amazing*. Source: *Smithsonian Institution*, accessed at http://seriouslyamazing.si.edu on June 22, 2014

tions Alive is never made explicit, the portal embodies the ethos of reference librarianship.

A notable feature of Questions Alive is social integration, which allows readers to share their discoveries via e-mail, Twitter, Facebook, Tumblr, and Pinterest. From a user experience perspective, the site is responsive and visually appealing in its presentation of content from the Smithsonian's collections and tweets from the museums' Twitter handles. Taken together, the social media integration and usability of the site allow users to navigate the content seamlessly and create their own collections of information.

There is a strong likelihood that information seekers' preference for self-help and inclination toward readily available and easily accessible information sources will continue into the future, which is important for librarians and information professionals to consider as they evaluate and make changes to their existing reference service offerings. Certainly, an advantage of affording information seekers to self-help with library information sources and channels is that the librarians' expertise is scaled to accommodate many more individuals than librarians can handle on a one-on-one basis. The self-help reference tools described here make apparent that the crucial success factors involved in this type of service provision include:

- Technical Expertise: Librarians used their advanced knowledge of interface design and system development or developed strong working relationships with technologists.
- Understanding of Design: Librarians utilized user-centered methodologies and techniques to design tools and interfaces required to serve the needs of their intended users.

DESCRIPTIONS OF INNOVATION IN LIBRARIES

In addition to the examples of innovative reference services, libraries and information organizations are transforming in other ways. Widespread library developments include, for example, *makerspaces* and similar participatory learning environments that provide access to materials, tools, and technologies for individual and collaborative tinkering, designing, inventing, and creating; centers of *digital scholarship* for the humanities and across disciplines, with efforts focused on leveraging computing and communication technologies for digital practices in the production, publication, curation, and use of scholarship for fundamental research and pedagogy; initiatives in *linked open data* aimed at designing or developing library infrastructure to enhance discoverability and interoperability of data, information, and knowledge; and *user experience* and the application of user-centered design principles for building usable, useful, and enjoyable library physical spaces and in-person interactions and digital interfaces and systems. These transformative changes, among others, are refining the identity of the library in our modern and evolving information age.

To promote a strategic culture for innovation and library renewal and to coordinate entrepreneurial efforts internally, some libraries and information organizations have established research and development (R&D) labs to conceptualize and launch novel, experimental library products and services. Harvard University has two centers of library innovation, the Harvard Library Lab and the Harvard Library Innovation Lab, poised to deliver scalable solutions to enhance library services. Harvard's labs projects include StackLife, a prototype of a community-based way-finding tool to navigate collections across Harvard's seventy-three libraries, and a geospatial mapping application to visualize, analyze, and prioritize library resource preservation needs.[38] Similarly, the New York Public Library's NYPL Labs is a cross-functional, experimental design and technology team working to reimagine the library's services, tools, and experiences. NYPL Labs projects include Map Warper, a resource that aligns historical maps to current digital maps to research New York City history, and What's on the Menu?, a culinary menu archive and crowd-sourcing project to "research the tastes, appetites, and social fabric of the past."[39] Other libraries and information organizations are readying for innovation and organizational success by hiring agents for change charged to lead thinking and visioning around ways to revitalize the library and its services and assigning them job titles like innovation catalyst librarian at the Trenton (New Jersey) Public Library and technology innovation librarian at the Nebraska Library Commission.

Further, hackathons or codefests are taking place at libraries and library technology conferences (e.g., Code4Lib, Access[40]), providing opportunities to explore new ideas and develop technical solutions. The Digital Public Library of America (DPLA) held an Appfest at the Chattanooga Public Library in November 2012 to derive ideas and functional examples of engaging ways to use the content and metadata in the DPLA back-end platform.[41] In the true spirit of hackathons, the process was open and the designs and draft code were shared on GitHub.[42] While it is difficult to determine the exact impact of this event, many of the ideas presented have certainly influenced the apps available as part of DPLA's platform and inspired further development.[43] Likewise, Mozilla's offices in Toronto held a fifty-four-hour hackathon event in April 2014 as part of the global Startup Weekend. Programming focused on challenges experienced by libraries and resulted in such developments as gesture-based way-finding technology for use in libraries, an application for parents to connect with the library and track reading milestones for children aged zero to five years, and a mobile tool to help college students select a library or learning space and determine the availability of student study space.[44]

Industries across business sectors are focused on shifting mind sets, seizing new opportunities, and thriving in a landscape of continual change, so it is unsurprising that libraries and information organizations are doing the same. Events like the DPLA Appfest and library hackathons are happening with increasing regularity, and professional organizations are beginning to recognize these and other innovative initiatives in libraries and information organizations. For instance, the Stanford Prize for Innovation in Research Libraries looks at "programs, projects, and/or new or improved services that directly or indirectly benefit readers and users" and awards and celebrates "functionally significant results of the innovative impulses in research libraries worldwide."[45] Also, the Urban Libraries Council's annual Innovation Initiative showcases libraries and information organizations that are adapting and leading "best" and "next" practices, ideas, and approaches.[46] In light of these initiatives and in this environment of openness and exploration, librarians and information professionals are primed to shape their future and the nature of their work in libraries in exciting and original ways.

Chapter 4

NEXT STEPS FOR REFERENCE INNOVATION

The examples described in this chapter illustrate librarians' search for new possibilities and their creativity directed at reimagining and delivering new library reference services. As was noted earlier, the success factors involved in these entrepreneurial reference services are manyfold, from organizational readiness and librarians prepared with the competencies needed to perform the new service to timing and ease of adoption by the libraries' user communities to available and flexible technologies and community entities for partnerships.

However, while the examples show that there is some movement toward bold ideas for reconceptualizing reference services, no paradigm shift is evident; rather, the examples point to incremental changes, and there are many opportunities and areas of untapped potential. For example, an environmental scan of existing library reference services determined that there are not any libraries found to be crowd-sourcing questions and answers. This is despite librarians' deep involvement in collaborative question-answering through Slam the Boards! since 2007[47] and librarians in the United Kingdom as part of the Enquire collaborative who have been a knowledge partner for Yahoo! Answers (UK and Ireland) since 2008, answering questions for the Q&A service.[48] Further, many library reference services still do not have a searchable, open repository of question answers to serve as a knowledge base that captures the expertise of the librarian and makes the information shared as part of the reference interaction available for reuse.[49]

Additionally, it appears that work undertaken on transforming libraries is concurrent with efforts to transform reference services: all of the examples of innovative reference described in this chapter were conceived independently and without any connection to a hackathon or R& D department, which rarely (if ever) focus exclusively on enhancing reference services. This is a missed opportunity, as revitalizing reference services should be part of the conversation around enhancing and modernizing libraries, not only because reference innovations need to be integrated with other library changes in order to increase their impact and ensure sustainability, but also because reference librarians have a role to play in makerspaces, linked open data initiatives, user experience projects, and the like. However, just making recommendations is not sufficient; ideas actually need to be developed and implemented, and the resulting project or tool needs to be tracked and tested to see if any change occurs. Without this assessment component, it won't be clear if improvements actually took place or the extent of its impact. Reference innovation is not just about getting more out of the reference services already offered—it is about an entirely new paradigm of reference.

Securing future changes to library reference services will require library and information professionals in practice who express future-oriented perspectives. In the curriculum of LIS graduate education, aside from student internships and practicum experiences (a requirement for some programs), there are few opportunities to teach new skills to prepare practitioners to be creative, risk-taking, and inventive professionals. Two examples from a review of the curriculum of ALA-accredited graduate LIS programs in the United States are "Innovation in Public Libraries" taught at Syracuse University and "Change Management" taught at the University of Illinois at Urbana–Champaign. The "Innovation in Public Libraries" course has students "identify, develop, and participate in new and creative approaches to and practices of public libraries," with assignments on environmental scanning, interviewing an innovator in the public library field, and conceptualizing an innovation for a library or to enhance services for a library community.[50] The "Change Management" course provides students with an awareness and understanding on the causes and nature of change across diverse organizations and focuses on "managing the impact of change, and [the] practical application of the tools and skills required to enable successful leadership in response to a rapidly changing workplace."[51] LIS educators need to be involved in conversations about "reskilling" and also in enhancing LIS education so that new graduates are prepared to take on new roles and those seeking to retool have the appropriate educational options available to them.

More is needed to develop entrepreneurial leaders with the necessary skills. As Luanne Freund learned from a survey of LIS graduate students, students are less likely to feel they are leaders or innovators at the time of graduation than they did when entering the program.[52] Freund suggests an emphasis on a "curriculum of practice" and an LIS school environment that is a place for exploration and experimentation, a place to test "wild ideas that fail" as part of the process for developing graduates who are truly ready to innovate once they reach the workplace. Outside of LIS, Harvard University's Graduate School of Design offers a course titled "Library Test Kitchen" that has resulted in prototypes for new library machines, architecture, and services to contribute to new directions for public and academic libraries.[53] The multidisciplinary approach and user-centered design methodologies central to the "Library Test Kitchen" course could serve as a model for LIS educators.

NO TURNING BACK

There are several exciting innovations in libraries and information organizations, though the truly transformative changes appear to be tangential to reference services. However, there are developments underway that point to reimagined reference services in academic and public libraries. Examples of these pockets of innovation are described in this chapter to demonstrate how librarians and information professionals are thinking outside of the box and implementing changes to traditional library reference services. Chapter 5 delves into environmental scanning, which is one method available to help librarians be proactive instead of reactive and to cultivate and act on their entrepreneurial spirits. In addition, LIS curriculum needs to keep pace with changes to prepare library and information science practitioners to lead future transformations for library reference services.

NOTES

1. Barbara Stripling, "Summit on the Future of Libraries," *ALA Connect,* last modified May 19, 2014, http://connect.ala.org/node/223667.

2. "Dialogue on Public Libraries: Communications and Society Program," *The Aspen Institute,* accessed June 17, 2014, http://www.aspeninstitute.org/policy-work/communications-society/our-work/dialogue-public-libraries.

3. "ACRL/NY Annual Symposium 2012: Cultivating Entrepreneurship in Academic Libraries," *Association for College and Research Libraries, Greater New York Metropolitan Chapter,* accessed June 16, 2014, http://acrlnysymp2012.wordpress.com.

4. Justine, "Call for Participation—A Reference Renaissance 2010: Inventing the Future," *LISWire,* February 3, 2010, http://liswire.com/content/call-participation-reference-renaissance-2010-inventing-future.

5. "LibAnalytics Insight," *Springshare,* accessed June 8, 2014, http://www.springshare.com/libanalytics.

6. Eric Schurenberg, "What's an Entrepreneur? The Best Answer Ever," *Inc.,* last updated January 9, 2012, http://www.inc.com/eric-schurenberg/the-best-definition-of-entepreneurship.html; and Thomas R. Eisenmann, "Entrepreneurship: A Working Definition," *HRB Blog Network* (blog), *Harvard Business Review,* January 10, 2013, http://blogs.hbr.org/2013/01/what-is-entrepreneurship.

7. Peter F. Drucker, *Innovation and Entrepreneurship: Practice and Principles* (New York: HarperBusiness, 2001), 27–28.

8. "NPR Librarian's Take on Fact-Checking and Research with Katie Daugert," Vimeo video, 54:47, 2012, posted by *NPR Digital Services,* accessed May 23, 2014, http://vimeo.com/43998624.

9. "Information Center," *Catalyst,* accessed May 19, 2014, http://www.catalyst.org/what-we-do/services/information-center.

10. "JoCo Librarians Fact Check Debate," YouTube video, 2:07, posted by NBCActionNews, October 22, 2012, https://www.youtube.com/watch?v=VsCCBiGRVeU.

11. Dave C., "Join Us for a Live Viewing of the Final Presidential Debate," *Johnson County Library,* last updated October 4, 2012, http://www.jocolibrary.org/templates/JCL_NewsListItem.aspx?id=24181&epslanguage=EN.

12. Mitch Weber, "JoCo Librarians Fact Check Presidential Debate," *KSHB-41 Action News Kansas City,* last updated October 22, 2012, http://www.kshb.com/news/political/joco-librarians-fact-check-presidential-debate.

13. "Living Voters Guide," *Seattle CityClub,* accessed April 11, 2014, https://livingvotersguide.org.

14. Travis Kriplean, Caitlin Bonnar, Alan Borning, Bo Kinney, and Brian Gill, "Integrating On-Demand Fact-Checking with Public Dialogue," presented at ACM Conference on Computer Supported Cooperative Work (CSCW), February 15–19, 2014, Baltimore, MD, accessed June 14, 2014, http://homes.cs.washington.edu/~borning/papers/kriplean-cscw2014.pdf.

15. Kriplean et al., "Integrating On-Demand Fact-Checking," 4.

16. Ibid.

17. Jie Zhang and Nevin Mayer, "Proactive Chat Reference: Getting in the Users' Space," *College and Research Libraries News* 75, no. 4 (2014): 202–5, http://crln.acrl.org/content/75/4/202.full.pdf+html.

18. Zhang and Mayer, "Proactive Chat Reference," 205.

19. Cinthya Ippoliti to ili-l@ala.org, April 22, 2014, RSS Management of Reference Committee Spring e-Forum: New Models of Reference (May 6–7, 2014), http://lists.ala.org/sympa/info/rss-eforum.

20. "Book A Librarian," *Arapahoe Library District*, accessed May 10, 2014, http://arapahoelibraries.org/book-a-librarian.

21. "Book-A-Librarian: Sno-Isle Libraries," *Urban Libraries Council*, accessed May 2, 2014, http://www.urbanlibraries.org/book-a-librarian-innovation-177.php?page_id=38.

22. Kelly House, "Your Own Personal Librarian: Multnomah County Library Allows Patrons to Pick Professional Book Advisors Online," *The Oregonian*, April 30, 2014, http://www.oregonlive.com/portland/index.ssf/2014/04/your_own_personal_librarian_mu.html.

23. Ellen Forsyth, "Fancy Walkie Talkies, Star Trek Communicators or Roving Reference?" paper presented at VALA—Libraries, Technology and the Future, Inc., February 5–7, 2008, Melbourne, Australia, accessed May 2, 2014, http://www.valaconf.org.au/vala2008/papers2008/148_Forsyth_Final.pdf.

24. "Retooling Reference for Relevant Service @ Dallas Public Library," *Urban Libraries Council*, accessed May 3, 2014, http://www.urbanlibraries.org/retooling-reference-for-relevant-service-dallas-public-library-innovation-151.php?page_id=38.

25. Fiona May, "Roving Reference, iPad-Style," *The Idaho Librarian: A Publication of the Idaho Library Association*, November 23, 2011, http://theidaholibrarian.wordpress.com/2011/11/23/roving-reference-ipad-style/; and Megan Lotts and Stephanie Graves, "Using the iPad for Reference Services: Librarians Go Mobile," *College and Research Libraries News* 72, no. 4 (2011): 217–20, http://crln.acrl.org/content/72/4/217.full.pdf+html.

26. Catherine Fraser Riehle and Michael Witt, "Librarians in the Hall: Instructional Outreach in Campus Residences," *Purdue University: Purdue e-Pubs*, paper 107, http://docs.lib.purdue.edu/lib_research/107.

27. "AskAway Chat Now in Moodle," *Emily Carr University of Art + Design Teaching and Learning Centre*, June 25, 2012, http://tlc.ecuad.ca/askaway-chat-now-in-moodle.

28. "Books on Bikes," *The Seattle Public Library*, accessed May 2, 2014, http://www.spl.org/using-the-library/library-on-the-go/books-on-bikes.

29. Renee Wilson, "Ask a Librarian: Now Virtually Everywhere!" *Behind the Scenes* (blog), *National Library of Australia*, May 7, 2014, http://www.nla.gov.au/blogs/behind-the-scenes/2014/05/07/ask-a-librarian-now-virtually-everywhere; and "Template: WikiProject Australia/AAL/What," *Wikipedia*, accessed June 12, 2014, http://en.wikipedia.org/wiki/Template:WikiProject_Australia/AAL/What.

30. The ed17, "'Ask a Librarian'—Connecting Wikimedians with the National Library of Australia," *Wikipedia: The Signpost*, May 14, 2014, http://en.wikipedia.org/wiki/Wikipedia:Wikipedia_Signpost/2014-05-14/News_and_notes.

31. *Answerland*, accessed April 28, 2014, http://www.answerland.org.

32. "Our Favorite Sites," *Answerland*, accessed April 28, 2014, https://www.answerland.org/our-favorite-sites.

33. *Library Extension*, accessed May 2, 2014, http://www.libraryextension.com.

34. "The Right Service at the Right Time," *Florida Department of State, State Library and Archives of Florida*, accessed May 2, 2014, http://www.rightservicefl.org.

35. Kathryn Zickuhr, "Innovative Library Services 'In the Wild,'" *Libraries in the Digital Age* (blog), *Pew Internet and American Life Project*, January 29, 2013, http://libraries.pewinternet.org/2013/01/29/innovative-library-services-in-the-wild.

36. "SI—Q," *Smithsonian: Seriously Amazing*, accessed April 26, 2014, http://seriouslyamazing.si.edu.

37. G. Wayne Clough, "What Does It Mean to Be Seriously Amazing?" *Smithsonian Magazine*, November 2012, http://www.smithsonianmag.com/arts-culture/what-does-it-mean-to-be-seriously-amazing-79778715/?no-ist.

38. "Harvard Library Lab: About the Library Lab," *Harvard University Library: Office for Scholarly Communication*, accessed June 3, 2014, https://osc.hul.harvard.edu/liblab; and "Harvard Library Innovation Lab," *The President and Fellows of Harvard College*, accessed June 2, 2014, http://librarylab.law.harvard.edu.

39. "NYPL Labs," *New York Public Library*, accessed May 26, 2014, http://www.nypl.org/collections/labs.

40. Margaret Heller, "Creating Quick Solutions and Having Fun: The Joy of Hackathons," *ACRL TechConnect* (blog), *Association of College and Research Libraries*, June 23, 2012, http://acrl.ala.org/techconnect/?p=1443.

41. "Appfest," *Digital Public Library of America*, accessed April 30, 2014, http://dp.la/wiki/Appfest; and "DPLA Appfest Hackathon in Chattanooga, TN," *Berkman Center for Internet and Society at Harvard University*, last updated October 17, 2012, http://cyber.law.harvard.edu/events/2012/11/dpla.

42. "Digital Public Library of America," *GitHub*, accessed May 14, 2014, https://github.com/dpla.

43. "App Library," *Digital Public Library of America*, accessed May 20, 2014, http://dp.la/apps.

44. Elena Yunusov, "Winners Announced for Toronto's Startup Weekend: Library Edition," *Betakit Canadian Startup News and Emerging Technology*, April 4, 2014, http://www.betakit.com/winners-announced-for-torontos-startup-weekend-library-edition; and Gary Price, "First 'Library Edition' of Startup Weekend Held in Toronto," *Info-Docket* (blog), *Library Journal*, April 4, 2014, http://www.infodocket.com/2014/04/04/first-library-edition-of-startup-weekend-held-in-toronto.

45. "Stanford Prize for Innovation in Research Libraries (SPIRL)," *Stanford University Libraries*, accessed June 5, 2014, http://library.stanford.edu/projects/stanford-prize-innovation-research-libraries-spirl.

46. "2014 Innovations Initiative," *Urban Libraries Council*, accessed June 5, 2014, http://www.urbanlibraries.org/innovations-pages-268.php.

47. "Slam the Boards!" *Answer Board Librarians*, accessed May 20, 2014, http://answerboards.wikifoundry.com/page/Slam+the+Boards%21.

48. "Enquire: Ask a Librarian 24/7," *OCLC*, accessed May 15, 2014, http://www.oclc.org/content/dam/oclc/services/brochures/213584ukf_enquire.pdf.

49. Scott Nicholson and R. David Lankes, "The Digital Electronic Warehouse Project: Creating the Infrastructure for Digital Reference Research through a Multidisciplinary Knowledge Base," *Reference & User Services Quarterly* 46, no. 3 (2007): 45–59, doi:10.5860/rusq.46n3.45.

50. Alison Miller, "IST 600 Innovation in Public Libraries Syllabus," *Syracuse University*, accessed May 10, 2014, http://my.ischool.syr.edu/Uploads/CourseSyllabus/Innovation%20in%20Public%20Libraries%20general%20syllabus-1142.46026-5b028c70-d85b-4154-a3f1-17f730fe5698.pdf.

51. "Graduate School of Library and Information Science Full Catalog, Course Information," *University of Illinois at Urbana-Champaign*, accessed June 12, 2014, http://www.lis.illinois.edu/academics/courses/catalog#500level.

52. "Luanne Freund—Innovation and Library Leadership Pecha Kucha," YouTube video, 6:59, from Changing Times, Inspiring Libraries Summit on December 6–7, 2012, posted by "BCLibraries," December 17, 2012, http://youtu.be/1BN8DSfsOcA.

53. Jeff Goldenson, Ann Whiteside, and Jessica Yurkofsky, with Jeffrey Schnapp, "GSD 09125: Library Test Kitchen III: Library Machines Working Syllabus," *Harvard University*, accessed May 22, 2014, http://www.librarytestkitchen.org/assets/LTK-III-Syllabus_august.pdf.

FIVE

Leveraging Environmental Scanning for Repositioning

Throughout the earlier chapters, examples of change in the world around us have been given, primarily changes in information and communication technologies. The availability of new tools and information resources has resulted in changes to the expectations, preferences, and information behaviors of information seekers. Edward L. Ayers notes that "we have grown accustomed to a head-spinning pace of technological and social change. Innovations that would have amazed us ten years ago are now merely passing news."[1]

Not only are we experiencing constant change, but also the speed of change in information and communication technologies has greatly accelerated over time. Michael DeGusta presented data that documents the speed with which technologies are spreading.[2] He focused on the market penetration of nine technologies and the time it took them to reach saturation, which is the time it takes to go from 40 to 75 percent of the market. While it took almost a century for landline telephones to reach saturation, mobile phones achieved saturation in twenty years. Degusta predicts that smartphones will likely halve that time, and tablets may reach saturation even faster yet.

According to Twitter's blog, the first tweet was sent on March 21, 2006, and it took "3 years, 2 months and 1 day" to reach the billionth tweet.[3] By 2011, five years after the first tweet was sent, Twitter had 100 million active users. This is another example of the fact that, not only are we experiencing change in the way we communicate, but also the rate of change has greatly accelerated. Librarians need to monitor the environment, synthesize trends, and quickly assess and make decisions regarding new and existing services. A willingness to try and fail or change midstream is essential in the quick-moving environment around us.

These changes have in turn resulted in changes in the use of libraries, including a decline in traffic at the physical reference desk that are described in chapter 2. Yet, as is noted in earlier chapters, reference services have changed primarily in the modes of delivery but not in the nature of the service. In other words, libraries and reference services specifically have not kept pace with the monumental and rapid changes around us. However, as is seen in chapter 4, there are some examples of innovative services in libraries of all types. Such innovative practices as those highlighted in chapter 4 need to become the norm for librarians and information professionals. As Brian Mathews noted in his white paper, "what we really need right now are breakthrough, paradigm-shifting, transformative and disruptive ideas."[4]

This chapter introduces the concept of environmental scanning as a method that librarians and information professionals can use to identify trends to position themselves for the future, being proactive rather than reactive. Following the description of the process, an environmental scan is presented to demonstrate how librarians can go from identifying trends to creating innovative services, including some that are described in chapter 4.

A METHOD FOR MONITORING CHANGE: ENVIRONMENTAL SCANNING

Given the changes in information and communication technologies and the impact they have on library and information services, it is essential that librarians and information professionals stay abreast of trends and emerging trends and technologies, not only those applied in libraries and information centers but also in any field or discipline. Applying a new process, solution, or information technology that has been successful in other disciplines or industries will help move librarianship forward in innovative ways. Environmental or external scanning is one approach for routinely monitoring trends.

Environmental scanning is an ongoing process that includes both an internal environmental assessment and an external environmental scan. The internal environmental assessment identifies strengths and weaknesses of the organization. The external environmental scan identifies opportunities and threats in the environment. This analytical process helps organizations keep current with the external forces relevant to the institution, such as economic, social, and political trends and events. The results of environmental scanning provide administrators with the information needed for decision making and planning for the future.[5] Research suggests that environmental scanning improves the performance of an organization.[6] The strengths and weaknesses identified within the organization, along with the opportunities and threats in the external environment, may be used as the basis for a SWOT (strengths, weaknesses, opportunities, threats) analysis that is discussed later in this chapter.

Overview of the Environmental Process

John M. Bryson[7] outlines general steps for conducting an environmental scan based on a process presented by Pflaum and Delmont.[8] The following expands the steps recommended and then provides details on each step:

- Assess internal strengths and weaknesses.
- Identify the purpose, participants, and time constraints of the environmental scanning activity.
- Identify key issues.
- Select resources to include in the scan.
- Carry out the scanning activities.
- Analyze and interpret the strategic importance of issues and trends.
- Create information for decision making.
- Assess decisions.

Assess Internal Strengths and Weaknesses

An initial activity to be conducted prior to or along with the external scanning is an internal assessment of strengths and weaknesses. Without knowing the strengths and weaknesses of the organization, it will not be possible to take advantage of opportunities or to minimize threats. Generally, the internal assessment focuses on inputs and outputs. Inputs include the number of employees, budgets for wages, supplies, equipment, facilities, and resources. Outputs include the services offered or the products produced. In a library, outputs might include the number of databases available, number of consultations of each database, hours of operation, number of patrons visiting the facilities, pathfinders created, books circulated, reference questions asked and answered, and a technology inventory.

When examining internal inputs and outputs, strengths and weaknesses will come to light. Strengths could include a unique product or service, the unique skill set of staff members, or the high quality of a product or service. Weaknesses could include a lack of quality or poor customer service, a lack of access to resources, or undifferentiated products or services. Once the external scan begins, these strengths and weaknesses will be brought into the analysis.

Identify the Purpose, Participants, and Time Constraints of the
Environmental Scanning Activity

In keeping with the theme of this book, the overall objective or purpose of environmental scanning is to identify trends and technologies
that can be applied for the continual repositioning of reference services
provided by librarians and information professionals. Note that the focus
is on services provided *by* librarians and information professionals and
not *in* libraries and information centers. Environmental scanning is
meant to assist librarians in thinking beyond the reference desk and even
outside of the library as they imagine and create innovative and entrepreneurial initiatives.

Environmental scanning activities are most effective if undertaken by
a team of staff members with a team leader. However, environmental
scanning is crucial even in a one-person library or information center.
Regardless of the setting, external scanning provides insights for planning for the future. Scanning needs to be considered as part of the work
obligations of individuals or team members.[9] While environmental scanning may seem to be peripheral to one's job responsibilities, it is in fact
essential to future success. Regardless of the level of environmental scanning put into place, the efforts must be ongoing and routine for the organization. Without these efforts, opportunities will be missed, and as
Bryson notes, the organization "will be in a reactive rather than anticipa-
tory position."[10] The missed opportunities may result in an organization's failure to succeed.

Identify Key Issues

An important step in environmental scanning is the identification of
external events that impact an industry. As one prepares the plan for an
environmental scan, common areas to consider include competitors, technology, regulatory activity, political events, and the economy. While the
range of topics or key issues selected will depend upon the library or
information center and the resources available to conduct the scan, for
repositioning reference services, all scans need to focus on:

- Competitors,
- Information users, and
- Information technology.

These categories need to be viewed from the broadest perspective
possible. Competitors would include any organization or individual offering access to information or services similar to those provided by libraries and information organizations. Monitoring activities of competitors and new product launches is ongoing. In many ways, the new and
emerging technologies are competitors to libraries in that they present
information seekers new ways of finding, organizing, storing, creating,

and sharing information. Notice that the focus is on information users and not on library users, as all individuals seek and use information but do not necessarily use the library or consult with a librarian.

Because this is an ongoing process, there are events that will have an impact on the external environment. Changes in regulations may be important to some librarians in terms of the services that they provide. Predictable periodic events, such as elections that may have an impact on budgets and information service provision, need to be monitored. Then, there are other events that are unpredictable and may have far-reaching and enduring impacts. These become part of the environmental scan when they occur. In 2013, for example, when the government shut down, citizens were left without access to resources from libraries, archives, museums, and government agencies for weeks.

Select Resources to Include in the Scan

The next step involves the selection of resources to scan. The number and range of resources will vary upon the level of scanning being undertaken, and it is an iterative process. These resources will provide information that will be used to chart the future course of the organization. The resources may include research studies, newspapers, magazines, journal literature, demographic data, benchmarking initiatives, blogs, wikis, websites, and Twitter feeds. For each item selected, the frequency of scanning needs to be determined. Lists of resources need to be monitored by their useful contributions to the scan. New resources may be identified, and items on the list may be removed.

Research studies and reports are time-saving resources in that they often provide environmental scans and analysis of data. Some reports lend themselves best to particular types of libraries and information centers. For example, the New Media Consortium (NMC), a community of hundreds of leading universities, colleges, museums, and research centers, produces the Horizon Project.[11] This report, which identifies and describes emerging technologies likely to have a large impact over the coming five years in higher education, is a key resource for academic librarians. Another useful report for academic settings is Ithaka S+R,[12] cited in chapter 1. Ithaka is a research and consulting firm helping organizations transition into the digital world. Universities, libraries, museums, and scholarly publishers are part of their target audience.

There are other trend reports that will be most helpful to public libraries. The American Library Association (ALA) produces a variety of reports on trends on a regular basis, including the annual *State of America's Libraries Report*[13] that presents facts and figures for public libraries, school libraries, and academic libraries along with other general trends in libraries. One section of the ALA website focuses on advocacy, legislation, and issues.[14] Associations in general are excellent resources for the identification of trends and technologies through their websites, social media outlets, and conferences.

Other organizations prepare reports that are of interest to all types of libraries and information professionals. The *IFLA Trend Report*[15] identifies trends that "shape the information society." The Pew Internet Research Project[16] conducts regular surveys related to the evolution of the Internet and the impact of the Internet on the general public. OCLC Research[17] produces a variety of reports of interest to librarians and information professionals. Its membership reports[18] include in-depth research as well as surveys on a variety of topics and issues. OCLC also produces *Above the Fold*[19] to expose readers to literature that they might not encounter on a regular basis. Written from a business perspective, Forrester Research identifies technological trends that can help librarians think more broadly.[20]

In addition to these reports that are updated at least annually, several associations and organizations will issue environmental scans from time to time. For example, the Association of College and Research Libraries (ACRL) produced *Environmental Scan 2013* based on a two-phase project. Its purpose was to "support the planning and positioning of academic libraries for the future."[21] In 2003, OCLC produced *Environmental Scan: Pattern Recognition*, which identified issues and trends having an impact on libraries, museums, archives, and other related fields.[22]

Depending upon the scope of the environmental scan, a list of resources can be compiled, including some of the reports mentioned here and other resources, including:

- News outlets, such as the *New York Times*,[23] the *Wall Street Journal*,[24] and the *Chronicle of Higher Education*[25];
- Magazines, either print or electronic, including, among others, the *MIT Technology Review*,[26] which identifies and reviews emerging technologies and analyzes their impact;
- Conferences or proceedings, such as entrelib: The Conference for Entrepreneurial Librarians,[27] Computers in Libraries,[28] Internet Librarian,[29] and Association for Computing Machinery[30];
- Association websites, including American Library Association,[31] Special Libraries Association,[32] and EDUCAUSE[33];
- Blogs, such as ACRLog[34] and Harvard Library Innovation Lab[35]; and
- Twitter hashtags, for example, #libchat or #innovation.

Because of the importance of currency, scanning some resources that are updated at least once a day is important to complement annual or quarterly reports. As thought leaders are identified, their Twitter feeds, blogs, or other publications can be added to the list. The appendix contains a spreadsheet of resources that have been used for environmental scanning for reference services.

Carry Out the Scanning Activities

Scanning activities can range from very simple to very complex. In a simple environmental scan, keeping up with news and the literature may be sufficient. Environmental scanning does not involve searching for specific terms but rather scanning the selected resources to identify trends. It is not possible to search because trends emerge. In many ways, scanning is about "knowing it when you see it." Having questions in mind will help to shape the scanning process: What information technologies are information users adopting? What issues arise with the use of the new technologies? Where can information seekers obtain answers to questions? What kinds of resources are information users consulting? What factors influence information seeking? What new technologies are other industries adopting? What will the next disruptive technology be? What innovative features are competitors adding to their products?

Analyze and Interpret the Strategic Importance of Issues and Trends

Once the scanning is underway, some type of system is needed to track findings. This can be as simple as a list, a short report on each reading of interest, a spreadsheet, or a database. The key is to determine the potential strategic importance of the various trends. Techniques can range from informal brainstorming to scenario building or any of a variety of strategic planning techniques available.[36] Ann M. Pflaum and Timothy J. Delmont suggest three courses of action for each item scanned: (1) a trend worthy of specific future scanning, (2) a trend that requires action, and (3) a trend that can be dropped from further consideration.[37] Tracking these trends is important because a trend that is rejected today may come back in the future and due to circumstances be worthy of consideration at that time.

For issues and trends that require additional information, the information-gathering technique changes. At this point, targeted searching is performed on the specific trend. The search would likely go beyond the sources used for scanning, including an organization's website and databases.

Trends that are either worthy of additional scanning or those that require action become part of a SWOT analysis. This draws on the internal assessment described earlier. The selected trends that represent opportunities and threats are placed in the context of the specific organization in terms of the *strengths* and *weaknesses* of the organization based on the internal assessment of inputs and outputs. In many cases, a trend will be an opportunity if the organization is poised to take advantage of it, and it will be a threat if the organization is too weak to capitalize on it.

During this analysis, four different strategies may emerge, as strengths and weaknesses are associated with opportunities and threats. These strategies are described here:

Strength—Opportunity: In this case, opportunities match the strengths of the organization. This is highly desirable, as the organization is well positioned to take advantage of the opportunity.

Weakness—Opportunity: On occasion, the environmental scan might reveal an opportunity that the organization cannot take advantage of due to its weaknesses. This is problematic because the organization is not in a good position to take advantage of the opportunity.

Strength—Threat: In this case, the organization is in a good position to deal with the threat and can reduce its vulnerability because of its strength. This is a nonproblematic situation for the organization.

Weakness—Threat: Of all of the situations, this is clearly the most challenging, as the organization is not in a strong position to deal with the threat. This is a distressing situation for the organization.

To help in the analysis, the trends may be placed on a SWOT matrix, shown in figure 5.1.

Create Information for Decision Making

The key to environmental scanning is to create actionable information. There are various options to accomplish this. Issue or trend summaries may be created and distributed to stakeholders. Regular newsletters can be created and distributed. However, distribution of the information is not sufficient. Follow-up discussions that result in action items will help move the organization in the right direction.

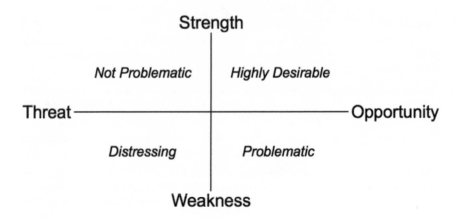

Figure 5.1.   SWOT Matrix

This is a continual process as is stated earlier because new technologies, trends, service models, and solutions will emerge constantly. Decisions need to involve all constituencies, making the idea of a newsletter or blog an attractive means of keeping them informed.

Assess Decisions

Environmental scanning, coupled with interaction with constituencies, positions a library or information center to provide the most valuable services. However, decisions made on the basis of the environmental scan need to be assessed. Is the new service or product meeting the intended need? Are the users of the service satisfied? Is the new service or product achieving the stated objectives? Is the service or product providing value? Librarians need to know what the goals of the new service are and then plan to collect data to determine if they are meeting those goals, using these questions as a guide. If they are meeting the goals, they might set new goals. If they are not meeting their goals, they need to determine why and decide whether to change their approach, reallocate resources, or discontinue the service.

MONITORING TRENDS AND EMERGING TECHNOLOGIES FOR LIBRARIES: A SAMPLE ENVIRONMENTAL SCAN

Some librarians have made environmental scanning part of their daily work for quite some time. Leigh Buchanan described this process at Highsmith in 1999. She noted that the president and CEO of the company met for two hours twice a week with the librarian to "sift through stacks of articles" on a wide range of topics. The purpose of these efforts was to identify "nascent trends, provocative contradictions, and most important, connections that could eventually reshape his business."[38]

The innovative services described in chapter 4 also provide evidence that librarians are engaging in environmental scanning. These services can be linked to trends that have been reported in the resources described earlier, demonstrating the power of scanning the environment to advance libraries and information services. Table 5.1 links some of the innovative services in chapter 4 to trends that are identified in these resources. The items in the table are organized by the date that the trend was identified, starting with the earlier trends. As appropriate, multiple resources are listed to show that trends can be identified at different times by different resources and some resources track trends on a regular basis. Finding that a trend is listed in multiple sources or that it appears year after year helps to solidify the notion that this is a long-term trend rather than a temporary one.

In his white paper that was posted in 2012, Brian Mathews reflected on the adoption of new technologies.[39] Consider the following reflections

Table 5.1.   Environmental Scan: Mapping Trends to Library Innovation

Date and Source(s)	Trend	Innovative Service
2005 Pew Research Internet Project[1] 2012 Pew Research Internet Project[2] 2014 Horizon Report 2014[3]	Self-serve Self-tracking Quantified self	Self-help reference tools
2008 Mashable[4] 2009 Nielsen[5] 2010 Pew Research Internet Project[6] 2011 Pew Research Internet Project[7] 2013 Pew Research Internet Project[8] 2014 Horizon Report[9]	Ubiquity of social media	Questions Alive (Smithsonian)
2012 Computerworld[10] 2012 Horizon Report[11] 2014 EDUCAUSE[12]	Gesture-based computing	Gesture-based way- finding
2012 Horizon Report[13] 2013 Horizon Report[14]	Tablet computing	Roving reference using tablets
2012 Horizon Report[15] 2012 Forbes[16]	Mobile apps	Codefests and appfests
2012 Horizon Report[17] 2014 Pew Research Internet Project[18]	Internet of Things	Full potential still to be realized
2013 ACRL[19] 2014 Horizon Report[20]	Shift to creators of information	Makerspaces
2013 Horizon Report[21] 2014 Horizon Report[22]	3D printers	Makerspaces

1. Lee Rainie, Susannah Fox, and Janna Anderson, "The Predictions and Respondents' Reactions," *Pew Research Internet Project*, January 9, 2005, http://www.pewinternet.org/2005/01/09/the-predictions-and-respondents-reactions.
2. Susannah Fox, "What's the Future for Self-Tracking?" *Pew Research Internet Project*, March 9, 2012, http://www.pewinternet.org/2012/03/09/whats-the-future-for-self-tracking-2.
3. Larry Johnson, Samantha Adams Becker, Victoria Estrada, and Alex Freeman, *NMC Horizon Report: 2014 Higher Education Edition* (Austin, TX: The New Media Consortium, 2014).
4. Adam Ostrow, "My 2008 Predictions Rocked; So What's on Tap for Next Year?" *Mashable*, December 29, 2008, http://mashable.com/2008/12/29/2009-tech-predictions.
5. "Global Faces and Networked Places: A Nielsen Report on Social Networking's New Global Footprint," *Nielsen*, March 2009, http://www.nielsen.com/content/dam/corporate/us/en/newswire/uploads/2009/03/nielsen_globalfaces_mar09.pdf.
6. "Global Publics Embrace Social Networking," *Pew Research Internet Project*, December 15, 2010, http://www.pewinternet.org/2010/12/15/global-publics-embrace-social-networking.
7. Mary Madden and Kathryn Zickuhr, "65% of Online Adults Use Social Networking Sites," *Pew Research Internet Project*, August 26, 2011, http://www.pewinternet.org/2011/08/26/65-of-online-adults-use-social-networking-sites.
8. Maeve Duggan and Aaron Smith, "Social Media Update 2013: 42% of Online Adults Use Multiple Social Networking Sites, but Facebook Remains the Platform of

Choice," *Pew Research Internet Project*, December 30, 2013, http://www.pewinternet.org/2013/12/30/social-media-update-2013.

9. Johnson et al., *NMC Horizon Report: 2014*.

10. Jonny Evans, "Apple's Next Innovation: 3D Gesture-Based Computing Puts the 'Post' in Post-PC," *AppleHolic* (blog), *Computerworld*, August 10, 2012, http://blogs.computerworld.com/mac-os-x/20821/apples-next-innovation-3d-gesture-based-computing-puts-post-post-pc.

11. Larry Johnson, Samantha Adams, and Michele Cummins, *NMC Horizon Report: 2012 Higher Education Edition* (Austin, TX: The New Media Consortium, 2012).

12. "7 Things You Should Know about Gesture-Based Computing," *EDUCAUSE Learning Initiative (ELI)*, January 8, 2014, http://www.educause.edu/library/resources/7-things-you-should-know-about-gesture-based-computing.

13. Johnson, Adams, and Cummins, *NMC Horizon Report: 2012*.

14. Larry Johnson, Samantha Adams Becker, Michele Cummins, Victoria Estrada, Alex Freeman, and Holly Ludgate, *NMC Horizon Report: 2013 Higher Education* (Austin, TX: The New Media Consortium, 2013), http://www.nmc.org/pdf/2013-horizon-report-HE.pdf.

15. Johnson, Adams, and Cummins, *NMC Horizon Report: 2012*.

16. Eric Savitz, "Gartner: Top 10 Strategic Technology Trends for 2013," *Forbes*, October 23, 2012, http://www.forbes.com/sites/ericsavitz/2012/10/23/gartner-top-10-strategic-technology-trends-for-2013.

17. Johnson, Adams, and Cummins, *NMC Horizon Report: 2012*.

18. Janna Anderson and Lee Rainie, "The Internet of Things Will Thrive by 2025: Many Experts Say the Rise of Embedded and Wearable Computing Will Bring the Next Revolution in Digital Technology," *Pew Research Internet Project*, May 14, 2014, http://www.pewinternet.org/2014/05/14/internet-of-things.

19. ACRL Research Planning and Review Committee, "Environmental Scan 2013," *Association of College and Research Libraries*, April 2013, http://www.ala.org/acrl/sites/ala.org.acrl/files/content/publications/whitepapers/EnvironmentalScan13.pdf.

20. Johnson et al., *NMC Horizon Report: 2014*.

21. Johnson et al., *NMC Horizon Report: 2013*.

22. Johnson et al., *NMC Horizon Report: 2014*.

from Mathews in light of the trends identified in table 5.1. According to Mathews, at that time, if a library was planning a Facebook page, it was lagging behind. If the library was offering text reference, it was part of the late majority at that time. However, if the library was building visualization services, it would be considered an early adopter. An innovation service according to Mathews would be one that experimented with 3D printing. Horizon identified 3D printing as a technology to adopt in the next two to three years. While the Horizon Report identified 3D printing in the 2014 edition, Mathews recognized the potential of 3D printing in his 2012 white paper.

An examination of the trends in table 5.1 provides insight into the environmental-scanning process and the benefits of identifying trends that are appropriate for a particular library or information organization and its users in terms of the creation of innovation services or products.

Self-Serve

As is discussed in chapter 2, the self-serve trend has been emerging for quite some time with the desire of members of the general public to do things by themselves, whether it is banking, arranging for travel, pumping gasoline, shopping, or finding information. The trend has been referred to as self-serve, self-help, and DIY (Do It Yourself). In table 5.1, another term, *quantified self*, is included. This refers to the trend for individuals to track and measure their health and physical activities using wearable technology. The self-serve trend relates closely to the 24/7 trend, the expectation that services are available every day of the week and every hour of the day. Chapter 2 includes a discussion of the popularity of search engines or search tools that have made information self-help the primary way that most Americans find information. According to Pew, search engines have been popular since 2002.[40] Chapter 4 dedicates a section to self-help reference tools, showing that librarians have embraced the self-help trend. Rather than trying to restrict access to information seekers, librarians have created searchable websites, database-driven web applications that connect people to information and services, and searchable knowledge bases.

Social Media

Social media technologies have been around since the late 1960s, when CompuServe was founded. Over time, the number and type of social media technologies have grown and include blogs, microblogs (Twitter), podcasts, social bookmarking (Delicious, Evernote), content communities (YouTube), collaborative projects (Wikipedia), social networking (Facebook, LinkedIn), and music sharing (Pandora, Spotify), among others. These technologies have changed the way we communicate, find information, and share information. "Social Media Update 2013" reported that 42 percent of adults who engage in the online environment use multiple social networking sites, with 73 percent of "online adults" using at least one social networking site.[41] Libraries of all types have incorporated social media tools into their services. The American Library Association noted that Facebook, Twitter, and YouTube were among the most used social media tools in public libraries.[42] In many cases, libraries use these social media tools to market their services or to communicate with library users. In chapter 4, the Smithsonian project Questions Alive was featured as a service that encourages website visitors to share discoveries using a variety of social media tools. This resource also addresses the trend of information user as information creator because the readers create their own collections.

Gesture-Based Computing

Gesture-based technology involves a new kind of interaction between people and technology. Control is through the movement of the hand without actually having to touch a mouse, keyboard, or switch. Fashion shows have used gesture-based technologies to dim or brighten lights. The potential of gesture-based technologies for libraries was identified in 2011 in the Wolbach User Experience Lab at Harvard University.[43] While still in the experimental stage for the most part in libraries, chapter 4 describes a gesture-based way-finding technology for connecting with the library that was developed during a hackathon in 2014.

Tablets

Tablets, noted in table 5.1, are just one type of mobile device. Pew Research reported the following for American adults as of January 2014: 90 percent had a cell phone, 58 percent had a smartphone, 32 percent owned an e-reader, and 42 percent owned a tablet computer.[44] The popularity of tablet computing became evident in 2012 when the Pew Internet and American Life Project reported that tablet and e-book reader ownership nearly doubled during the holiday season in 2011.[45] As is pointed out in chapter 4, several libraries are transitioning to using tablets and other contemporary mobile devices for roving reference services. Libraries have been adopting mobile technologies and apps. At around that same time, Barile noted that librarians "should be exploring mobile devices as a way to connect with patrons."[46] As trends on a fast track, according to the Horizon Report, both tablets and mobile technologies need to be well embedded into service delivery in libraries at this point.

Mobile Apps

The growth of mobile technology has been accompanied by a proliferation of mobile applications, or apps. The iTunes App Store offered approximately 1.2 million apps, with 75 billion downloads as of June 2, 2014.[47] Apps are available for a wide variety of categories, including, among others, business, education, entertainment, finance, games, health, music, news, sports, and travel. In chapter 4, several examples are given of codefests and appfests sponsored by libraries, library association conferences, and the Digital Public Library of America. As noted in table 5.1, one trend that has been identified is the ubiquity of mobile technology and specifically of mobile apps.

Internet of Things

The Oxford Dictionary defines the *Internet of things* as a "proposed development of the Internet in which everyday objects have network connectivity, allowing them to send and receive data." [48] The term *ubiquitous computing* is often used to describe this concept; that is, computing is everywhere. Janna Anderson and Lee Rainie, who predict that the "Internet of Things will thrive in 2025," summarize where one finds these devices: wearable technology, remote controls in homes, embedded devices or "smart systems" that enable the infrastructure (e.g., transportation, electricity), sensors and readers that improve the distribution of goods and services, and real-time monitors of the environment.[49] Jim Hahn proposed various applications of the Internet of things in libraries, including having "your smart phone interact with the library building; smart digital shelving units; digital library integration with physical objects."[50] Hahn indicated that the integration of the Internet of things is still a few years off, and he asked the important question of the reader: "What is your plan for smart objects in the library environment?"[51] This is an example of a recently identified trend whose potential for libraries has been recognized. Libraries need to turn their imagination to the variety of devices that fall under the umbrella of the Internet of things.

Shift to Creators of Information

The notion of students as creators rather than consumers of information mentioned in the Horizon Report translates easily to members of the general public as noted in reference to the Smithsonian website, which facilitates this in a virtual environment. Members of the general public are creating content, and as the NMC Horizon Report notes, libraries are facilitating this in many cases. As noted in chapter 4, some public and academic libraries are offering "makerspaces" with a variety of tools and equipment. Ellyssa Kroski created "A Librarians' Guide to Makerspaces: 16 Resources" to help librarians create makerspaces in their libraries or information centers.[52] The guide was produced in March 2013, showing that librarians have been following this trend and have initiated activities in response to the trend. A blog post on June 8, 2014, entitled "Apps for Content Creation"[53] describes mobile apps available for content creation that can be used by librarians. This blog post also includes articles that highlight libraries that are offering users the opportunity to create content.

3D Printers

The 3D printer is one of the more common technologies found in makerspaces in libraries. These printers in libraries allow patrons to be creative. Teaching library patrons to use technology, such as 3D printers, also increases their digital literacy. Libraries with 3D printers will often hold workshops or programs. This technology is clearly an example of libraries embracing the "creation rather than consumption" trend mentioned in the Horizon Report.[54]

EMBRACING CHANGE

Given the monumental changes in information and communication technologies and the speed of the changes, librarians and information professionals need to begin to monitor change, if they haven't already done so, in order to be able to act quickly. Not all trends or innovations are appropriate for all organizations. The decision to adopt a given trend depends on the strengths and weaknesses of the institution as well as the information needs and preferences of the constituencies associated with the institution.

Rather than rule out a trend or innovation due to a lack of resources, librarians might consider collaborating with others. Some of the examples given throughout this book have cited collaborations between software developers and librarians. In other cases, libraries have worked within library consortia to offer innovative services. Harvard Business School professor Rosabeth Moss Kanter reminds us that we don't all have to design and build the innovation. She notes, "Innovation is putting new ideas into use. It isn't necessarily invention. Making it happen, that's innovation."[55]

Innovation results in change, and change is necessary for success in libraries. However, change brings with it challenges. Environmental scanning will provide decision makers with information on trends and emerging technologies for sound actions regarding the future of reference and library services. Chapter 6 focuses on all aspects of managing change in libraries and information centers.

NOTES

1. Edward L. Ayers, "Does Digital Scholarship Have a Future?" *EDUCAUSE Review Online*, August 5, 2013, http://www.educause.edu/ero/article/does-digital-scholarship-have-future.

2. Michael DeGusta, "Are Smart Phones Spreading Faster Than Any Technology in Human History?" *MIT Technology Review*, May 9, 2012, http://www.technologyreview.com/news/427787/are-smart-phones-spreading-faster-than-any-technology-in-human-history.

3. Twitter, "#numbers," *The Official Twitter Blog* (blog), *Twitter*, March 14, 2011, https://blog.twitter.com/2011/numbers.

4. Brian Mathews, "Think Like a Startup: A White Paper to Inspire Library Entrepreneurialism," *Virginia Tech University Libraries*, April 3, 2012, accessed July 7, 2014, http://hdl.handle.net/10919/18649.

5. James L. Morrison, "Environmental Scanning," in *A Primer for New Institutional Researchers*, ed. M. A. Whitely, J. D. Porter, and R. H. Fenske (Tallahassee, FL: The Association for Institutional Research, 1992), 86–99, http://horizon.unc.edu/courses/papers/enviroscan/index.html.

6. Chun Wei Choo, "Environmental Scanning as Information Seeking and Organizational Learning," *Information Research* 7, no. 1 (October 2001), accessed July 7, 2014, http://informationr.net/ir/7-1/paper112.html.

7. John M. Bryson, "Resource A: An Ongoing Approach for Identifying External Threats and Opportunities," in *Strategic Planning for Public and Nonprofit Organizations: A Guide to Strengthening and Sustaining Organizational Achievement*, rev. ed., ed. John M. Bryson (San Francisco: Jossey-Bass, 1995), 245–44.

8. Ann M. Pflaum and Timothy J. Delmont, "External Scanning: A Tool for Planners," *Journal of the American Planning Association* 53, no. 1 (1987): 56–67.

9. Ibid., 63.

10. Bryson, "Resource A," 245.

11. "NMC Horizon Project," *New Media Consortium*, accessed July 13, 2014, http://www.nmc.org/horizon-project.

12. *Ithaka S+R*, accessed June 8, 2014, http://www.sr.ithaka.org.

13. "The State of America's Libraries: A Report from the American Library Association," *American Library Association*, accessed June 15, 2014, http://www.ala.org/news/mediapresscenter/americaslibraries/soal_archive.

14. "Advocacy, Legislation and Issues," *American Library Association*, accessed June 14, 2014, http://www.ala.org/advocacy.

15. "IFLA Trend Report," *International Federation of Library Associations and Institutions*, last updated August 16, 2013, accessed June 14, 2014, http://trends.ifla.org.

16. *Pew Research Internet Project*, accessed June 8, 2014, http://www.pewinternet.org.

17. *OCLC Research*, accessed June 8, 2014, http://www.oclc.org/research.html.

18. "Membership Reports," *OCLC*, accessed June 22, 2014, http://www.oclc.org/reports.en.html.

19. "Above the Fold," *OCLC Research*, accessed June 15, 2014, http://www.oclc.org/research/publications/newsletters/abovethefold.html.

20. Brian Hopkins' Blog (blog), *Forrester*, accessed July 13, 2014, http://blogs.forrester.com/brian_hopkins.

21. ACRL Research Planning and Review Committee, "2012 Top Ten Trends in Academic Libraries: A Review of the Trends Affecting Academic Libraries in Higher Education," *College and Research Libraries News* 73, no. 6 (2012): 311–20, http://crln.acrl.org/content/73/6/311.full; and ACRL Research Planning and Review Committee, "Environmental Scan 2013," *Association of College and Research Libraries*, April 2013, accessed June 14, 2014, http://www.ala.org/acrl/sites/ala.org.acrl/files/content/publications/whitepapers/EnvironmentalScan13.pdf.

22. "Environmental Scan: Pattern Recognition (2003)," *OCLC*, accessed June 15, 2014, http://www.oclc.org/reports/escan.en.html.

23. *New York Times*, accessed June 16, 2104, http://www.nytimes.com.

24. *Wall Street Journal*, accessed June 16, 2014, http://online.wsj.com/home-page.

25. *Chronicle of Higher Education*, accessed June 16, 2014, http://chronicle.com/section/Home/5.

26. *MIT Technology Review*, accessed June 16, 2014, www.technologyreview.com.

27. *entrelib: The Conference for Entrepreneurial Librarians*, accessed July 15, 2014, http://entrelib.org.

28. "29th Annual Computers in Libraries 2014," *Information Today, Inc.*, http://www.infotoday.com/cil2014.

29. "Internet Librarian 2014," *Information Today, Inc.*, http://www.infotoday.com/il2014.

30. "Conferences," *Association for Computing Machinery*, http://www.acm.org/conferences.

31. *American Library Association*, http://www.ala.org.

32. *Special Libraries Association*, http://www.sla.org.

33. *EDUCAUSE*, http://www.educause.edu.

34. *ACRLog*, accessed July 15, 2014, http://acrlog.org.

35. *Harvard Library Innovation Lab*, http://librarylab.law.harvard.edu/blog.

36. John M. Bryson, Fran Ackermann, Edin Colin, and Charles Finn, "Resource C: Using the 'Oval Mapping Process' to Identify Strategic Issues and Formulate Effective Strategies," in *Strategic Planning for Public and Nonprofit Organizations: A Guide to Strengthening and Sustaining Organizational Achievement*, rev. ed., ed. John M. Bryson (San Francisco: Jossey-Bass, 1995), 257–75.

37. Pflaum and Delmont, "External Scanning," 65.

38. Leigh Buchanan, "The Smartest Little Company in America," *Inc.* (January 1999): 43.

39. Mathews, "Think Like a Start-Up."

40. Kristen Purcell, Joanna Brenner, and Lee Rainie, "Search Engine Use 2012," *Pew Research Internet Project*, March 9, 2012, http://www.pewinternet.org/2012/03/09/search-engine-use-2012.

41. Maeve Duggan and Aaron Smith, "Social Media Update 2013: 42% of Online Adults Use Multiple Social Networking Sites, but Facebook Remains the Platform of Choice," *Pew Research Internet Project*, December 30, 2013, http://www.pewinternet.org/2013/12/30/social-media-update-2013.

42. "Social Networking: Public Libraries' Use of Social Media Is Up Sharply, Especially among Large Libraries," *American Library Association*, accessed June 14, 2014, http://www.ala.org/news/state-americas-libraries-report-2014/social-networking.

43. Christopher Erdmann, "The Wolbach User Experience Lab," *Harvard University Library: Office for Scholarly Communication*, February 10, 2011, https://osc.hul.harvard.edu/liblab/proj/wolbach-user-experience-lab.

44. "Mobile Technology Fact Sheet," *Pew Research Internet Project*, accessed June 14, 2014, http://www.pewinternet.org/fact-sheets/mobile-technology-fact-sheet.

45. "A Snapshot of E-Reader and Tablet Owners (Infographic)," *Pew Research Internet Project*, January 27, 2014, accessed June 14, 2014, http://libraries.pewinternet.org/2012/01/27/a-snapshot-of-ereader-and-tablet-owners.

46. Lori Barile, "Mobile Technologies for Libraries: A List of Mobile Applications and Resources for Development," *College and Research Libraries News* 72 no. 4 (2011): 222, accessed June 14, 2014, http://crln.acrl.org/content/72/4/222.full.

47. Sarah Perez, "iTunes App Store Now Has 1.2 Million Apps, Has Seen 75 Billion Downloads to Date," *Techcrunch*, June 2, 2014, accessed June 14, 2014, http://techcrunch.com/2014/06/02/itunes-app-store-now-has-1-2-million-apps-has-seen-75-billion-downloads-to-date.

48. "Internet of Things," *Oxford Dictionaries*, accessed June 14, 2014, http://www.oxforddictionaries.com/definition/english/Internet-of-things.

49. Janna Anderson and Lee Rainie, "The Internet of Things Will Thrive by 2025: Many Experts Say the Rise of Embedded and Wearable Computing Will Bring the Next Revolution in Digital Technology," *Pew Research Internet Project*, May 14, 2014, http://www.pewinternet.org/2014/05/14/internet-of-things.

50. Jim Hahn, "The Internet of Things Meets the Library of Things," *ACRL TechConnect*, March 19, 2012, http://acrl.ala.org/techconnect/?p=474.

51. Hahn, "Internet of Things."

52. Ellyssa Kroski, "A Librarian's Guide to Makerspaces: 16 Resources," *OEDb: Open Education Database*, March 12, 2013, accessed June 23, 2014, http://oedb.org/ilibrarian/a-librarians-guide-to-makerspaces.

53. Nicole Hennig, "Apps for Content Creation," *Unbound* (blog), *Simmons GSLIS*, June 8, 2014, accessed June 16, 2014, http://gslis.simmons.edu/blogs/unbound/06/08/apps-for-content-creation.

54. Larry Johnson, Samantha Adams Becker, Michele Cummins, Victoria Estrada, Alex Freeman, and Holly Ludgate. *NMC Horizon Report: 2013 Higher Education* (Austin, TX: The New Media Consortium, 2013), accessed July 15, 2014, http://www.nmc.org/pdf/2013-horizon-report-HE.pdf.

55. Rosabeth Moss Kanter, "3 Ways to Innovate in a Stagnant Environment," interview by Brian Kenny, *The Business*, podcast transcript, March 11, 2014, http://www.hbs.edu/news/articles/Pages/three-ways-to-innovate.aspx.

SIX

Leading and Managing Change for Organizational Renewal

John P. Kotter, Harvard Business School professor, researches transformation efforts in organizations and is widely regarded as one of the foremost experts on the topics of leadership and change. The following excerpt is taken from Kotter's interview with an organization's staff about the organization's transformation efforts: "'A sense of urgency is important of course,' he tells [Kotter]. 'Complacency is a disaster these days. But complacency is a relatively minor issue for us. Better execution of our innovation initiative is our challenge.'"[1] The last sentence of the interview passage is fundamental. Essentially, this staff member's astute observation is that, while identifying change ideas and upending the status quo matter, so does the "how" of change—making certain the change ideas come to life. Without attention directed at the process and possibilities for implementation, the promising change ideas remain ideas rather than become a reality.

Taking a feasible, relevant, and desirable change idea and making it work in practice is considered the most challenging part of the innovation process.[2] For some organizations, change efforts are getting increasingly difficult to execute in that organizations have less money, less time, and fewer staff to implement innovation initiatives. From a survey of academic library deans and directors conducted in 2013, Ithaka S+R reported that the primary constraints on the deans' and directors' ability to make desired change in their libraries are lack of financial resources (90 percent of respondents), as well as lack of staff skills in key areas, challenges in implementing new technologies, and general resistance to change among library staff.[3] The survey's open-ended responses illustrated the diversity among the academic libraries on their plans for the future, with some respondents expressing that they have the opportunity

111

to innovate extensively in their organizations, while others noted the many constraints their organizations are saddled with. These results lead to an obvious question: How can libraries implement innovative changes, big or small, despite the many apparent obstacles to doing so?

This chapter focuses on the "how" of change. Models of change management and change leadership are outlined, and lessons learned and best practices for securing success with change efforts are provided. Central to implementation are aspects around approaches to innovation and processes for leading and managing change. Additional sections address issues of staffing and education, including how to help staff through transitions and adopt a culture of innovation.

PILLARS OF INNOVATION

A powerful combination of environmental change forces has been bearing down on libraries and information organizations. These forces, detailed in the previous chapters, include rapid increase in competition in the information sector, decrease in funding, and increase in the spread of communication and proclivity of information technologies into every aspect of daily lives. The use of environmental scanning as a method of identifying change opportunities, being proactive rather than reactive, is covered in chapter 5. The ways in which librarians and information professionals recognize and respond to these forces is vital to the innovation process. Steven J. Bell suggested that librarians and information professionals utilize a design thinking process, which takes a "more deliberate and thoughtful approach to problem resolution" by fully understanding the problem before formulating possible solutions rather than "jump[ing] on bandwagons."[4] Design thinking can be traced to Silicon Valley–based IDEO, a leading design firm, and the creation of their products and services from reinventing the Apple mouse to the Palm handheld. IDEO's design thinking process begins with assessing the gap between what exists and what needs to change. Then, the process follows five steps— understanding, observing, visualizing, evaluating/refining, and implementing—to catalyze suitable solutions and sustain them.[5] Design thinking has been credited with fostering cultures and processes for continuous improvement and innovation.

Google's Susan Wojcicki, senior vice president of advertising, discussed how the company has committed to innovation and risk taking from year to year. Eight principles of innovation guide Google's efforts:

1. Have a mission that matters.
2. Think big, but start small.
3. Strive for continual innovation, not instant perfection.
4. Look for ideas everywhere.
5. Share everything.

6. Spark with imagination, fuel with data.
7. Be a platform.
8. Never fail to fail.[6]

As is evident from its first placement in the list of innovation principles, Google's mission guides all decisions. For most organizations, there are not enough resources to address all change ideas, so adopting a strategic mindset is important: focusing on those directional choices that will move the organization toward its desired future. Erika Andersen explained that being strategic about change "implies that you know where you're starting from, that you're clear about where you want to go and that you will make core choices about how to get there, with a consistent, focused effort to travel down your clear path."[7] Having a balanced and accurate picture of the organization's current reality relative to that challenge is a key aspect, as it allows the organization to identify and invest in only those change ideas that are most potentially impactful.

THE CHANGE PROCESS

Change is cyclical and nonlinear, an ongoing and rising spiral of design, implementation, tracking, and redesign of the desired innovation. Despite all of the focus on innovation and managing change efforts across industries and organization types, studies have shown that only approximately 30 percent of all change efforts succeed. The 60 to 70 percent failure rate for change projects is a statistic that has stayed constant since the 1970s.[8] In addition, it has been reported that a majority of change-related failures are caused by implementation failures rather than a failure of the initial idea.[9] Consequently, the steps undertaken to execute change initiatives are significantly important.

The terms *change management* and *change leadership* are not interchangeable. Change management is a "set of tools and a set of mechanisms that are designed to make sure that when you do try to make some changes, A, it doesn't get out of control, and B, the number of problems associated with it . . . doesn't happen," whereas change leadership is "much more associated with putting an engine on the whole change process, and making it go faster, smarter, and more efficiently."[10] A key distinction between the two terms is that change leadership is about visions and empowering people to take the big leaps necessary to transform organizations, whereas change management is about minimizing disruption. These processes can happen simultaneously, or one can flow from the other.

John P. Kotter's eight-step model is one often-cited process for leading change in an ever-changing, global information economy.[11] Kotter's model has been used in educational settings for transformation initiatives, though less frequently applied in libraries and information organizations to facilitate change.[12] The steps of Kotter's model are:

1. **Establish a Sense of Urgency.** The first step of the model is to establish a sense of urgency, and by that Kotter is not advising frenetic activity. Rather, this essential step involves creating and sustaining a highly positive, highly focused force on an organization's crucial opportunities and threats in the immediate. In libraries and information organizations, as with any mature organization, this would include ways to overcome complacency. It also might require shifting the staff's focus toward seeing their work from a different perspective (e.g., from reference interactions to information seekers' contextualized search behaviors).

2. **Form a Guiding Coalition.** The second step is to form a guiding coalition, meaning putting together a group of people with a shared objective. Individuals in this group should possess the power, expertise, leadership, and credibility to direct the change initiative. Members of the organization's administration do not necessarily have to lead the change effort, though they do have to support the change idea and path. In libraries and information organizations, it may not be necessary to assemble a representative or diverse group for a task force but instead to gather the right people who embody the aforementioned qualities.

3. **Create a Change Vision.** The third step is to create a vision that will clarify how the future will be different from the past. This vision—focused, feasible, and easy to communicate—motivates people to take action and helps to coordinate action. When visions lack clarity, librarians and information professionals may experience confusion about the seemingly disconnected nature of the change initiative to their work or to their organization, and this reduces the possibility of empowering action.

4. **Communicate the Vision for Buy-In.** The fourth step is to communicate the vision, making certain that as many people at the organization as possible understand and accept the vision. This is where resistance can be expected, and Kotter cautions that not communicating the vision enough or communicating the vision inconsistently could create a stalled transformation. In libraries and information organizations, the dialog between the task force and the organization's stakeholders pertains to the potential impact of the change vision and what specific skills librarians and information professionals will need to have to be effective in doing their work and carrying out the change effort. Any skepticism or resistance to the proposed change should be addressed by the organization's change leadership, and thus the vision may be refined before the change initiative proceeds.

5. **Empower Others to Act on the Vision.** The fifth step is to empower others to act on the vision. At this stage, it is imperative that leaders and administrators encourage experimentation and remove as many obstacles as possible to allow people to do their best work. In certain libraries and information organizations, tenure, promotion, and reappointment systems might influence employees' willingness to experiment, with employees fearing that a failed experiment would impact job security. Additionally, time is needed for experimentation. For reference librarians, this may warrant time spent away from the in-person or digital reference desk to develop and conduct experiments, assess results, and reflect and communicate about methods and outcomes to inform the subsequent aspects of the change initiative.

6. **Generate Short-Term Wins.** The sixth step is to generate short-term wins. This means creating recognizable, unmistakable success as soon as possible to increase motivation and momentum toward the bigger vision. As an example, in chapter 4, the Book-A-Librarian personalized reference services at the Sno-Isles Libraries in Washington began with a six-month beta test at the library system's five largest and busiest libraries. The beta test included an assessment of the change effort, which showed positive results: "significant customer interest and positive staff adaptation to the one-to-one instruction model."[13] The next iteration was to beta-test with the smaller community libraries, and because the assessment results were shown to be consistent with the larger library test group, the Book-A-Librarian service was fully implemented across all of Sno-Isle's twenty-one community libraries.

7. **Consolidate Gains.** The seventh step is to consolidate gains and improvements to create further change. The caution here is letting up and declaring victory too soon. Instead, new practices and behaviors must be driven into the culture of the organization to ensure long-term success. In libraries and information organizations, data can be shared with stakeholders to demonstrate the status of the change effort. Some type of assessment or judgment is examined to determine if the change is moving in a positive direction based on the intended goals of the change idea. Evidence is used to chart the course forward, aiding decisions about continuing with or deviating from the original plan.

8. **Institutionalize New Approaches for Sustained Change.** Last, the eighth step in Kotter's model is to institutionalize new approaches for sustained change. For libraries and information organizations, this could mean using the innovation to inspire additional change efforts and inculcating new staff with what the organization now values. In this way, the change effort is sustainable beyond the organization's change leadership.

Certainly, there is no one-size-fits-all approach to managing or leading change in organizations, and change strategies can often be tailored to the organization's situation. Aside from Kotter's model, Erika Andersen promoted a strategic change map, accomplished through five steps, intended to position an organization for future success.[14] The five steps, outlined here, provide a path to act strategically in the face of external or internal challenges:

1. Decide what you're solving for.
2. Know where you're starting from.
3. Get clear about your hoped-for future.
4. Face the obstacles.
5. Make core directional choices, and then get specific.

In addition, alternative change strategies have been used in libraries and information organizations. For example, Andrew Wells utilized Birkinshaw's five ways of agile management at the library of the University of New South Wales, a research-intensive Australian university, to reflect on library innovation directed at meeting the challenges of changes in higher education, digital libraries, and the scholarly information environment.[15] Further, Brinley Franklin described the shift at the University of Connecticut Libraries, which strategically aligned the libraries with the objectives in the campus academic plan and organizational structure, an approach that generated buy-in from campus stakeholders for library transformation and supported institutional outcomes.[16]

SOME KEY CHANGE LESSONS

In the modern era, the pressure to innovate is accelerating. As a result, leading change is a complex undertaking. What are some key lessons that have been learned about managing and leading change in organizations? One key lesson is that organizations should pay attention to the hard factors of change management as well as the soft factors. Boston Consulting Group (BCG) researchers have reported that soft factors alone, such as culture, leadership, and motivation, do not directly influence the outcomes of many change programs.[17] Hard factors, those that can be measured directly or indirectly, communicated internally or externally, or influenced quickly, should not be neglected in transformation initiatives. The research finding reported by BCG is that four hard factors, forming the DICE framework, have predicted the outcomes of more than one thousand change management initiatives around the world:

- **Duration:** The time between formal project review of milestones. This is more crucial for success than a project's life span. A long project that is reviewed frequently is more likely to succeed than a short project that isn't reviewed frequently.

- **Integrity:** The quality of the team, skills, knowledge and social networks of team members, and their proven ability to complete innovation initiatives.
- **Commitment:** Top-level commitment from influential executives and support from the people who ultimately deal with new systems, processes, and ways of working.
- **Effort:** The percentage of increased effort that the employees must make to implement the change initiative.

Other key lessons learned pertain to an organization's human resources. First, collaborative workplace and systems cultures will not emerge spontaneously within organizations; they must be coached and modeled.[18] Successful work cultures ask "Why don't we?" more than "Why don't they?" Second, when a decision is made to implement a change idea, staff is faced with having to do something new, and this identifies a capability gap that practitioners must learn. Ultimately, innovation can only be achieved if the individuals responsible for their implementation learn how to do what's needed and actually implement the change. This issue is discussed in greater detail later in the chapter and specific to reference librarianship. Third, crucial issues are how to build consensus and how to make changes generally acceptable to or accepted by the majority within the organization. Issues of participation and resistance become of some significance when conceptualizing and implementing a change effort. And in relation, managers are not the only change leaders, which means that staff will come up with ideas on their own and pursue them. Therefore, everyone will need to pay attention to emergent best practices on effective change leadership.

Further, another key lesson is to assess and articulate clearly the obstacles that will have to be overcome to implement the change idea.[19] As the topic of collaboration is discussed in chapter 5, given extensive resource shortages, libraries and information organizations can develop innovation projects with like organizations that have similar change priorities, forming collaborative partnerships.

Finally, chapter 5 explains the increasing speed in advances to information and communication technologies and in their prevalence. A by-product is that organizations are testing new ideas at speeds that were unimaginable even a decade ago due to rapid and continual technological developments, meaning that innovation initiatives that used to take months and money to coordinate and launch are now starting more quickly.[20] Because experiments can be initiated more readily for concept testing, it is easier to get feedback from customers and incorporate the input into organizations' decisions. Greg Linden, an entrepreneur who has been an innovator at both Amazon and Microsoft, remarked that the ease of obtaining customer feedback makes iteration a central feature of the new era of innovation: "In each failed test, you learn something that helps you find something that works. Constant, continuous, ubiquitous experimentation is the most important thing."[21]

GETTING THE STAFF ON BOARD

As noted earlier, organizational and cultural change can cause discomfort and even resistance among staff. And yet, if staff do not buy into and work to implement the necessary change, it is unlikely to succeed, regardless of how good the initial vision is. Brian Mathews notes, "We can't hire a few creative and improvisational individuals and expect them to deliver new service models if the work culture is not ready for new service models."[22] As the paradigm of reference shifts and reference librarianship becomes increasingly multifunctional, managers will need to grapple with how to manage change, including reorganizing, and perhaps retraining, staff and encouraging commitment to innovation. Further, they might need to recruit new professionals who can fulfill the demands of these positions. Human resources are among the most important assets of any organization. A key part of innovation involves ensuring that staff are organized and deployed in the most efficient and effective ways and that they have the skills and knowledge necessary to fulfill their responsibilities. There is not likely to be a single framework for all institutions, as the specific changes will depend on the strategic directions and goals of each institution. However, some general approaches to managing staff change should be applicable to most places.

Changes with Current Staff

In many cases, the changes in reference services will not necessarily lead to new hires but in the restructuring of an existing position. The new job description might require significant changes of the current employee, as most reference librarians and information professionals will be spending less time "sitting and waiting" at a desk and more time focused on other areas. As described in chapters 2 through 4, most reference positions have become multifunctional, with new areas of responsibility often involving creating and implementing new services and assessing the success of those services. The "University Libraries Section" of the Association for College and Research Libraries (ACRL) outlines five examples of restructuring initiatives in order to meet challenges, such as changing priorities and budget and staff cuts.[23] For instance, McGill University described the retraining and redeployment of staff in order to bridge the gap after losing 31 of its 130 staff members. In part, the library consolidated service desks to a single point and trained all staff to work at that desk, thereby allowing librarians and information professionals more time to focus on outreach, instruction, and content creation. Harvard University Libraries describe using a skills assessment check-in to help access services staff identify their strengths and areas of contribution. New working groups were then organized around functional areas drawing on these strengths.

In managing restructuring, it will be important for the library director or manager to work with affected staff to establish expectations and priorities for restructured positions by drawing on the change management techniques described here. Some positions might require training in order for staff to address the capability gap addressed earlier, and employers might need to provide time and resources for their staff to engage in continuing education or professional development to develop or refine skills to meet the demands of their new positions. Part of the success of managing this change requires library directors or managers to identify existing staff who exhibit the capacity to innovate and to cultivate them for new positions. Such staff members are likely to be attractive to other organizations who are looking to create change, so directors and managers will need to work to retain their talent by providing them with ample opportunities to apply their abilities and contribute to the mission and vision of the organization.

For existing staff who are used to staffing the reference desk as a substantial portion of their duties, the transition might be difficult, possibly expressed as resistance to the proposed change. Some librarians and information professionals express concern that staffing the desk with paraprofessionals will result in lower levels of service and that reference questions might go unanswered if they are not identified and referred to the professional on call. Others whose professional identity is strongly tied to the reference desk might be unsure of their new roles and how they fit into the larger library once their desk duties are reduced or eliminated. The job analysis described earlier can help employees to see how their new positions align with the overall structure and mission of the institution. Michael A. Crumpton emphasized the importance of communication in helping staff to adapt to organizational change. He stressed that managers should show empathy and be supportive of staff, offer staff opportunities to provide input and feedback, and create a framework to keep the conversation productive.[24] He also acknowledged that the manager has to maintain an appropriate sense of pressure in order to create the energy to move forward, which is similar to Kotter's sense of urgency described earlier. Resistance to change is natural, and Kevin Craine pointed out that it can even lead to anger or depression. But managers can assist staff in transition by listening empathetically, being clear about expectations, and providing them with a consistent vision of the intended outcome.[25]

Overall, library managers should focus on the benefits that restructuring can have for users, staff, and the organization as a whole. New delivery models should provide users with improved service that better meets their expectations, as described in chapter 2. Studies have shown that paraprofessionals can be very effective at answering questions,[26] which frees up professionals to pursue other important activities, such as outreach, assessment, instruction, and so on. This flexibility should also provide librarians and information professionals with more time and space to be creative and to envision and implement innovative services along the lines of those described in chapter 4. Finally, when reference librarians and information professionals are only answering questions that are referred to them, they might feel a greater sense of job satisfaction because they tend to get more complex research questions that draw on their professional skills and expertise.[27]

New Positions and New Hires

Changing reference services will lead to restructured positions and might provide the opportunity to hire new staff. Deborah Jakubs encouraged library managers to view these changes as opportunities to "engage in fresh thinking about how we are organized, what skills we seek in new hires, and what leadership we provide."[28] There are several considerations for designing new jobs and recruiting for new positions. Ann Jerabek offered a detailed overview of the process of writing a job description and underscored the various purposes of the job description, including detailing job activities, creating a shared understanding between employer and employee of the position, locating the position within the larger structure of the organization, and serving as the basis for a job posting.[29] To ensure that the job description achieves its functions effectively, Jerabek recommended undertaking a job analysis in which the employer defines the core activities of the position, as well as the skills, knowledge, and qualifications required to perform those activities. When the position is a restructuring of an existing one, she recommended interviewing and observing the current employee to better understand the work being done.

In addition, and perhaps especially when creating a new position, the employer should review job descriptions and vacancy postings of similar positions at other institutions.[30] During times of innovation, however, there might not be an equivalent position either within or outside of the organization on which to base the job description. In such cases, managers will need to focus the description based on their perceived needs and be willing to change as the position and needs evolve. Chapter 3 of this book outlines some of the new competency areas that librarians and information professionals will need to meet the demands of the different service models (such as those highlighted in chapter 2) and in order to initiate innovative services, such as those described in chapter 4. The specific competencies and qualifications will depend on the needs and vision of the particular library and position. For instance, while technology will be a big part of both positions, a data management librarian will need a different set of technical skills from an instructional design librarian. A full job analysis should include:

- What is/should be happening on the job;
- How the job should be performed;
- Required knowledge, education background, experience, and skills;
- How the requirements are applied in making decisions and solving problems;
- Outcomes or results expected from the person performing the job; and
- Employee accountability (for what and to whom is the job holder accountable?).[31]

The job analysis will lead to a lengthy position description. The level of detail is necessary for defining the parameters of the job and creating that shared understanding with the employee.

Recruiting employees who are a good match for the position and the organization is obviously important. Hiring for a completely new position is especially challenging, as the employer does not have historical knowledge to guide decision making. Several strategies can help ensure a smooth and successful process. A primary consideration is where to post the vacancy. While general job boards like the American Library Association's (ALA) "Job List" will reach a wide audience, employers might also want to choose outlets targeted specifically to job seekers with relevant qualifications. These outlets might include the job banks of specific professional associations and job banks associated with library and information science (LIS) programs, especially those programs offering classes or concentrations related to the job area. Employers can also source candidates at conferences and other professional venues.[32] In addition to recruiting for "hard skills," such as technology skills, library managers should be looking for new hires who exhibit "soft skills," or personal attributes, such as creativity, flexibility, and curiosity, which are key to innovative thinking and adapting to change.[33] In some cases, libraries are hiring individuals who do not have a library background but do have the specific skills in other crucial areas, such as technology, marketing, assessment, and budgeting.[34] Although people without an LIS degree can bring a much-needed outside perspective, integrating staff who do not have a library background can be a challenge, as they will need to become familiar with some foundational library concepts. Similarly, staff with a more traditional background might feel threatened by the recruitment of people without a library degree and might feel their education and skills are not valued. Managers will need to pay particular attention to integrating and enculturating all staff in order to move forward successfully.

IMPLICATIONS OF A REFERENCE PARADIGM SHIFT
FOR LIS EDUCATION

The changing reference paradigm will necessarily impact LIS education. Faculty members will need to rethink the curriculum in order to ensure students are prepared for the new world of reference. Chapter 3 outlines some of the new competency areas for LIS. Among these are the ability to work with data sets; comfort with instruction, including some knowledge of pedagogy and teaching methods; ability to manage people, projects, and change; and ability to assess services and resources, both for continuous improvement and to demonstrate value to stakeholders. These specific skill sets will vary by the type of organization and the particular position. Chapter 3 also touches on some of the implications of changes in the field for LIS curricula, such as technology and instruction. Beyond the skills for individual positions, however, this book identifies additional competency areas that are surfacing as necessary and points to a need for LIS curricula to broadly address areas related to innovation and change. The following paragraphs outline skill areas that have emerged over the course of this book as key areas for innovative library and reference services.

As noted throughout this chapter, librarians and information professionals are now finding themselves in the roles of change managers and change leaders. Such positions require them not only to be able to proactively monitor external change forces and envision innovative new services, but also to manage and lead their staff through the transitions. While creativity and vision are important aspects of implementing change, ideas will not enact themselves. Change leaders and managers will need to create buy-in and support among their staff and develop a culture of innovation and change. While general management courses are common in LIS programs, as noted in chapter 4, few seem to focus on change management in particular. Currently, Illinois and Pratt are the only programs found with a course devoted to change management. Considering that change is a constant in the field and resistance to change among staff is also natural, it will be very important for LIS students to learn how to create, implement, and manage change in their organizations.

Similarly, LIS programs might offer more courses, or integrate more attention to, entrepreneurship. Technology has been changing at an enormous rate, and this has affected our users' expectations of how they can access and use information. This book has demonstrated that most libraries and reference departments have still only made incremental changes in response to these trends. As Mathews noted, "now is not the time to find new ways of doing old things," and "we don't just need change, we need break-through, paradigm-shifting, transformative, disruptive ideas."[35] Such ideas involve risk. If we expect library and information professionals to be able to envision and implement such ideas, then LIS programs have a responsibility to teach the processes and practices of visioning and risk management, as well as such practical aspects as budgeting, human resource management, and planning.

Chapter 5 introduces the concept of environmental scanning, which is one way for librarians and information professionals not only to keep abreast of but also actually anticipate changes in the field. While librarians and information professionals, especially reference librarians, are trained to find information, environmental scanning entails more than just searching for specific information. Rather, as described in chapter 5, it involves scanning the literature, not for specific keywords or topics, but to get an overall sense of trends. It also requires analysis of the content to determine which trends might present challenges and opportunities, which trends to monitor, and which to act on. Nevertheless, as far back as 2000, Kathy Shelfer and Abby Goodrum noted that such practices as "benchmarking, product costing, technical forecasting, sophisticated database development and data mining techniques are infrequently offered in library and information science (LIS) programs."[36] Because environmental scanning is such a powerful tool for understanding and meeting emerging trends in the field, it makes sense for LIS programs to teach the process of environmental scanning, along with such related skills as SWOT analysis and scenario planning.

Although assessment and evaluation are already mentioned in chapter 3 as an important area for LIS education, it bears repeating here. The processes associated with assessment and evaluation, from setting goals to collecting and analyzing data in order to gauge progress toward those goals, cut across all areas of library and information science and are perhaps especially important for areas of innovation. Brian Mathews acknowledged the importance of the testing and measuring of a concept. As he put it, "the aim isn't to develop a finished product, but to continuously [sic] evaluate and evolve the concept."[37] Assessment is also identified repeatedly in chapter 4 as a factor in the success of innovative programs and services. The key is for librarians and information professionals to be clear about their goals and then check in on an ongoing basis to see how well they are meeting those goals. Data gathered in this way can be used to make incremental adjustments to services and programs, set new goals, or make decisions about continuing or cutting services and programs. To that end, it is important for LIS students to understand how to conduct evaluation research, including understanding various methodologies and having at least a basic knowledge of statistics.[38] Even those librarians and information professionals who are not conducting their own research need this knowledge in order to be informed consumers of published research, but only 61 percent of LIS programs require a research methods course.[39] As a result, many practicing librarians and information professionals feel unprepared to undertake evaluation research.[40]

Related to assessment and evaluation research is the ability to conduct community or user needs assessment. As noted throughout this book, our users' habits, tastes, and expectations have changed drastically over time and will likely continue to change as new technologies impact their abilities to access, manipulate, and create information. If librarians and information professionals hope to remain relevant, they will need a clear understanding of their users' wants and needs, which will involve reaching out to their communities and continuously gathering data on their users in order to respond to or anticipate those changing needs.

All of these suggested curricular changes have implications for LIS faculty as well. Needless to say, LIS faculty need to stay abreast of changes, including technological changes, in order to ensure that their courses and programs are preparing students to fulfill the current needs and responsibilities in the field. Sharon Hu noted that changes to LIS curricula will entail different knowledge and skills among LIS faculty.[41] Traditionally, there has been some tension between LIS practitioners and programs with regard to how well students are prepared for practice and what the right balance is between theory and practice, training and education. Michael Gorman suggested that a "gap between what is being taught in many LIS schools and what is being practiced in most libraries is wide and widening,"[42] prompting ALA to convene a task force to address this "perceived gap between what is taught in ALA-accredited LIS programs and the knowledge, skills and competences needed for work in the libraries of the 21st century."[43] It would seem there is pressure on LIS faculty to demonstrate their relevance just as there is for practitioners. The key is for curricular review to be an ongoing and iterative process. In order to be responsive to the demands of employers, LIS faculty members will need to engage in the same environmental scanning, assessment and evaluation, and continuous learning as their counterparts in the field.

MAKING CHANGE BUSINESS AS USUAL

If change is a constant, not only in libraries and information organizations, but also in the wider world, then libraries must be ready to make the business of change part of their everyday practice. Essentially, innovation and change need to become an expected part of the regular practice of librarians and information professionals, and in many places this might involve a cultural shift. The Kotter model, described earlier, considers culture throughout its process, thereby ensuring that the changes being addressed will be embedded into the culture.[44] Julia Leong and Craig Anderson noted that successful cultural change depends on both the example of managers and the buy-in of general staff.[45] As such, change leaders need to model innovative thinking and appreciate risk taking and failure, but they must also find ways to engage all employees in the process.

Innovation has been slow to come to reference. The traditional reference service model has remained virtually unchanged for more than one hundred years. While this model may have served well in a time of information scarcity, many have already questioned the relevance and effectiveness of the model in a world of ubiquitous remote access to information. This book highlights several libraries that have met the challenges of changing expectations and technologies by developing innovative new services that move beyond that traditional reference service model. While the examples in chapter 4 offer some exciting ideas, they are only a start. In order for reference services to remain relevant into the future, more libraries will need to draw inspiration from these examples and build on their knowledge of their local communities and the strengths of their organizations to develop their own innovations.

The environmental scanning process outlined in chapter 5 is one way for librarians and information professionals to keep abreast of trends and to identify those trends that are likely to have an impact on the field, for better or worse. Combined with a SWOT analysis, environmental scans can assist librarians and information professionals in anticipating challenges and opportunities to their organization and to position themselves to take advantage of their strengths and minimize the effect of threats. One important aspect of environmental scanning is reading—scholarly literature, trade journals, blogs, among others—across difference disciplines in order to get a sense of what is being talked about and which trends are emerging. These scans of the literature can also keep us informed of what ideas our colleagues are implementing and how well they succeed.

Books are necessarily static, but in order to assist our readers with their literature and environmental scans, we have also initiated a living blog entitled *Unbound: Library Futures Unfettered* (http://gslis.simmons.edu/blogs/unbound). While not a substitute for ongoing environmental scanning, this blog features regular posts about trends, ideas, and innovations throughout the field of library science and specifically within the area of reference services. Contributors to the blog include LIS faculty, practitioners, and students, and readers of this book are invited to submit posts as well. We hope *Unbound* will serve as a mechanism for keeping up with the trends and new ideas that this book has identified.

We hope that this book helps to create the sense of urgency identified by Kotter as necessary to spur change and innovation. Indeed, change is coming to the library field already. The choice is ours whether to let that change be driven by forces outside the field or to take the lead and shape the change. While big ideas are needed, it is important to remember that no innovation is too small. Rather, what is important is focusing on the future and continuously working toward our vision of that future. With that in mind, we encourage our readers to start (or continue) to implement new ideas. We also encourage you to report back to the community, perhaps using the *Unbound* blog, so that we can learn from and build on each other's successes.

NOTES

1. John P. Kotter, *A Sense of Urgency* (Boston: Harvard Business Press, 2008).

2. Geoff Scott, "Effective Change Management in Higher Education," *EDUCAUSE Review* 38, no. 5 (November/December 2003): 64–80, https://net.educause.edu/ir/library/pdf/erm0363.pdf.

3. Matthew P. Long and Roger C. Schonfeld, "Ithaka S+R US Library Survey 2013," *Ithaka S+R*, March 11, 2014, accessed June 22, 2014, http://sr.ithaka.org/sites/default/files/reports/SR_LibraryReport_20140310_0.pdf.

4. Steven J. Bell, "Design Thinking," *American Libraries* 41, nos. 6/7 (June/July 2010): 50.

5. Ibid.

6. Susan Wojcicki, "The Eight Pillars of Innovation," *Think Newsletter*, July 2011, accessed June 23, 2014, http://www.thinkwithgoogle.com/articles/8-pillars-of-innovation.html.

7. Erika Andersen, "The Basics of Being Strategic about Change" (blog), *Forbes*, September 8, 2010, accessed June 27, 2014, http://www.forbes.com/2010/09/08/change-strategy-management-leadership-managing-human-capital-10-steps.html.

8. Scott Keller and Carolyn Aiken, "The Inconvenient Truth about Change Management: Why It Isn't Working and What to Do about It," *McKinsey and Company*, 2008, 1–18, accessed July 1, 2014, http://www.mckinsey.com/app_media/reports/financial_services/the_inconvenient_truth_about_change_management.pdf.

9. Myungweon Choi, "Employees' Attitudes toward Organizational Change: A Literature Review," *Human Resource Management* 50, no. 4 (July/August 2011): 479–500, doi:10.1002/hrm.20434.

10. John P. Kotter, "Change Management vs. Change Leadership—What's the Difference?" (blog), *Forbes*, July 12, 2011, accessed June 26, 2014, http://www.forbes.com/sites/johnkotter/2011/07/12/change-management-vs-change-leadership-whats-the-difference.

11. "The 8-Step Process for Leading Change," *Kotter International*, accessed June 21, 2014, http://www.kotterinternational.com/our-principles/changesteps.

12. Meredith Gorran Farkas, "Building and Sustaining a Culture of Assessment: Best Practices for Change Leadership," *Reference Services Review* 41, no. 1 (2012): 18, doi:10.1108/00907321311300857.

13. "Book-A-Librarian, Sno-Isle Libraries," *Urban Libraries Council*, accessed July 5, 2014, http://www.urbanlibraries.org/book-a-librarian-innovation-177.php?page_id=38.

14. Andersen, "Basics of Being Strategic."

15. Andrew Wells, "Agile Management: Strategies for Success in Rapidly Changing Times—an Australian University Library Perspective," *IFLA Journal* 40, no. 1 (2014): 30–34, doi:10.1177/0340035214526539.

16. Brinley Franklin, "Surviving to Thriving: Advancing the Institutional Mission," *Journal of Library Administration* 52, no. 1 (2012): 94–107, doi:10.1080/01930826.2012.630244.

17. Harold L. Sirkin, Perry Keenan, and Alan Jackson, "The Hard Side of Change Management," *Harvard Business Review* 83, no. 10 (October 2005): 108–18, accessed June 20, 2014, http://hbr.org/2005/10/the-hard-side-of-change-management/ar/1.

18. Scott, "Effective Change Management."

19. Andersen, "Basics of Being Strategic."

20. Erik Brynjolfsson and Michael Schrage, "The New, Faster Face of Innovation: Thanks to Technology, Change Has Never Been So Easy or So Cheap," *Wall Street Journal*, August 17, 2009, accessed June 25, 2014, http://online.wsj.com/news/articles/SB10001424052970204830304574130820184260340

21. Ibid.

22. Brian Mathews, "Think Like a Startup: A White Paper to Inspire Library Entrepreneuralism," *Virginia Tech University Libraries*, April 3, 2012, http://hdl.handle.net/10919/18649.

23. "Reorganizing for the Future: Five Stories for an Online Discussion," *ALA Connect*, last modified June 6, 2014, http://connect.ala.org/node/224120.

24. Michael A. Crumpton, "Talk about Change," *The Bottom Line: Managing Library Finances* 25, no. 4 (2012): 140–42, accessed July 7, 2014, http://0-www.emeraldinsight.com.library.simmons.edu/journals.htm?issn=0888-045x&volume=25&issue=4&articleid=17065522&show=html.

25. Kevin Craine, "Managing the Cycle of Change," *Information Management Journal* 41, no. 5 (2007): 44–50, accessed July 7, 2014, http://0-search.ebscohost.com.library.simmons.edu/login.aspx?direct=true&db=lls&AN=27200121&site=ehost-live&scope=site.

26. Christy R. Stevens, "Reference Reviewed and Re-Envisioned: Revamping Librarian and Desk-Centric Services with LibStARs and LibAnswers," *The Journal of Academic Librarianship* 39, no. 2 (2013): 202–14, accessed May 24, 2014, doi:10.1016/j.acalib.2012.11.006.

27. Megan Dempsey, "Blending the Trends: A Holistic Approach to Reference Services," *Public Services Quarterly* 7, nos. 1/2 (2011): 3–17, accessed July 8, 2014, http://0-search.ebscohost.com.library.simmons.edu/login.aspx?direct=true&db=lls&AN=60735577&site=ehost-live&scope=site.

28. Deborah Jakubs, "Out of the Gray Times: Leading Libraries into the Digital Future," *The Journal of Library Administration* 48, no. 2 (2008): 235–48, accessed July 7, 2014, http://0-search.ebscohost.com.library.simmons.edu/login.aspx?direct=true&db=lls&AN=502938322&site=ehost-live&scope=site.

29. Ann Jerabek, "Job Descriptions: Don't Hire without Them," *Journal of Interlibrary Loan, Document Delivery, and Information Supply* 13, no. 3 (2003): 113–26, accessed May 24, 2014, http://0-web.a.ebscohost.com.library.simmons.edu/ehost/pdfviewer/pdfviewer?sid=8367d61f-a405-4760-9dfd-0462d45bb055%40sessionmgr4003&vid=9&hid=4112.

30. Gail M. Staines, "Finding the Best People in a Tough Economy," *Library Leadership and Management* 26, nos. 3/4 (2012): 1–13, accessed May 25, 2014, http://0-web.b.ebscohost.com.library.simmons.edu/ehost/pdfviewer/pdfviewer?sid=2a385174-f5a1-42d7-9e81-3e6a351c1db7%40sessionmgr112&vid=2&hid=120.

31. R. I. Henderson, "Job Descriptions—Critical Documents, Versatile Tools. Part 3: Conducting a Job Analysis," *Supervisory Management* 21 (1976): 26–34.

32. Leo S. Lo, "New Perspectives in Leadership," *Library Leadership and Management* 27, no. 4 (2013): 1–4, accessed July 15, 2013, http://0-web.b.ebscohost.com.library.simmons.edu/ehost/pdfviewer/pdfviewer?vid=17&sid=05565469-9a24-4d87-8ede-9ec16e7e7059%40sessionmgr114&hid=123.

33. Mathews, "Think Like a Startup"; Jakubs, "Out of the Gray Times."

34. Jakubs, "Out of the Gray Times."

35. Mathews, "Think Like a Startup," 12.

36. Kathy Shelfer and Abby Goodrum, "Competitive Intelligence as an Extension of Library Education," *The Journal of Education for Library and Information Science* 41, no. 4

(2000): 353–61, accessed July 7, 2014, http://0-www.jstor.org.library.simmons.edu/stable/40324050?seq=2.

37. Mathews, "Think Like a Startup," 6.

38. Amy S. Van Epps, "Librarians and Statistics: Thoughts on a Tentative Relationship," *Practical Academic Librarianship: The International Journal of the SLA* 2, no. 1 (2012): 25–32, accessed July 8, 2014, http://0-search.ebscohost.com.library.simmons.edu/login.aspx?direct=true&db=lls&AN=76435802&site=ehost-live&scope=site.

39. Lili Luo, "Fusing Research into Practice: The Role of Research Methods Education," *Library and Information Science Research* 33, no. 3 (2011): 191–201, http://0-www.sciencedirect.com.library.simmons.edu/science/article/pii/S0740818811000338.

40. Catherine Sassen and Diane Wahl, "Fostering Research and Publication in Academic Libraries," *College and Research Libraries* 75, no. 4 (2014): 458–91, accessed July 8, 2014, http://crl.acrl.org/content/75/4/458.full.pdf+html.

41. Sharon Hu, "Technology Impacts on Curriculum of Library and Information Science (LIS)—a United States (US) Perspective," *LIBRES: Library and Information Science Electronic Journal* 23, no. 2 (2013): 1–9, accessed July 8, 2014, http://0-search.ebscohost.com.library.simmons.edu/login.aspx?direct=true&db=lls&AN=92616179&site=ehost-live&scope=site.

42. Michael Gorman, "Special Feature: Whither Library Education," *New Library World* 105, no. 9 (2004): 376–80, accessed July 8, 2014, http://0-search.proquest.com.library.simmons.edu/docview/229671844/1409710CAB2160936C7/10?accountid=13870.

43. American Library Association, President's Task Force on Library Education, "Final Report," *American Library Association*, January 2009, http://www.ala.org/aboutala/sites/ala.org.aboutala/files/content/governance/officers/eb_documents/2008_2009ebdocuments/ebd12_30.pdf.

44. Farkas, "Building and Sustaining."

45. Julia Leong and Craig Anderson, "Fostering Innovation through Cultural Change," *Library Management* 33, nos. 8/9 (2012): 490–97, accessed July 8, 2014, doi:10.1108/01435121211279858.

Appendix

Table A.1 Resources That Have Been Used for Environmental Scanning for Reference Services

Source	Source Type	Location
Academic Librarian (Wayne Bivens-Tatum)	blog	https://blogs.princeton.edu/librarian
ACRLog	blog	http://acrlog.org
ALA TechSource	blog	http://www.alatechsource.org
American Libraries	Twitter	http://twitter.com/amlibraries
The Atlantic Technology	online magazine	http://www.theatlantic.com/technology
Bits: The Business of Technology (*New York Times*)	blog	http://bits.blogs.nytimes.com
Confessions of a Science Librarian	blog	http://scienceblogs.com/confessions
D-Lib Magazine	journal	http://www.dlib.org
Dan Cohen	Twitter	https://twitter.com/dancohen
The Daring Librarian (Gwyneth Jones)	blog	http://www.thedaringlibrarian.com
David Weinberger	Twitter	http://twitter.com/dweinberger
The Digital Shift	blog	http://thedigitalshift.com
Digital Reference (Stephen Francoeur)	blog	http://www.stephenfrancoeur.com/digitalreference
Disruptive Technology Library Jester	blog	http://dltj.org
District Dispatch	blog	http://www.districtdispatch.org
EDUCAUSE	blog	http://www.educause.edu/blogs
Emerging Technologies Librarian	blog	http://etechlib.wordpress.com/techtooltoy-sources
Engadget	blog	http://www.engadget.com
First Monday	journal	http://www.firstmonday.org
Forrester Research	Twitter	https://twitter.com/forrester

Freakonomics	blog	http://www.freakonomics.com/blog
Free Range Librarian	blog	http://freerangelibrarian.com
Gavia Libraria (The Library Loon)	blog	http://gavialib.com
Gigaom	blog	http://gigaom.com
Hack Library School	blog	http://hacklibschool.wordpress.com
Harvard Library Innovation Lab	blog	http://librarylab.law.harvard.edu/blog
Idea Lab (PBS; sponsored by Knight Foundation)	blog	http://www.pbs.org/idealab
InfoDocket (*Library Journal*)	blog	http://www.infodocket.com
Information Research	journal	http://informationr.net/ir
Information Wants to Be Free	blog	http://meredith.wolfwater.com/wordpress
Innovation Excellence	blog	http://www.innovationexcellence.com/blog
Internet Research	journal	http://www.emeraldinsight.com/journals.htm?issn=1066-2243
Jan Holmquist	blog	http://janholmquist.wordpress.com
Librarian.net (Jessamyn West)	blog	http://www.librarian.net
Library City	blog	http://librarycity.org
LifeHacker	blog	http://lifehacker.com
LISNews	blog	http://lisnews.org
LITA Blog	blog	http://litablog.org
Maria Popova	Twitter	http://twitter.com/brainpicker
Marshall Breeding	Twitter	https://twitter.com/mbreeding
Michael Schofield	blog	http://ns4lib.com
Miriam Posner: Blog	blog	http://miriamposner.com/blog
MIT Technology Review	online magazine	http://www.technologyreview.com
New York Public Library	blog	http://www.nypl.org/voices/blogs/blog-channels
New York Times (Technology)	online newspaper	http://www.nytimes.com/pages/technology/index.html
Next Big Future	blog	http://nextbigfuture.com
Pew Internet and American Life Project	blog	http://libraries.pewinternet.org
ReadWrite	blog	http://readwrite.com

Reference and User Services Quarterly	journal	http://rusa.metapress.com/home/main.mpx
Reference Services Review	journal	http://www.emeraldinsight.com/journals.htm?issn=0090-7324
Chasing Reference (RUSA)	blog	http://www.chasingreference.com
Tame the Web (Michael Stephen)	blog	http://tametheweb.com
TechCrunch	blog	http://techcrunch.com
Technically Philly	blog	http://technicallyphilly.com
TechSoup for Libraries	blog	http://www.techsoupforlibraries.org/blog
Transforming Libraries	blog	http://www.ala.org/transforminglibraries
The Ubiquitous Librarian	blog	http://chronicle.com/blognetwork/theubiquitouslibrarian
The UX—User Experience (Library Journal)	blog	http://lj.libraryjournal.com/category/opinion/aaron-schmidt
The Verge	blog	http://www.theverge.com
Virtual Dave . . . Real Blog (Dave Lankes)	blog	http://quartz.syr.edu/blog
Wall Street Journal (Technology)	online newspaper	http://online.wsj.com/public/page/news-tech-technology.html?mod=WSJ_topnav_tech_main
WIRED	online magazine	http://www.wired.com
	Twitter hashtag	#innovation
	Twitter hashtag	#libchat
	Twitter hashtag	#librarians
	Twitter hashtag	#libraries
	Twitter hashtag	#tech and #technology

Bibliography

"7 Things You Should Know about Gesture-Based Computing." *EDUCAUSE Learning Initiative (ELI)*. January 8, 2014. http://www.educause.edu/library/resources/7-things-you-should-know-about-gesture-based-computing.

"The 8-Step Process for Leading Change." *Kotter International*. Accessed June 21, 2014. http://www.kotterinternational.com/our-principles/changesteps.

"29th Annual Computers in Libraries 2014." *Information Today, Inc.* Accessed July 15, 2014. http://www.infotoday.com/cil2014.

"2014 Innovations Initiative." *Urban Libraries Council*. Accessed June 5, 2014. http://www.urbanlibraries.org/innovations—pages-268.php.

"Above the Fold." *OCLC Research*. Accessed June 15, 2014. http://www.oclc.org/research/publications/newsletters/abovethefold.html.

Abram, Stephen. "Social Libraries: The Librarian 2.0 Phenomenon." *Library Resources and Technical Services* 52, no. 2 (2008): 19–22.

"A*CENSUS Results." *Society of American Archivists*. Accessed September 16, 2013. http://www2.archivists.org/sites/all/files/ACENSUS-Final.pdf.

ACRL Research Planning and Review Committee. "2012 Top Ten Trends in Academic Libraries: A Review of the Trends Affecting Academic Libraries in Higher Education." *College and Research Libraries News* 73, no. 6 (2012): 311–20. Accessed January 16, 2014. http://crln.acrl.org/content/73/6/311.full.

ACRL Research Planning and Review Committee. "Environmental Scan 2013." *Association of College and Research Libraries*. April 2013. http://www.ala.org/acrl/sites/ala.acrl/files/content/publications/whitepapers/EnvironmentalScan13.pdf.

"ACRL/NY Annual Symposium 2012: Cultivating Entrepreneurship in Academic Libraries." *Association of College and Research Libraries, Greater New York Metropolitan Chapter*. Accessed June 16, 2014. http://acrlnysymp2012.wordpress.com.

ACRLog. Accessed July 15, 2014. http://acrlog.org.

"Advocacy, Legislation and Issues." *American Library Association*. Accessed July 15, 2014. http://www.ala.org/advocacy.

Agosto, Denise E., Lily Rozaklis, Craig MacDonald, and Eileen G. Abels. "A Model of the Reference and Information Service Process: An Educator's Perspective." *Reference and User Services Quarterly* 50, no. 3 (2011): 235–44. http://blog.rusq.org/wp-content/uploads/2011/04/Agosto-et-al.pdf.

"ALA's Core Competences of Librarianship." *American Library Association*. January 27, 2009. Accessed December 17, 2013. http://www.ala.org/educationcareers/sites/ala.org.educationcareers/files/content/careers/corecomp/corecompetences/finalcorecompstat09.pdf.

Al-Maskari, Azzah, and Mark Sanderson. "A Review of Factors Influencing User Satisfaction in Information Retrieval." *Journal of the American Society for Information Science and Technology* 61, no. 5 (2010): 859–68. doi:10.1002/asi.21300.

American Library Association. http://www.ala.org.

American Library Association, President's Task Force on Library Education. "Final Report." *American Library Association*. January 2009. http://www.ala.org/aboutala/sites/ala.org.aboutala/files/content/governance/officers/eb_documents/2008_2009ebdocuments/ebd12_30.pdf.

American Library Association Committee on Terminology. *A.L.A. Glossary of Library Terms*. Chicago: American Library Association, 1943.

Andersen, Erika. "The Basics of Being Strategic about Change." *Forbes* (blog). September 8, 2010. Accessed June 27, 2014. http://www.forbes.com/2010/09/08/change-strategy-management-leadership-managing-human-capital-10-steps.html.

Anderson, Janna, and Lee Rainie. "The Internet of Things Will Thrive by 2025: Many Experts Say the Rise of Embedded and Wearable Computing Will Bring the Next Revolution in Digital Technology." *Pew Research Internet Project.* May 14, 2014. http://www.pewinternet.org/2014/05/14/internet-of-things.

Andy. "KIA for QandA NJ." *Agnostic, Maybe* (blog). *WordPress.* April 21, 2011. http://agnosticmaybe.wordpress.com/2011/04/21/kia-for-qanda-nj.

Answerland. Accessed April 28, 2014. http://www.answerland.org.

"App Library." *Digital Public Library of America.* Accessed May 20, 2014. http://dp.la/apps.

"Appfest." *Digital Public Library of America.* Accessed April 30, 2014. http://dp.la/wiki/Appfest.

Applegate, Rachel. "Whose Decline? Which Academic Libraries Are "Deserted" in Terms of Reference Transactions?" *Reference and User Services Quarterly* 48, no. 2 (2008): 176–89. doi:10.5860/rusq.48n2.176.

"AskAway Chat Now in Moodle." *Emily Carr University of Art + Design Teaching and Learning Centre.* June 25, 2012. http://tlc.ecuad.ca/askaway-chat-now-in-moodle.

"Association of College and Research Libraries Standards for Proficiencies for Instruction Librarians and Coordinators." *Association of College and Research Libraries.* June 24, 2007. http://www.ala.org/acrl/standards/profstandards.

Ayers, Edward L. "Does Digital Scholarship Have a Future?" *EDUCAUSE Review Online.* August 5, 2013. http://www.educause.edu/ero/article/does-digital-scholarship-have-a-future.

Ball, Heather. *Core Competencies and Core Curricula for the Art Library and Visual Resources Professions.* Oak Creek, WI: ARLIS/NA, n.d.

Barile, Lori. "Mobile Technologies for Libraries: A List of Mobile Applications and Resources for Development." *College and Research Libraries News* 72, no. 4 (2011): 222–28. http://crln.acrl.org/content/72/4/222.full.pdf+html.

Bawden, David, and Polona Vilar. "Digital Libraries: To Meet or Manage User Expectations." *Aslib Proceedings* 58, no. 4 (2006): 346–54. doi:10.1108/00012530610687713.

Beile, Penny M., and Megan M. Adams. "Other Duties as Assigned: Emerging Trends in the Academic Library Job Market." *College and Research Libraries* 61, no. 4 (2000): 336–47.

Bell, Steven J. "Design Thinking." *American Libraries* 41, nos. 6/7 (June/July 2010): 50.

Bell, Steven J. "Who Needs a Reference Desk?" *Library Issues* 27, no. 6 (2007).

Bennett, Erika, and Jennie Simning. "Embedded Librarians and Reference Traffic: A Quantitative Analysis." *Journal of Library Administration* 50, nos. 5/6 (2010): 443–57. doi:10.1080/01930826.2010.491437.

Bias, Randolph G., Paul F. Marty, and Ian Douglas. "Usability/User-Centered Design in the iSchools: Justifying a Teaching Philosophy." *Journal of Education for Library and Information Science* 53, no. 4 (2012): 274–89.

Biddix, J. Patrick, Chung Joo Chung, and Han Woo Park. "Convenience or Credibility? A Study of College Student Online Research Behaviors." *The Internet and Higher Education* 14, no. 3 (2011): 175–82. doi:10.1016/j.iheduc.2011.01.003.

Blankenship, Emily F. "Who Holds the Keys to the Web for Libraries?" *Journal of Library Administration* 47, nos. 1–2 (2008): 55–66, doi:10.1080/01930820802110670.

Blau, Reuven. "Brooklyn Public Library Researchers Answered 3.5 Million Questions in 2013, Records Show." *New York Daily News*, March 26, 2014, 2:00 a.m. Accessed March 26, 2014. http://www.nydailynews.com/new-york/brooklyn-public-library-researchers-answered-3-5-million-questions-2013-records-show-article-1.1734547.

Blummer, Barbara A., and Olga Kristkaya. "Best Practices for Creating an Online Tutorial: A Literature Review." *The Journal of Web Librarianship* 3, no. 3 (2009): 199–216. doi:10.1080/19322900903050799.

Boissè, Joseph A., and Carla Stoffle. "Epilogue: Issues and Answers: The Participants' Views." In *The Information Society: Issues and Answers*, edited by E. J. Josey, 110–21. Phoenix, AZ: Oryx Press, 1978.

"Book A Librarian." *Arapahoe Library District*. Accessed May 10, 2014. http://arapahoe-libraries.org/book-a-librarian.

"Book a Librarian." *Skokie Public Library*. Accessed December 10, 2013. http://skokieli-brary.info/s_info/book_librarian.asp.

"Book-A-Librarian: Sno-Isle Libraries." *Urban Libraries Council*. Accessed May 2, 2014. http://www.urbanlibraries.org/book-a-librarian-innovation-177.php?page_id=38.

"Books on Bikes." *The Seattle Public Library*. Accessed May 2, 2014. http://www.spl.org/using-the-library/library-on-the-go/books-on-bikes.

Bopp, Richard E., and Linda C. Smith. *Reference and Information Services: An Introduction*. Santa Barbara, CA: Libraries Unlimited, 2011.

Bracke, Marianne Stowell, Michael Brewer, Robyn Huff-Eibl, Daniel R. Lee, Robert Mitchell, and Michael Ray. "Finding Information in a New Landscape: Developing New Service and Staffing Models for Mediated Information Services." *College and Research Libraries* 68, no. 3 (2007): 248–67. Accessed November 18, 2013. http://crl.acrl.org/content/68/3/248.full.pdf+html.

Brian Hopkins' Blog (blog). *Forrester*. Accessed July 13, 2014. http://blogs.forrester.com/brian_hopkins.

Brynjolfsson, Erik, and Michael Schrage. "The New, Faster Face of Innovation: Thanks to Technology, Change Has Never Been So Easy or So Cheap." *Wall Street Journal*, August 17, 2009. Accessed June 25, 2014. http://online.wsj.com/news/articles/SB10001424052970204830304574130820184260340.

Bryson, John M. "Resource A: An Ongoing Approach for Identifying External Threats and Opportunities." In *Strategic Planning for Public and Nonprofit Organizations: A Guide to Strengthening and Sustaining Organizational Achievement*, edited by John M. Bryson, 245–44. San Francisco: Jossey-Bass, 1995.

Bryson, John M., Fran Ackermann, Edin Colin, and Charles Finn. "Resource C: Using the 'Oval Mapping Process' to Identify Strategic Issues and Formulate Effective Strategies." In *Strategic Planning for Public and Nonprofit Organizations: A Guide to Strengthening and Sustaining Organizational Achievement*, edited by John. M. Bryson, 257–75. San Francisco: Jossey-Bass, 1995.

Buchanan, Leigh. "The Smartest Little Company in America." *Inc.* (January 1999): 43.

Budd, John M. *The Academic Library: Its Context, Its Purpose, and Its Operation*. Santa Barbara, CA: Libraries Unlimited, 1998.

Bunge, Charles A. "Reference Services." *The Reference Librarian* 31, no. 66 (1999): 185–99. doi:10.1300/J120v31n66_17.

Carlson, Scott. "Are Reference Desks Dying Out? Librarians Struggle to Redefine— and in Some Cases Eliminate—the Venerable Institution." *The Reference Librarian* 48, no. 2 (2007): 25–30. doi:10.1300/J120v48n02_06.

Cassell, Kay Ann, and Uma Hiremath. *Reference and Information Services in the 21st Century: An Introduction*. New York: Neal-Schuman, 2009.

Choi, Myungweon. "Employees' Attitudes toward Organizational Change: A Literature Review." *Human Resource Management* 50, no. 4 (July/August 2011): 479–500. doi:10.1002/hrm.20434.

Choo, Chun Wei. "Environmental Scanning as Information Seeking and Organizational Learning." *Information Research* 7, no. 1 (October 2001). Accessed July 7, 2014. http://informationr.net/ir/7-1/paper112.html.

Chow, Anthony S., Theresa L. Shaw, David Gwynn, Dan Martensen, and Margaret Howard. "Changing Times and Requirements: Implications for LIS Education." *LIBRES: Library and Information Science Research Electronic Journal* 21, no. 1 (2011): B1–23.

Chronicle of Higher Education. Accessed June 16, 2014. http://chronicle.com/section/Home/5.

Clark, Wendy. "Reference Service 2.0 Revisited." *Refer* 26, no. 2 (2010): 11–16.

Clough, G. Wayne. "What Does It Mean to Be Seriously Amazing? The Smithsonian's Secretary Introduces the Institution's New Campaign to Highlight Its Best and Most Innovative Work." *Smithsonian Magazine* (November 2012). http://www.smithsonianmag.com/arts-culture/what-does-it-mean-to-be-seriously-amaz-ing-79778715/?no-ist.

Coffman, Steve, and Linda Arret. "To Chat or Not to Chat—Taking Another Look at Virtual Reference, Part I." *Searcher* 12, no. 7 (2004). Accessed February 16, 2014. http://www.infotoday.com/searcher/jul04/arret_coffman.shtml.

"Competencies: Competencies for Information Professionals of the 21st Century." *Special Library Association*. Last updated June 2003. http://www.sla.org/about-sla/competencies.

"Competencies for Professional Success: Executive Summary." *Medical Library Association*. Accessed July 12, 2014. http://www.mlanet.org/education/policy/executive_summary.html#B.

"Competencies of Law Librarianship." *American Association of Law Libraries*. Last modified April 2010. http://www.aallnet.org/main-menu/Leadership-Governance/policies/PublicPolicies/competencies.html.

"Conferences." *Association for Computing Machinery*. Accessed July 15, 2014. http://www.acm.org/conferences.

Connaway, Lynn Sillipigni, Timothy J. Dickey, and Marie L. Radford. "If It's Too Inconvenient, I'm Not Going After It: Convenience as a Critical Factor in Information-Seeking Behaviors." *Library and Information Science Research* 33, no. 3 (2011): 179–90. doi:10.1016/j.lisr.2010.12.002.

Courtois, Martin P., Martha E. Higgins, and Aditya Kapur. "Was This Guide Helpful? Users' Perceptions of Subject Guides." *Reference Services Review* 33, no. 2 (2005): 188–96. doi:10.1108/00907320510597381.

Courtois, Martin P., and Maira Liriano. "Tips for Roving Reference: How to Best Serve Library Users." *College and Research Library News* 61, no. 4 (2000): 289–301.

Craine, Kevin. "Managing the Cycle of Change." *Information Management Journal* 41, no. 5 (2007): 44–50. Accessed July 7, 2014. http://0-search.ebscohost.com.library.simmons.edu/login.aspx?direct=true&db=lls&AN=27200121&site=ehost-live&scope=site.

Crumpton, Michael A. "Talk about Change." *The Bottom Line: Managing Library Finances* 25, no. 4 (2012): 140–42. Accessed July 7, 2014. http://0-www.emeraldinsight.com.library.simmons.edu/journals.htm?issn=0888-045x&volume=25&issue=4&articleid=17065522&show=html.

Cuillier, Cheryl. "Choosing Our Futures. .. Still." *The Journal of Library Administration* 52, no. 5 (2012): 436–51. doi:10.1080/01930826.2012.700806.

Cummings, Joel, Lara Cummings, and Linda Frederiksen. "User Preferences in Reference Services: Virtual Reference and Academic Libraries." *portal: Libraries and the Academy* 7, no. 1 (2007): 81–96. doi:10.1353/pla.2007.0004.

Cyrus, John W. W., and Mark P. Baggett. "Mobile Technology: Implications for Privacy and Librarianship." *The Reference Librarian* 53, no. 3 (2012): 284–96. doi:10.1080/02763877.2012.678765.

Davies-Hoffman, Kimberly, Michelle Costello, and Debby Emerson. "Keeping Pace with Information Literacy Instruction for the Real World." *Communications in Information Literacy* 7, no. 1 (2013): 9–23.

De Jager-Loftus, Danielle. "Value-Added Technologies for Liaison and Outreach." *Journal of Electronic Resources in Medical Libraries* 6, no. 4 (2009): 307–15, doi:10.1080/15424060903364800.

de Jong, Cees-Jan. "Undergraduate Students' Perspectives on the Reference Transaction: A Pilot Study." Proceedings of the Annual Conference of the Canadian Association for Information Science, Toronto, Canada, 2006. http://www.cais-acsi.ca/proceedings/2006/dejong_2006.pdf.

De Rosa, Cathy, Joanne Cantrell, Matthew Carlson, Peggy Gallagher, Janet Hawk, and Charlotte Sturtz. *Perceptions of Libraries 2010: Context and Community*. Dublin, OH:

OCLC, 2011. Accessed August 28, 2013. http://www.oclc.org/reports/2010percep-tions.en.html.

De Rosa, Cathy, Joanne Cantrell, Janet Hawk, and Alane Wilson. *College Students' Perceptions of Libraries and Information Resources: A Report to the OCLC Membership.* Dublin, OH: OCLC Online Computer Library Center, 2006. http://www.oclc.org/content/dam/oclc/reports/pdfs/studentperceptions.pdf.

Deeken, JoAnne, and Deborah Thomas. "Technical Services Job Ads: Changes since 1995." *College and Research Libraries* 67, no. 2 (2006): 136–45. http://crl.acrl.org/content/67/2/136.full.pdf+html.

"Definitions of Reference." *Reference and User Services Association.* January 14, 2008. Accessed August 15, 2013. http://www.ala.org/rusa/resources/guidelines/definitionsreference.

"The Degree Qualifications Profile." *Lumina Foundation.* January 2011. Accessed December 13, 2013. http://www.luminafoundation.org/publications/The_Degree_Qualifications_Profile.pdf.

DeGusta, Michael. "Are Smart Phones Spreading Faster Than Any Technology in Human History?" *MIT Technology Review.* May 9, 2012. http://www.technologyreview.com/news/427787/are-smart-phones-spreading-faster-than-any-technology-in-human-history.

Dempsey, Megan. "Blending the Trends: A Holistic Approach to Reference Services." *Public Services Quarterly* 7, nos. 1/2 (2011): 3–17.

D'Esposito, Joanne E., and Rachel M. Gardner. "University Students' Perceptions of the Internet: An Exploratory Study." *The Journal of Academic Librarianship* 25, no. 6 (1999): 456–61. doi:10.1016/S0099-1333(99)00078-6.

Detmering, Robert, and Claudene Sproles. "Forget the Desk Job: Current Roles and Responsibilities in Entry-Level Reference Job Advertisements." *College and Research Libraries* 73, no. 6 (2012): 543–55.

Dewey, Barbara I. "The Embedded Librarian: Strategic Campus Collaborations." *Resource Sharing and Information Networks* 17, nos. 1/2 (2004): 5–17. doi:10.1300/J121v17n01_02.

"Dialogue on Public Libraries: Communications and Society Program." *The Aspen Institute.* Accessed June 17, 2014. http://www.aspeninstitute.org/policy-work/communications-society/our-work/dialogue-public-libraries.

"Digital Public Library of America." *GitHub.* Accessed May 14, 2014. https://github.com/dpla.

"DPLA Appfest Hackathon in Chattanooga, TN." *Berkman Center for Internet and Society at Harvard University.* Last updated October 17, 2012. http://cyber.law.harvard.edu/events/2012/11/dpla.

Drewes, Kathy, and Nadine Hoffman. "Academic Embedded Librarianship: An Introduction." *Public Services Quarterly* 6, nos. 2/3 (2010): 75–82. doi:10.1080/15228959.2010.498773.

Drucker, Peter F. *Innovation and Entrepreneurship: Practice and Principles.* New York: HarperBusiness, 2001.

Duggan, Maeve, and Aaron Smith. "Cell Internet Use 2013." *Pew Research Internet Project.* September 16, 2013. http://www.pewinternet.org/Reports/2013/Cell-Internet.aspx.

Duggan, Maeve, and Aaron Smith. "Social Media Update 2013: 42% of Online Adults Use Multiple Social Networking Sites, but Facebook Remains the Platform of Choice." *Pew Research Internet Project.* December 30, 2013. http://www.pewinternet.org/2013/12/30/social-media-update-2013.

Durfee, Linda J. "Student Awareness of Reference Services in a Liberal Arts College Library." *Library Quarterly* 56, no. 3 (1986): 286–302. http://www.jstor.org/stable/4308017.

Eastwood, Terence M. "Public Services Education for Archivists." *The Reference Librarian* 26, no. 56 (1997): 27–38.

The ed17, "'Ask a Librarian'—Connecting Wikimedians with the National Library of Australia." *Wikipedia: The Signpost.* May 14, 2014. http://en.wikipedia.org/wiki/Wikipedia:Wikipedia_Signpost/2014-05-14/News_and_notes.

EDUCAUSE. http://www.educause.edu.

Eisenmann, Thomas R. "Entrepreneurship: A Working Definition." *HRB Blog Network* (blog). January 10, 2013. http://blogs.hbr.org/2013/01/what-is-entrepreneurship.

"Enquire: Ask a Librarian 24/7" *OCLC.* Accessed May 15, 2014. http://www.oclc.org/content/dam/oclc/services/brochures/213584ukf_enquire.pdf.

entrelib: The Conference for Entrepreneurial Librarians. Accessed July 15, 2014. http://entrelib.org.

"Environmental Scan: Pattern Recognition (2003)." *OCLC.* Accessed June 15, 2014. http://www.oclc.org/reports/escan.en.html.

Erdmann, Christopher. "Wolbach User Experience Lab." *Harvard University Library: Office for Scholarly Communication.* Last updated February 10, 2011. https://osc.hul.harvard.edu/liblab/proj/wolbach-user-experience-lab.

Evans, Jonny. "Apple's Next Innovation: 3D Gesture-Based Computing Puts the 'Post' in Post-PC." *AppleHolic* (blog). *Computer World.* August 10, 2012. http://blogs.computerworld.com/mac-os-x/20821/apples-next-innovation-3d-gesture-based-computing-puts-post-post-pc.

Fagan, Jody. "Students' Perceptions of Academic Librarians." *The Reference Librarian* 37 no. 78 (2002): 131–48. doi:10.1300/J120v37n78_09.

Fagan, Jody Condit, and Christina M. Desai. "Communication Strategies for Instant Messaging and Chat Reference Services." *The Reference Librarian,* nos. 79/80 (2003): 121–55. doi:10.1300/J120v38n79_09.

Faibisoff, Sylvia G., and Donald P. Ely. "Information and Information Needs." *Information Reports and Bibliographies* 5, no. 5 (1976): 2–16.

Fallows, Deborah. "Search Engine Users: Internet Users Are Confident, Satisfied, and Trusting, but They Are Also Unaware and Naïve." *Pew Internet and American Life Project.* January 23, 2005. Accessed November 21, 2013. http://www.pewinternet.org/~/media//Files/Reports/2005/PIP_Searchengine_users.pdf.pdf.

Farkas, Meredith. "Skills for the 21st Century Librarian." *One-Person Library* 24, no. 10 (2008): 6.

Farkas, Meredith Gorran. "Building and Sustaining a Culture of Assessment: Best Practices for Change Leadership." *Reference Services Review* 41, no. 1 (2013): 13–31. doi:10.1108/00907321311300857.

Fennewald, Joseph. "Same Questions, Different Venue: An Analysis of In-Person and Online Questions." *The Reference Librarian* 46, nos. 95–96 (2006): 21–35. doi:10.1300/J120v46n95_03.

Fister, Barbara. "The Research Processes of Undergraduate Students." *The Journal of Academic Librarianship* 18, no. 3 (1992): 163–69.

Ford, Barbara J. "Reference beyond (and without) the Reference Desk." *College and Research Libraries* 47, no. 5 (1986): 491–94. Accessed November 18, 2013. http://crl.acrl.org/content/47/5/491.full.pdf+html.

Forsyth, Ellen. "Fancy Walkie Talkies, Star Trek Communicators or Roving Reference?" Paper presented at VALA—Libraries, Technology and the Future, Inc., Melbourne, Australia, February 5–7, 2008. Accessed May 2, 2014. http://www.valaconf.org.au/vala2008/papers2008/148_Forsyth_Final.pdf.

Fox, Susannah. "What's the Future for Self-Tracking?" *Pew Research Internet Project.* March 9, 2012. http://www.pewinternet.org/2012/03/09/whats-the-future-for-self-tracking-2.

Franklin, Brinley. "Surviving to Thriving: Advancing the Institutional Mission." *Journal of Library Administration* 52, no. 1 (2012): 94–107. doi:10.1080/01930826.2012.630244.

Ganshorn, Heather. "A Librarian Consultation Service Improves Decision-Making and Saves Time for Primary Care Practitioners." *Evidence-Based Library and Informa-*

tion Practice 4, no. 2 (2009): 148–51. http://ejournals.library.ualberta.ca/index.php/EBLIP/article/view/6019.

Garrison, Julie. "What Do We Do Now? A Case for Abandoning Yesterday and Making the Future." *Reference and User Services Quarterly* 51, no. 1 (2011): 12–14.

Gazan, Rich. "Social Q & A." *Journal of the American Society for Information Science and Technology* 62, no. 12 (2011): 2301–12. doi:10.1002/asi.21562.

"Global Faces and Networked Places: A Nielsen Report on Social Networking's New Global Footprint." *Nielsen.* March 2009. http://www.nielsen.com/content/dam/corporate/us/en/newswire/uploads/2009/03/nielsen_globalfaces_mar09.pdf.

"Global Publics Embrace Social Networking." *Pew Research Internet Project.* December 15, 2010. http://www.pewinternet.org/2010/12/15/global-publics-embrace-social-networking.

Goldenson, Jeff, Ann Whiteside, and Jessica Yurkofsky, with Jeffrey Schnapp. "GSD 09125: Library Test Kitchen III: Library Machines Working Syllabus." *Harvard University.* Accessed May 22, 2014. http://www.librarytestkitchen.org/assets/LTK-III-Syllabus_august.pdf.

Goodchild, Lester, and Harold Weschler. *The History of Higher Education.* Boston: Pearson Custom Publishing, 2008.

Gorman, Michael. "Special Feature: Whither Library Education." *New Library World* 105, no. 9 (2004): 376–80. Accessed July 8, 2014. http://0-search.proquest.com.library.simmons.edu/docview/229671844/1409710CAB2160936C7/10?accountid=13870

"Graduate School of Library and Information Science Full Catalog, Course Information." *University of Illinois at Urbana-Champaign.* Accessed June 12, 2014, http://www.lis.illinois.edu/academics/courses/catalog#500level.

Gratz, Amy, and Julie Gilbert. "Meeting Student Needs at the Reference Desk." *Reference Services Review* 39, no. 3 (2011): 423–38. doi:10.1108/00907321111161412.

Green, Samuel Swett. "Personal Relations between Librarians and Readers." *American Library Journal* 1 (1876): 74–81.

Griffiths, Jillian R., and Peter Brophy. "Student Searching Behavior and the Web: Use of Academic Resources and Google." *Library Trends* 53, no. 4 (2005): 539–54. http://hdl.handle.net/2142/1749.

Griffiths, José-Marie, and Donald W. King. "InterConnections: The IMLS National Study on the Use of Libraries, Museums and the Internet: Conclusions." *Institute of Museum and Library Services.* February 2008. Accessed November 23, 2013. http://interconnectionsreport.org/reports/ConclusionsFullRptB.pdf.

Gross, Melissa, and Don Latham. "What's Skill Got to Do with It? Information Literacy Skills and Self-Views among First-Year College Students." *Journal of the American Society of Information Science and Technology* 63, no. 3 (2012): 547–83. doi:10.1002/asi.21681.

"Guidelines: Competencies for Special Collections Professionals." *Association of College and Research Libraries.* July 1, 2008. Accessed December 17, 2013. http://www.ala.org/acrl/standards/comp4specollect#msa.

"Guidelines for a Graduate Program in Archival Studies." *Society of American Archivists.* Accessed September 16, 2013. http://www2.archivists.org/gpas.

Gutsche, Betha. "Coping with Continual Motion." *Library Journal* 135, no. 4 (2010): 28–31.

Hahn, Jim. "The Internet of Things Meets the Library of Things." *ACRL TechConnect.* March 19, 2012. http://acrl.ala.org/techconnect/?p=474.

Hall, Russell A. "Beyond the Job Ad: Employers and Library Instruction." *College and Research Libraries* 74, no. 1 (2013): 24–38. http://crl.acrl.org/content/74/1/24.full.pdf+html.

Hardy, Quentin. "Quora and the Search for Truth." *Bits* (blog). *New York Times.* February 9, 2014. http://nyti.ms/1gal2Uu.

Harison, Elan, and Albert Boonstra. "Essential Competencies for Technochange Management: Towards an Assessment Model." *International Journal of Information Management* 29, no. 4 (2009): 283–94. doi:10.1016/j.ijinfomgt.2008.11.003.

Harrington, Sara. "'Library as Laboratory': Online Pathfinders and the Humanities Graduate Student." *Public Services Quarterly* 3, nos. 3/4 (2007): 37–52. doi:10.1080/15228950802110445.

Harvard Library Innovation Lab (blog). http://librarylab.law.harvard.edu/blog.

"Harvard Library Innovation Lab." *The President and Fellows of Harvard College*. Accessed June 2, 2014. http://librarylab.law.harvard.edu.

"Harvard Library Lab: About the Library Lab." *Harvard University Library: Office for Scholarly Communication*. Accessed June 3, 2014. https://osc.hul.harvard.edu/liblab.

Head, Alison J. "Beyond Google: How Do Students Conduct Academic Research?" *First Monday* 12, no. 8 (2007). Accessed August 28, 2013. http://www.uic.edu/htbin/cgiwrap/bin/ojs/index.php/fm/article/view/1998/1873.

Head, Alison J. "Project Information Literacy: What Can Be Learned about the Information-Seeking Behavior of Today's College Students?" In *Proceedings of the 2013 ACRL Conference: Imagine, Innovate, Inspire*, edited by Dawn Mueller, 472–82. Chicago: ACRL, 2013.

Head, Alison J., and Michael B. Eisenberg. "Finding Context: What Today's College Students Say about Conducting Research in the Digital Age." *Project Information Literacy Progress Report*. February 4, 2009. http://projectinfolit.org/pdfs/PIL_ProgressReport_2_2009.pdf.

Head, Alison J., and Michael B. Eisenberg. "Truth Be Told: How College Students Evaluate and Use Information in the Digital Age." *Project Information Literacy Progress Report*. November 1, 2010. Accessed January 24, 2014. http://projectinfolit.org/images/pdfs/pil_fall2010_survey_fullreport1.pdf.

Heinrichs, John H., and Jeen-Su Lim. "Emerging Requirements of Computer Related Competencies for Librarians." *Library and Information Science Research* 31, no. 2 (2009): 101–6. doi:10.1016/j.lisr.2008.11.001.

Heller, Margaret. "Creating Quick Solutions and Having Fun: The Joy of Hackathons." *ACRL TechConnect* (blog). *Association of College and Research Libraries*. June 23, 2012. http://acrl.ala.org/techconnect/?p=1443.

Henderson, R. I. "Job Descriptions—Critical Documents, Versatile Tools. Part 3: Conducting a Job Analysis." *Supervisory Management* 21 (1976): 26–34.

Hennig, Nicole. "Apps for Content Creation." *Unbound* (blog). *Simmons GSLIS*. June 8, 2014. http://gslis.simmons.edu/blogs/unbound/2014/06/08/apps-for-content-creation.

Henry, Jo. "Death of Reference or Birth of a New Marketing Age?" *Future Voices in Public Service* 7, nos. 1/2 (2011): 87–93. doi:10.1080/15228959.2011.572793.

Hinchliffe, Lisa Janicke. "Instruction." In *Reference and Information Services: An Introduction*, edited by Richard E. Bopp and Linda C. Smith, 221–60. Santa Barbara, CA: Libraries Unlimited, 2011.

Hines, Samantha Schmehl. "Outpost Reference: Meeting Patrons on Their Own Ground." *PNLA Quarterly* 72, no. 1 (2007): 12–26. http://scholarworks.umt.edu/cgi/viewcontent.cgi?article=1011&context=ml_pubs.

Hodge, Megan, and Nicole Spoor. "Congratulations! You've Landed an Interview: What Do Hiring Committees Really Want?" *New Library World* 113, nos. 3/4 (2012): 139–61. doi:10.1108/03074801211218534.

Hoffman, Starr. "Embedded Academic Librarians Experiences in Online Courses: Roles, Faculty Collaboration, and Opinion." *Library Management* 32, nos. 6/7 (2011): 444–56. doi:10.1108/01435121111158583.

Holman, Lucy. "Millennial Students' Mental Models of Search: Implications for Academic Librarians and Database Developers." *The Journal of Academic Librarianship* 37, no. 1 (2011): 19–27. doi:10.1016/j.acalib.2010.10.003.

Hopkins, Brian. "How Do New 'Systems of Insight' Power Great Mobile Moments and Customer Experiences?" *Forrester* (blog). May 28, 2014. http://blogs.forrester.com/brian_hopkins.

House, Kelly. "Your Own Personal Librarian: Multnomah County Library Allows Patrons to Pick Professional Book Advisors Online." *The Oregonian*, April 30, 2014. http://www.oregonlive.com/portland/index.ssf/2014/04/your_own_personal_librarian_mu.html.

"How Americans Use Online Sources and Their Libraries." *Perceptions of Libraries 2010*. Accessed August 28, 2013. http://www.oclc.org/content/dam/oclc/reports/2010perceptions/howamericansuse.pdf.

Hu, Sharon. "Technology Impacts on Curriculum of Library and Information Science (LIS)—A United States (US) Perspective." *LIBRES: Library and Information Science Electronic Journal* 23, no. 2 (2013): 1–9. Accessed July 8, 2014. http://0-search.ebscohost.com.library.simmons.edu/login.aspx?direct=true&db=lls&AN=92616179&site=ehost-live&scope=site.

Huber, Jeffrey T., Emily B. Kean, Philip D. Fitzgerald, Trina A. Altman, Zach G. Young, Katherine M. Dupin, Jacqueline Leskovec, and Ruth Holst. "Outreach Impact Study: The Case of the Greater Midwest Region." *Journal of the Medical Library Association* 99, no. 4 (2011): 297–303. doi:10.3163/1536-5050.99.4.007.

Hunter, Ben. "Dynamic Pathfinders: Leveraging Your OPAC to Create Resource Guides." *Journal of Web Librarianship* 2, no. 1 (2008): 75–90. doi:10.1080/19322900802186694.

Hurst, Susan, and Matthew Magnuson. "School Libraries and Academic Libraries, What We Can Learn from Each Other." *Chat, E-mail, and IM Reference*. May/June 2007. http://www.ala.org/aasl/aaslpubsandjournals/knowledgequest/kqwebarchives/v35/355/355hurstmagnuson.

Hutchinson, Alvin. "Creative Destruction in Library Services." *Issues in Science and Technology Librarianship* 73 (2013).

Huvila, Isto, Kim Holmberg, Maria Kronqvist-Berg, Outi Nivakoski, and Gunilla Widen. "What Is Librarian 2.0—New Competencies or Interactive Relations? A Library Professional Viewpoint." *Journal of Librarianship and Information Science* 45, no. 3 (2013): 198–205. doi:10.1177/0961000613477122.

"IFLA Trend Report." *International Federation of Library Associations and Institutions*. Last updated August 16, 2013. Accessed June 14, 2014. http://trends.ifla.org.

"Information Center: Access and the Latest Research on Women and Work." *Catalyst*. Accessed May 19, 2014. http://www.catalyst.org/what-we-do/services/information-center.

"Information Literacy Competency Standards for Higher Education." *Association of College and Research Libraries*. Accessed August 15, 2013. http://www.ala.org/acrl/standards/informationliteracycompetency.

"Information Services and Use: Metrics and Statistics for Library and Information Providers—Data Dictionary." *National Information Standards Organization*. March 26, 2013. http://www.niso.org/apps/group_public/download.php/11283/Z39-7-2013_metrics.pdf.

"Internet Librarian 2014." *Information Today, Inc.* Accessed July 15, 2014. http://www.infotoday.com/il2014.

"Internet of Things." *Oxford Dictionaries*. Accessed July 14, 2014. http://www.oxforddictionaries.com/definition/english/Internet-of-things.

Ithaka S+R. Accessed June 8, 2014. http://www.sr.ithaka.org.

Jaeger, Paul T., John Carlo Bertot, and Mega Subramaniam. "Preparing Future Librarians to Effectively Serve Their Communities." *Library Quarterly* 83, no. 3 (2013): 243–48.

Jaguszewski, Janice M., and Karen Williams. *New Roles for New Times: Transforming Liaison Roles in Research Libraries*. Washington, DC: Association of Research Libraries, 2013. Accessed September 30, 2013. http://www.arl.org/storage/documents/publications/NRNT-Liaison-Roles-final.pdf.

Jakubs, Deborah. "Out of the Gray Times: Leading Libraries into the Digital Future." *The Journal of Library Administration* 48, no. 2 (2008): 235–48. Accessed July 7, 2014. http://0-search.ebscohost.com.library.simmons.edu/login.aspx?direct=true& db=lls&AN=502938322&site=ehost-live&scope=site.

Jenkins, Sandra. "Undergraduate Perceptions of the Reference Collection and the Reference Librarian in an Academic Library." *The Reference Librarian* 35, no. 73 (2001): 229–41. doi:10.1300/J120v35n73_01.

Jerabek, Ann. "Job Descriptions: Don't Hire without Them." *Journal of Interlibrary Loan, Document Delivery, and Information Supply* 13, no. 3 (2003): 113–26. Accessed May 24, 2014. http://0-web.a.ebscohost.com.library.simmons.edu/ehost/pdfviewer/pdfviewer?sid=8367d61f-a405-4760-9dfd-0462d45bb055%40sessionmgr4003&vid=9& hid=4112.

Jimerson, Randall C. "Archives and Manuscripts: Reference, Access, and Use." *OCLC Systems and Services* 19, no. 1 (2003): 13–16. doi:10.7560/IC49103.

Jimerson, Randall C. *Archives Power: Memory, Accountability, and Social Justice.* Chicago: Society of American Archivists, 2009.

Johnson, Corey M. "Online Chat Reference: Survey Results from Affiliates at Two Universities." *Reference and User Services Quarterly* 43, no. 3 (2004): 237–47. http://www.jstor.org/stable/20864205.

Johnson, Larry, Samantha Adams, and Michele Cummins. *NMC Horizon Report: 2012 Higher Education Edition.* Austin, TX: The New Media Consortium, 2012.

Johnson, Larry, Samantha Adams Becker, Michele Cummins, Victoria Estrada, Alex Freeman, and Holly Ludgate. *NMC Horizon Report: 2013 Higher Education.* Austin, TX: The New Media Consortium, 2013. Accessed July 15, 2014. http://www.nmc.org/pdf/2013-horizon-report-HE.pdf.

Johnson, Larry, Samantha Adams Becker, Victoria Estrada, and Alex Freeman. *NMC Horizon Report: 2014 Higher Education Edition.* Austin, TX: The New Media Consortium, 2014.

Julien, Heidi, and Shelagh K. Genuis. "Librarians' Experiences of the Teaching Role: A National Survey of Librarians." *Library and Information Science Research* 33, no. 2 (2011): 103–11. doi:10.1016/j.lisr.2010.09.005.

Julien, Heidi, and David Michels. "Source Selection among Information Seekers: Ideals and Realities." *Canadian Journal of Library and Information Science* 25, no. 1 (2000): 1–18. http://www.cais-acsi.ca/proceedings/2000/julien_2000.pdf.

Justine. "Call for Participation—A Reference Renaissance 2010: Inventing the Future." *LISWire* (blog). February 3, 2010. http://liswire.com/content/call-participation-reference-renaissance-2010-inventing-future.

Kanter, Rosabeth Moss. "3 Ways to Innovate in a Stagnant Environment." By Brian Kenny. *The Business.* Podcast transcript. March 11, 2014. http://www.hbs.edu/news/articles/Pages/three-ways-to-innovate.aspx.

Keller, Scott, and Carolyn Aiken. "The Inconvenient Truth about Change Management: Why It Isn't Working and What to Do about It." *McKinsey and Company.* 2008. http://www.mckinsey.com/app_media/reports/financial_services/the_inconvenient_truth_about_change_management.pdf.

Kennan, Mary Anne, Patricia Williard, and Concepcion Wilson. "What Do They Want? A Study of Changing Employer Expectations of Information Professionals." *Australian Academic and Research Libraries* 37, no. 1 (2006): 17–37.

Kennedy, Marie R., and Kristine R. Brancolini. "Academic Librarian Research: A Survey of Attitudes, Involvement and Perceived Capabilities." *College and Research Libraries* 73, no. 5 (2012): 431–48. http://crl.acrl.org/content/73/5/431.full.pdf+html.

Kennedy, May G., Laura Kiken, and Jean P. Shipman. "Addressing Underutilization of Consumer Health Information Resource Centers." *Journal of the Medical Library Association* 96, no. 1 (2008): 42–49. doi:10.3163/1536-5050.96.1.42.

Kennedy, Scott. "Farewell to the Reference Librarian." *The Journal of Library Administration* 51, no. 4 (2011): 323, 324. doi:10.1080/01930826.2011.556954.

Kim, Kyung-Sun, and Sei-Ching Joanna Sin. "Perception and Selection of Information Sources by Undergraduate Students: Effects of Avoidance Style, Confidence, and Personal Control in Problem-Solving." *The Journal of Academic Librarianship* 33, no. 6 (2007): 655–65. doi:10.1016/j.acalib.2007.09.012.

Kimok, Debra, and Holly Heller-Ross. "Visual Tutorials for Point-of-Need Instruction in Online Courses." *Journal of Library Administration* 48, nos. 3/4 (2008): 527–43. doi:10.1080/01930820802289656.

King, David Lee. "Basic Competencies of a 2.0 Librarian, Take 2." *davidleeking.com*. Accessed January 9, 2014http://www.davidleeking.com/2007/07/11/basic-competencies-of-a-20-librarian-take-2/#.U_FJvfldWSp.

Kinkus, Jane. "Project Management Skills: A Literature Review and Content Analysis of Librarian Position Announcements." *College and Research Libraries* 68, no. 4 (2007): 352–63.

Kolowich, Steve. "Embedded Librarians." *Inside Higher Ed*. June 9, 2010. http://www.insidehighered.com/news/2010/06/09/hopkins.

Kotter, John P. "Change Management vs. Change Leadership—What's the Difference?" *Forbes* (blog). July 12, 2011. Accessed June 26, 2014. http://www.forbes.com/sites/johnkotter/2011/07/12/change-management-vs-change-leadership-whats-the-difference.

Kotter, John P. *A Sense of Urgency*. Boston: Harvard Business Press, 2008.

Kriplean, Travis, Caitlin Bonnar, Alan Borning, Bo Kinney, and Brian Gill. "Integrating On-Demand Fact-Checking with Public Dialogue." Paper presented at ACM Conference on Computer Supported Cooperative Work (CSCW), Baltimore, February 15–19, 2014. Accessed June 14, 2014. http://homes.cs.washington.edu/~borning/papers/kriplean-cscw2014.pdf.

Kroski, Ellyssa. "A Librarians' Guide to Makerspaces: 16 Resources." *OEDb: Open Education Database*. March 12, 2013. http://oedb.org/ilibrarian/a-librarians-guide-to-makerspaces.

Kuchi, Triveni, Larua Bowering Mullen, and Stephanie Tama-Bartels. "Librarians without Borders: Reaching out to Students at a Campus Center." *Reference and User Services Quarterly* 43, no. 4 (2004): 310–17. https://rucore.libraries.rutgers.edu/rutgers-lib/37172.

Kwon, Nahyun. "A Mixed-Methods Investigation of the Relationship between Critical Thinking and Library Anxiety among Undergraduate Students in their Information Search Process." *College and Research Libraries* 69, no. 2 (2008): 117–31.

Lee, Jee Yeon, Woojin Paik, and Soohyung Joo. "Information Resource Selection of Undergraduate Students in Academic Search Tasks." *Information Research* 17, no. 1 (2012): 1–19.

Lee, Michelle. "Reference on the Road." *Library Journal* 138, no. 18 (2013): 18–20. http://reviews.libraryjournal.com/2013/11/reference/reference-on-the-road.

Lefevre, Julie, and Terence K. Huwe. "Digital Publishing from the Library: A New Core Competency." *Journal of Web Librarianship* 7, no. 2 (2013): 190–214. doi:10.1080/19322909.2013.780519.

Leong, Julia, and Craig Anderson. "Fostering Innovation through Cultural Change." *Library Management* 33, nos. 8/9 (2012): 490–97. Accessed July 8, 2014. doi:10.1108/01435121211279858.

"LibAnalytics Insight." *Springshare*. Accessed June 8, 2014. http://www.springshare.com/libanalytics.

"Liberal Education and America's Promise (LEAP): Essential Learning Outcomes." *Association of American Colleges and Universities*. Accessed December 13, 2013. http://www.aacu.org/leap/vision.cfm.

Library Extension. Accessed May 2, 2014. http://www.libraryextension.com.

"Living Voters Guide." *Seattle CityClub*. Accessed April 11, 2014. https://livingvotersguide.org.

Lo, Leo S. "New Perspectives in Leadership." *Library Leadership and Management* 27, no. 4 (2013): 1–4. Accessed July 15, 2013. http://0-

web.b.ebscohost.com.library.simmons.edu/ehost/pdfviewer/pdfviewer?vid=17&
  sid=05565469-9a24-4d87-8ede-9ec16e7e7059%40sessionmgr114&hid=123.
Lombardo, Shawn V., and Kristine S. Condic. "Convenience or Content: A Study of
  Undergraduate Periodical Use." *Reference Services Review* 29, no. 4 (2001): 327–38.
  doi:10.1108/EUM0000000006494.
Long, Matthew P., and Roger C. Schonfeld. "Ithaka S+R US Library Survey 2013."
  Ithaka S+R. March 11, 2014. Accessed June 22, 2014. http://sr.ithaka.org/sites/default/
  files/reports/SR_LibraryReport_20140310_0.pdf.
Lotts, Megan, and Stephanie Graves. "Using the iPad for Reference Services: Librar-
  ians Go Mobile." *College and Research Libraries News* 72, no. 4 (2011): 217–20. http://
  crln.acrl.org/content/72/4/217.full.pdf+html.
"Luanne Freund—Innovation and Library Leadership Pecha Kucha." YouTube video,
  6:59. From Changing Times, Inspiring Libraries Summit, December 6–7, 2012.
  Posted by "BCLibraries," December 17, 2012. http://youtu.be/1BN8DSfsOcA.
Luo, Lili. "Fusing Research into Practice: The Role of Research Methods Education."
  Library and Information Science Research 33, no. 3 (2011): 191–201. http://0-
  www.sciencedirect.com.library.simmons.edu/science/article/pii/
  S0740818811000338.
Luo, Lili. "Toward Sustaining Professional Development: Identifying Essential Com-
  petencies for Chat Reference Service." *Library and Information Science Research* 30, no.
  4 (2008): 298–311. doi:10.1016/j.lisr.2008.02.009.
Maatta, Stephanie L. "A Job by Any Other Name: A Few Bright Spots Shine for the
  Class of 2011." *Library Journal* 137, no. 17 (2012): 18–25.
Madden, Mary, and Kathryn Zickuhr. "65% of Online Adults Use Social Networking
  Sites." *Pew Research Internet Project.* August 26, 2011. http://www.pewinternet.org/
  2011/08/26/65-of-online-adults-use-social-networking-sites.
Magi, Trina J., and Patricia E. Mardeusz. "Why Some Students Continue to Value
  Individual, Face-to-Face Instruction in a Technology-Rich World." *College and Re-
  search Libraries* 74, no. 6 (2013): 605–18. http://crl.acrl.org/content/74/6/
  605.full.pdf+html.
Malbin, Susan L. "The Reference Interview in Archival Literature." *College and Research Libraries* 58, no. 1 (1997): 69–80. http://crl.acrl.org/content/58/1/
  69.full.pdf+html.
Malnati, Karen, and Ronnie Boseman. "Embedded Librarian Program Insights." *Community and Junior College Libraries* 18, nos. 3/4 (2012): 127–36. doi:10.1080/
  02763915.2012.792214.
Mardis, Lori A., and Connie Jo Ury. "Innovation—An LO Library: Reuse of Learning
  Objects." *Reference Services Review* 36, no. 4 (2008): 389–413. doi:10.1108/
  00907320810920360.
Martell, Charles. "The Absent User: Physical Use of Academic Library Collections and
  Services Continues to Decline 1995–2006." *The Journal of Academic Librarianship* 34,
  no. 5 (2008): 400–407. doi:10.1016/j.acalib.2008.06.003.
Martin, Pamela N., and Lezlie Park. "Reference Desk Consultation Assignment: An
  Exploratory Study of Students' Perceptions of Reference Service." *Reference and User
  Services Quarterly* 49, no. 4 (2010): 333–40. http://digitalcommons.usu.edu/lib_pubs/
  91.
Massey-Burzio, Virginia. "From the Other Side of the Reference Desk: A Focus Group
  Study." *The Journal of Academic Librarianship* 24, no. 3 (2010): 208–15. doi:10.1016/
  S0099-1333(98)90041-6.
Massey-Burzio, Virginia. "Reference Encounters of a Different Kind: A Symposium."
  The Journal of Academic Librarianship 18, no. 5 (1992): 276–86.
Mathews, Brian. "Think Like a Startup: A White Paper to Inspire Library Entrepreneu-
  rialism." *Virginia Tech University Libraries.* April 3, 2012. http://hdl.handle.net/10919/
  18649.
Mathews, Janie M., and Harold Pardue. "The Presence of IT Skill Sets in Librarian
  Position Announcements." *College and Research Libraries* 70, no. 3 (2009): 250–57.

Maxfield, David Kemp. *Counselor Librarianship: A New Departure*. Chicago: University of Illinois, Occasional Papers, 1954.

May, Fiona. "Roving Reference, iPad-Style." *The Idaho Librarian*, November 23, 2011. http://theidaholibrarian.wordpress.com/2011/11/23/roving-reference-ipad-style.

McCarthy, Jenny. "Planning a Future Workforce: An Australian Perspective." *New Review of Academic Librarianship* 11, no. 1 (2005): 41–56. doi:10.1080/13614530500417669.

"Membership Reports." *OCLC*. Accessed June 22, 2014. http://www.oclc.org/reports.en.html.

Miles, Dennis B. "Shall We Get Rid of the Desk?" *Reference and User Services Quarterly* 52, no. 4 (2013): 320–33. doi:10.5860/rusq.52n4.320.

Miller, Alison. "IST 600 Innovation in Public Libraries Syllabus." *Syracuse University*. Accessed May 10, 2014. http://my.ischool.syr.edu/Uploads/CourseSyllabus/Innovation%20in%20Public%20Libraries%20general%20syllabus-1142.46026-5b028c70-d85b-4154-a3f1-17f730fe5698.pdf.

Miller, Kim A., Deanne W. Swan, Terri Craig, Suzanne Dorinski, Michael Freeman, Natasha Isaac, Patricia O'Shea, Peter Schilling, and Jennifer Scotto. *Public Libraries Survey: Fiscal Year 2009* (IMLS-2011-PLS-02). Washington, DC: Institute of Museum and Library Services, 2011. http://www.imls.gov/assets/1/News/PLS2009.pdf.

Miner, Jonathon, and Ross Alexander. "LibGuides in Political Science: Improving Student Access, Research, and Information Literacy." *Journal of Information Literacy* 4, no. 1 (2010): 40–54.

MIT Technology Review. Accessed June 16, 2014. http://www.technologyreview.com.

Mitchell, Megan S., Cynthia H. Comer, Jennifer M. Starkey, and Eboni A. Francis. "Paradigm Shift in Reference Services at the Oberlin College Library: A Case Study." *Journal of Library Administration* 51, no. 4 (2011): 359–74. doi:10.1080/01930826.2011.556959.

"Mobile Technology Fact Sheet." *Pew Research Internet Project*. Accessed June 14, 2014. http://www.pewinternet.org/fact-sheets/mobile-technology-fact-sheet.

Moffett, Billie, and Melissa Ziel. "Librarians on the Loose: Serving Patrons beyond the Building." *Refer* 29, no. 1 (2013): 15–18.

Mon, Lorri, and Ebrahim Randeree. "On the Boundaries of Reference Services: Questioning and Library 2.0." *Journal for Education for Library and Information Science* 50, no. 3 (2009): 164–75.

Mooney, Hailey, and Breezy Silver. "Spread the News: Promoting Data Services." *College and Research Libraries News* 71, no. 9 (2010): 480–83.

Morrison, James L. "Environmental Scanning." In *A Primer for New Institutional Researchers*, edited by M. A. Whitely, J. D. Porter, and H. R. Fenske, 86–99. Tallahassee, FL: The Association for Institutional Research, 1992. Accessed July 15, 2014. http://horizon.unc.edu/courses/papers/enviroscan/index.html.

Mount, Ellis. *Special Libraries and Information Centers: An Introductory Text*. Washington, DC: Special Libraries Association, 1995.

Murray, Janet, and Cindy Tschernitz. "The Internet Myth: Emerging Trends in Reference Enquiries." *APLIS* 17, no. 2 (2004): 80–88.

Naylor, Sharon, Bruce Stoffel, and Sharon Van Der Laan. "Why Isn't Our Chat Reference Used More: Findings of Focus Group Discussions with Undergraduate Students." *Reference and User Services Quarterly* 47, no. 4 (2008): 342–54. doi:10.5860/rusq.47n4.342.

New York Times. Accessed June 16, 2104. http://www.nytimes.com.

Nicholson, Scott, and R. David Lankes. "The Digital Electronic Warehouse Project: Creating the Infrastructure for Digital Reference Research through a Multidisciplinary Knowledge Base." *Reference and User Services Quarterly* 46, no. 3 (2007): 45–59. doi:10.5860/rusq.46n3.45.

Niemla, Karen. "Libraries and the Telephone: A Look Back and a Look Around." *CODEX (2150-086X)* 2, no. 2 (2012): 5–16. http://journal.acrlla.org/index.php/codex/article/view/70.

"NMC Horizon Project." *New Media Consortium.* Accessed July 13, 2014. http://www.nmc.org/horizon-project.

Nonthacumjane, Pussadee. "Key Skills and Competencies of a New Generation of LIS Professionals." *IFLA Journal* 37, no. 4 (2011): 280–88. doi:10.1177/0340035211430475.

"NPR Librarian's Take on Fact-Checking and Research with Katie Daugert." *NPR Digital Services.* Vimeo video, 54:47. Posted by NPR Digital Services, 2012. Accessed May 23, 2014. http://vimeo.com/43998624.

"NYPL Labs." *New York Public Library.* Accessed May 26, 2014. http://www.nypl.org/collections/labs.

Oakleaf, Megan. *The Value of Academic Libraries: A Comprehensive Research Review and Report.* Chicago: ACRL, 2010. Accessed December 18, 2013. http://www.ala.org/acrl/sites/ala.org.acrl/files/content/issues/value/val_report.pdf.

OCLC Research. Accessed June 8, 2014. http://www.oclc.org/research.html.

Okamoto, Karen, and Mark Aaron Polger. "Off to Market We Go." *Library Leadership and Management* 26, no. 2 (2012): 1–20.

Ostrow, Adam. "My 2008 Predictions Rocked; So What's on Tap for Next Year?" *Mashable.* December 29, 2008. http://mashable.com/2008/12/29/2009-tech-predictions.

"Our Favorite Sites." *Answerland.* Accessed April 28, 2014. https://www.answerland.org/our-favorite-sites.

Overall, Patricia Montiel. "Cultural Competence: A Conceptual Framework for Library and Information Science Professionals." *Library Quarterly* 79, no. 2 (2009): 175–204.

Paisley, William J. "Information Needs and Uses." *Annual Review of Information Science and Technology* 3 (1967): 1–30.

Partlo, Kristin. "The Pedagogical Data Reference Interview." *IASSIST Quarterly* 33/34, nos. 4/1 (Winter 2009/Spring 2010): 6–10.

Partridge, Helen, Julie Lee, and Carrie Munro. "Becoming 'Librarian 2.0': The Skills, Knowledge, and Attributes Required by Library and Information Science Professionals in a Web 2.0 World (and Beyond)." *Library Trends* 59, nos. 1–2 (2010): 315–35.

Peltier-Davis, Cheryl. "Web 2.0, Library 2.0, Library User 2.0, Librarian 2.0: Innovative Services for Sustainable Libraries." *Computers in Libraries* 29, no. 10 (2009): 16–21.

Perez, Sarah. "iTunes App Store Now Has 1.2 Million Apps, Has Seen 75 Billion Downloads to Date." *Techcrunch.* June 2, 2014. http://techcrunch.com/2014/06/02/itunes-app-store-now-has-1-2-million-apps-has-seen-75-billion-downloads-to-date.

Peters, Thomas A. "Left to Their Own Devices: The Future of Reference Services on Personal, Portable Information, Communication, and Entertainment Devices." *The Reference Librarian* 52, nos. 1/2 (2011): 88–97. doi:10.1080/02763877.2011.520110.

Pew Research Internet Project. Accessed June 8, 2014. http://www.pewinternet.org.

Pflaum, Ann M., and Timothy J. Delmont. "External Scanning: A Tool for Planners." *Journal of the American Planning Association* 53, no. 1 (1987): 56–67.

Phan, Tai, Laura Hardesty, and Jaime Hug. *Academic Libraries: 2012* (NCES 2014-038). Washington, DC: U.S. Department of Education, National Center for Education Statistics, 2014. http://nces.ed.gov/pubs2014/2014038.pdf.

Poland, Jean. "Adapting to Changing User Expectations." Paper 31, Proceedings of the IATUL Conferences, Krakow, Poland, 2004. http://docs.lib.purdue.edu/iatul/2004/papers/31.

Ponsford, Bennett Claire, and Wyoma vanDuinkerken. "User Expectations in the Time of Google: Usability Testing of Federated Searching." *Internet Reference Services Quarterly* 12, nos. 1/2 (2007): 159–78. doi:10.1300/J136v12n01_08.

Prado, Javier Calzada, and Miguel Angel Marzal. "Incorporating Data Literacy into Information Literacy Programs: Core Competencies and Content." *LIBRI: International Journal of Libraries and Information Science* 63, no. 2 (2013): 123–34. doi:10.1515/libri-2013-0010.

"Presidential Committee on Information Literacy: Final Report." *Association of College and Research Libraries.* January 10, 1989. Accessed December 13, 2013. http://www.ala.org/acrl/publications/whitepapers/presidential.

Price, Gary. "First 'Library Edition' of Startup Weekend Held in Toronto." *InfoDocket* (blog). *Library Journal.* April 4, 2014. http://www.infodocket.com/2014/04/04/first-library-edition-of-startup-weekend-held-in-toronto.

Purcell, Kristen. "Search and Email Still Top the List of Most Popular Online Activities." *Pew Research Internet Project.* August 9, 2011. http://www.pewinternet.org/Reports/2011/Search-and-email.aspx.

Purcell, Kristen, Joanna Brenner, and Lee Rainie. "Search Engine Use 2012." *Pew Research Internet Project.* March 9, 2012. Accessed August 27, 2013. http://pewinternet.org/Reports/2012/Search-Engine-Use-2012.aspx.

Rabner, Lanell, and Suzanne Lorimer, comps. "Definitions of Reference Service: A Chronological Bibliography." *Reference and User Services Association.* Accessed August 15, 2013. http://www.ala.org/rusa/sites/ala.org.rusa/files/content/sections/rss/rsssection/rsscomm/evaluationofref/refdefbibrev.pdf.

Radford, Marie L., and M. Kathleen Kern. "A Multiple-Case Study Investigation of the Discontinuation of Nine Chat Reference Services." *Library and Information Science Research* 28, no. 4 (2006): 521–47. doi:10.1016/j.lisr.2006.10.001.

Rainie, Lee, Leigh Estabrook, and Evans Witt. "Information Searches That Solve Problems." *Pew Research Internet Project.* December 30, 2007. http://pewinternet.org/Reports/2007/Information-Searches-That-Solve-Problems.aspx.

Rainie, Lee, Susannah Fox, and Janna Anderson. "The Predictions and Respondents' Reactions." *Pew Research Internet Project.* January 9, 2005. http://www.pewinternet.org/2005/01/09/the-predictions-and-respondents-reactions.

Ralph, Lynn L., and Timothy J. Ellis. "An Investigation of a Knowledge Management Solution for the Improvement of Reference Services." *Journal of Information, Information Technology, and Organizations,* 4 (2009): 17–38.

RASD Ad Hoc Committee on Behavioral Guidelines for Reference and Information Services. "Guidelines for Behavioral Performance of Reference and Information Service Providers." *Reference and User Services Association.* Last updated May 28, 2013. Accessed January 13, 2014. http://www.ala.org/rusa/resources/guidelines/guidelinesbehavioral.

Read, Eleanor J. "Data Services in Academic Libraries: Assessing Needs and Promoting Services." *Reference and User Services Quarterly* 46, no. 3 (2007): 61–75.

Reed, Vivian. "Is the Reference Desk No Longer the Best Point of Reference?" *The Reference Librarian* 48, no. 2 (2007): 77–82. doi:10.1300/J120v48n02_12.

"Reference and Access." *Society of American Archivists.* Accessed October 3, 2013. http://www2.archivists.org/gpas/curriculum/reference-access.

Reid, Ian. "The Public Library Data Service 2012 Statistical Report: Characteristics and Trends." *Public Libraries* 51, no. 6 (2012): 36–46. Accessed February 28, 2014. http://publiclibrariesonline.org/2014/05/2013-plds.

Reinsfelder, Thomas L. "Citation Analysis as a Tool to Measure the Impact of Individual Research Consultations." *College and Research Libraries* 73, no. 3 (2012): 263–77. doi:10.5860/crl-261.

"Reorganizing for the Future: Five Stories for an Online Discussion." *ALA Connect.* Last modified June 6, 2014. http://connect.ala.org/node/224120.

"Research and Publications." *Ithaka S+R.* Last modified May 2012. http://sr.ithaka.org/research-publications.

Resnick, Taryn. "Core Competencies for Electronic Resources Access Services." *Journal of Electronic Resources in Medical Libraries* 6, no. 2 (2009): 101–22. doi:10.1080/15424060902932185.

"Retooling Reference for Relevant Service @ Dallas Public Library." *Urban Libraries Council.* Accessed May 3, 2014. http://www.urbanlibraries.org/retooling-reference-for-relevant-service—dallas-public-library-innovation-151.php?page_id=38.

Rettig, Jim. "The Reference Question—Where Has Reference Been? Where Is Reference Going?" *The Reference Librarian* 48, no. 2 (2007): 15–20. doi:10.1300/J120v48n02_04.

Richardson, John V., and Matthew L. Saxton. *Understanding Reference Transactions: Turning an Art into a Science.* San Diego: Academic Press, 2002.

Rieh, Soo Young, Brian Hilligoss, and Jiyeon Yang. "Toward an Integrated Framework of Information and Communication Behavior: College Students' Information Resources and Media Selection." *ASLIB Proceedings* 44, no. 1 (2007): 1–15. http://rieh.people.si.umich.edu/~rieh/papers/rieh_asist2007.pdf.

Riehle, Catherine Fraser, and Michael Witt. "Librarians in the Hall: Instructional Outreach in Campus Residences." *Purdue University: Purdue ePubs.* Paper 107. http://docs.lib.purdue.edu/lib_research/107.

"The Right Service at the Right Time." *Florida Department of State, State Library, and Archives of Florida.* Accessed May 2, 2014. http://www.rightservicefl.org.

Rothstein, Samuel. *The Development of Reference Services through Academic Traditions, Public Library Practice, and Special Librarianship.* Chicago: Association of College and Reference Libraries, 1955.

RUSA Task Force on Professional Competencies. "Professional Competencies for Reference and User Services Librarians." *Reference and User Services Association.* Accessed August 28, 2013. http://www.ala.org/rusa/resources/guidelines/professional.

Russell, Philip, Gerard Ryder, Gillian Kerins, and Margaret Phelan. "Creating, Sharing, and Re-Using Learning Objects to Enhance Information Literacy." *Journal of Information Literacy* 7, no. 2 (2013): 60–79. doi:10.11645/7.2.1744.

Ryan, Susan M. "Reference Transactions Analysis: The Cost-Effectiveness of Staffing a Traditional Academic Reference Desk." *The Journal of Academic Librarianship* 34, no. 5 (2008): 389–99. doi:10.1016/j.acalib.2008.06.002.

Sassen, Catherine, and Diane Wahl. "Fostering Research and Publication in Academic Libraries." *College and Research Libraries* 75, no. 4 (2014): 458–91. Accessed July 8, 2014. http://crl.acrl.org/content/75/4/458.full.pdf+html.

Saunders, Laura. "Professional Perspectives on Library and Information Science Education." *Library Quarterly* (forthcoming).

Saunders, Laura. "Regional Accreditation Organizations' Treatment of Information Literacy: Definitions, Collaboration, and Assessment." *The Journal of Academic Librarianship* 33, no. 3 (2007): 317–26. doi:10.1016/j.acalib.2007.01.009.

Saunders, Laura, and Mary Wilkins Jordan. "Significantly Different? Reference Services Competencies in Public and Academic Libraries." *Reference and User Services Quarterly* 52, no. 3 (2013): 216–23.

Savitz, Eric. "Gartner: Top 10 Strategic Technology Trends for 2013." *Forbes*, October 23, 2012. http://www.forbes.com/sites/ericsavitz/2012/10/23/gartner-top-10-strategic-technology-trends-for-2013.

Schonfeld, Roger C., and Ross Housewright. "US Faculty Survey 2012." *Ithaka S+R.* April 8, 2013. http://sr.ithaka.org/research-publications/us-faculty-survey-2012.

Schulte, Stephanie J. "Embedded Academic Librarianship: A Review of the Literature." *Evidence Based Library and Information Practice* 7, no. 4 (2012): 122–38. http://ejournals.library.ualberta.ca/index.php/EBLIP/article/view/17466/14483.

Schurenberg, Eric. "What's an Entrepreneur? The Best Answer Ever." *Inc.* Last updated January 9, 2012. http://www.inc.com/eric-schurenberg/the-best-definition-of-entepreneurship.html.

Schwartz, Meredith, Michelle Lee, and Bob Warburton. "Ithaka Survey: Humanities Faculty Love the Library; Scientists Less Enthusiastic." *Library Journal* 138, no. 8 (May 1, 2013): 8.

Scott, Geoff. "Effective Change Management in Higher Education." *EDUCAUSE Review* 38, no. 5 (November/December 2003): 64–80. https://net.educause.edu/ir/library/pdf/erm0363.pdf.

Shachaf, Pnina, Lokman Meho, and Noriko Hara. "Cross-Cultural Analysis of E-Mail Reference." *The Journal of Academic Librarianship* 33, no. 2 (2007): 243–53. doi:10.1016/j.acalib.2006.08.010.

Shah, Chirag, and Vanessa Kitzie. "Social Q & A and Virtual Reference: Comparing Apples and Oranges with the Help of Experts and Users." *Journal of the American Society for Information Science and Technology* 63, no. 10 (2011): 2020–36. doi:10.1002/asi.22699.

Shelfer, Kathy, and Abby Goodrum. "Competitive Intelligence as an Extension of Library Education." *The Journal of Education for Library and Information Science* 41, no. 4 (2000): 353–61. Accessed July 7, 2014. http://0-www.jstor.org.library.simmons.edu/stable/40324050?seq=2.

Shumaker, David. "Who Let the Librarians Out? Embedded Librarianship and the Library Manager." Edited by Judith M. Nixon. *Reference and User Services Quarterly* 48, no. 3 (2009): 239–42. http://blog.rusq.org/2009/05/29/who-let-the-librarians-out.

Si, Li, Xiaozhe Zhuang, Wenming Xing, and Weining Guo. "The Cultivation of Scientific Data Specialists: Development of LIS Education Oriented to e-Science Service Requirements." *Library Hi Tech* 31, no. 4 (2013): 700–724. doi:10.1108/LHT-06-2013-0070.

Singh, Vandana, and Bharat Mehra. "Strengths and Weaknesses of the Information Technology Curriculum in Library and Information Science Graduate Programs." *Journal of Librarianship and Information Science* 45, no. 3 (2012): 219–31. doi:10.1177/0961000612448206.

"SI—Q." *Smithsonian: Seriously Amazing.* Accessed April 26, 2014. http://seriouslyamazing.si.edu.

Sirkin, Harold L., Perry Keenan, and Alan Jackson. "The Hard Side of Change Management." *Harvard Business Review* 83, no. 10 (October 2005): 108–18. Accessed June 20, 2014. http://hbr.org/2005/10/the-hard-side-of-change-management/ar/1.

"Slam the Boards!" *Answer Board Librarians.* Accessed May 20, 2014. http://answerboards.wikifoundry.com/page/Slam+the+Boards%21.

Smolovik, Cindy C. "Role Delineation Statement." *Academy of Certified Archivists.* 2008–2009. http://www.certifiedarchivists.org/get-certified/role-delineation-statement.

"A Snapshot of E-Reader and Tablet Owners (Infographic)." *Pew Research Internet Project.* January 27, 2012. Accessed June 14, 2014. http://libraries.pewinternet.org/2012/01/27/a-snapshot-of-ereader-and-tablet-owners.

Sobel, Karen D. "Promoting Library Reference Services to First-Year Undergraduate Students: What Works?" *Reference and User Services Quarterly* 48, no. 4 (2009): 362–71. doi:10.5860/rusq.48n4.

"Social Media Trends." *Experian Marketing Services.* Accessed November 24, 2013. http://www.experian.com/marketing-services/online-trends-social-media.html.

"Social Networking: Public Libraries' Use of Social Media Is Up Sharply, Especially among Large Libraries." *American Library Association.* Accessed June 14, 2014. http://www.ala.org/news/state-americas-libraries-report-2014/social-networking.

Solorzano, Ronald Martin. "Adding Value at the Desk: How Technology and User Expectations Are Changing Reference Work." *The Reference Librarian* 54, no. 2 (2013): 89–102. doi:10.1080/02763877.2013.755398.

Sonntag, Gabriela, and Felicia Palsson. "No Longer the Sacred Cow—No Longer a Desk: Transforming Reference Service to Meet 21st Century User Needs." *Library Philosophy and Practice* (2007). Accessed December 10, 2013. http://www.webpages.uidaho.edu/~mbolin/sonntag-palsson.htm.

Sorensen, Karen, and Nancy R. Glassman. "From Desktop to Cloud: A Primer on Internet-Based Computing for Librarians." *Journal of Electronic Resources in Medical Libraries* 8, no. 3 (2011): 243–55. doi:10.1080/15424065.2011.601991.

Special Library Association. http://www.sla.org.

Sproles, Claudene, Anna Marie Johnson, and Leslie Farison. "What the Teachers Are Teaching: How MLIS Programs Are Preparing Academic Librarians for Instructional Roles." *Journal of Education for Library and Information Science* 49, no. 3 (2008): 195–209.

Sproles, Claudene, and David Ratledge. "An Analysis of Entry-Level Job Ads Published in *American Libraries*, 1982–2002." *Electronic Journal of Academic and Special Librarianship* 5, nos. 2/3 (2004). http://southernlibrarianship.icaap.org/content/v05n02/sproles_c01.htm.

Stahr, Beth. "Text Message Reference Service: Five Years Later." *The Reference Librarian* 52, nos. 1/2 (2010): 9–19. doi:10.1080/02763877.2011.524502.

Staines, Gail M. "Finding the Best People in a Tough Economy." *Library Leadership and Management* 26, nos. 3/4 (2012): 1–13. Accessed May 25, 2014. http://0-web.b.ebscohost.com.library.simmons.edu/ehost/pdfviewer/pdfviewer?sid=2a385174-f5a1-42d7-9e81-3e6a351c1db7%40sessionmgr112&vid=2&hid=120.

Standards and Guidelines Committee, Reference and User Services Association. "Guidelines for Information Services." *Reference and User Services Association.* Last updated July 2000. Accessed December 18, 2013. http://www.ala.org/rusa/resources/guidelines/guidelinesinformation.

"Standards for Libraries in Higher Education." *Association of College and Research Libraries.* October 2011. http://www.ala.org/acrl/standards/standardslibraries.

"Stanford Prize for Innovation in Research Libraries (SPIRL)." *Stanford University Libraries.* Accessed June 5, 2014. http://library.stanford.edu/projects/stanford-prize-in-novation-research-libraries-spirl.

"The State of America's Libraries." Special issue. *American Libraries* (2013). Accessed January 22, 2014. http://www.ala.org/news/sites/ala.org.news/files/content/2013-State-of-Americas-Libraries-Report.pdf.

"The State of America's Libraries: A Report from the American Library Association." *American Library Association.* Accessed June 15, 2014. http://www.ala.org/news/mediapresscenter/americaslibraries/soal_archive.

Stephens, Michael. "Essential Soft Skills: Office Hours." *Library Journal* 138, no. 3 (2013): 39. Accessed January 13, 2014. http://lj.libraryjournal.com/2013/02/opinion/michael-stephens/essential-soft-skills.

Stephens, Michael. "Into a New World of Librarianship: Sharpen These Skills for Librarian 2.0." *Next Space,* no. 2 (2006): 8. Accessed January 11, 2014. http://www.oclc.org/content/dam/oclc/publications/newsletters/nextspace/nextspace_002.pdf.

Stern, David. "User Expectations and the Complex Realities of Online Research Efforts." *Science and Technology Libraries* 22, nos. 3–4 (2002): 137–48. doi:10.1300/J122v22n03_11.

Stevens, Christy R. "Reference Reviewed and Re-Envisioned: Revamping Librarian and Desk-Centric Services with LibStARs and LibAnswers." *The Journal of Academic Librarianship* 39, no. 2 (2013): 202–14. doi:10.1016/j.acalib.2012.11.006.

Stiwinter, Katherine. "Using an Interactive Online Tutorial to Expand Library Instruction." *Internet Reference Services Quarterly* 18, no. 1(2013): 15–41. doi:10.1080/10875301.2013.777010.

Stover, Mark. "The Reference Librarian as Non-Expert: A Post-Modern Approach to Expertise." *The Reference Librarian,* nos. 87/88 (2004): 273–300. doi:10.1300/J120v42n87_10.

Stripling, Barbara. "Summit on the Future of Libraries." *ALA Connect.* Last modified May 19, 2014. http://connect.ala.org/node/223667.

Sung, Myung Gi. "Ten Essential Qualities for Success: A New Cataloging Librarian's Guide from a Supervisor's Perspective." *Public Libraries* 52, no. 3 (2013): 32–35.

Swanson, Jennifer. "Start Learning Project Management Skills." *Information Outlook* 17, no. 4 (2013): 18.

Swope, Mary Jane, and Jeffrey Katzer. "The Silent Majority: Why Don't They Ask Questions." *RQ* 12, no. 2 (1972): 161–66.

Taylor, Robert S. "Question-Negotiation and Information Seeking in Libraries." *College and Research Libraries* 29, no. 3 (1968): 178–94. http://hdl.handle.net/2142/38236.

"Template: WikiProject Australia/AAL/What." *Wikipedia*. Accessed June 12, 2014. http://en.wikipedia.org/wiki/Template:WikiProject_Australia/AAL/What.

Tenopir, Carol, Ben Birch, and Suzie Allard. "Academic Libraries and Research Data Services: Current Practices and Plans for the Future: An ACRL White Paper." *Association of College and Research Libraries*. June 2012. Accessed January 16, 2014. http://www.ala.org/acrl/sites/ala.org.acrl/files/content/publications/whitepapers/Tenopir_Birch_Allard.pdf.

Thompson, Samantha. "I Wouldn't Normally Ask This. ... : Or, Sensitive Questions and Why People Seem More Willing to Ask Them at a Virtual Reference Desk." *The Reference Librarian* 51, no. 2 (2010): 171–74. doi:10.1080/02763870903579869.

Trace, Ciaran B., and Carlos J. Ovalle. "Archival Reference and Access: Syllabi and a Snapshot of the Archival Canon." *The Reference Librarian* 53, no. 1 (2012): 76–94. doi:10.1080/02763877.2011.596364.

"Trend Data (Adults)." *Pew Research Internet Project*. Accessed November 21, 2013. http://www.pewinternet.org/Static-Pages/Trend-Data-(Adults)/Device-Ownership.aspx.

Twitter. "#numbers." *The Official Twitter Blog* (blog). *Twitter*. March 14, 2011. https://blog.twitter.com/2011/numbers.

Tyckoson, David A. "History and Functions of Reference Service." In *Reference and Information Services: An Introduction*, edited by Richard E. Bopp and Linda C. Smith, 3–22. Santa Barbara, CA: Libraries Unlimited, 2011.

Tyckoson, David A. "What Is the Best Model of Reference Service?" *Library Trends* 50, no. 2 (2001): 183–96. https://www.ideals.illinois.edu/bitstream/handle/2142/8398/librarytrendsv50i2d_opt.pdf?sequence=1.

Van Epps, Amy S. "Librarians and Statistics: Thoughts on a Tentative Relationship." *Practical Academic Librarianship: The International Journal of the SLA* 2, no. 1 (2012): 25–32. Accessed July 8, 2014. http://0-search.ebscohost.com.library.simmons.edu/login.aspx?direct=true&db=lls&AN=76435802&site=ehost-live&scope=site.

VanScoy, Amy. "Page Us! Combining the Best of In-Person and Virtual Reference Service to Meet In-Library Patron Needs." *Internet Reference Services Quarterly* 11, no. 2 (2006): 15–25. doi:10.1300/J136v11n02_02.

VanScoy, Amy Dianne. "Practitioner Experiences in Academic Research Libraries: An Interpretative Phenomenological Analysis of Reference Work." PhD diss., University of North Carolina, Chapel Hill, 2012. Accessed November 18, 2013. http://search.proquest.com/docview/1024564087.

Varvel, Virgil E., Jr. "The Public Library Data Service 2011 Statistical Report Characteristics and Trends." *Public Libraries* 50, no. 5 (2011): 26–34. Accessed February 28, 2014. http://www.ala.org/pla/sites/ala.org.pla/files/content/publications/plds/varvel_pl_50n5_sepoct11.pdf.

Vondracek, Ruth. "Comfort or Convenience? Why Students Choose Alternatives to the Library." *portal: Libraries and the Academy* 7, no. 3 (2007): 277–93. doi:10.1353/pla.2007.0039.

Wall Street Journal. Accessed June 16, 2014. http://online.wsj.com/home-page.

Walter, Scott. "Librarians as Teachers: A Qualitative Inquiry into Professional Identity." *College and Research Libraries* 69, no. 1 (2008): 51–71.

Wang, Hanrong, Yingqi Tang, and Carley Knight. "Contemporary Development of Academic Reference Librarianship in the United States: A 44-Year Content Analysis." *The Journal of Academic Librarianship* 36, no. 6 (2010): 489–94. doi:10.1016/j.acalib.2010.08.004.

Watstein, Sarah Barbara, and Stephen Bell. "Is There a Future for the Reference Desk? A Point-Counterpoint Discussion." *The Reference Librarian* 49, no. 1 (2008): 1–20. doi:10.1080/02763870802103258.

Weber, Mitch. "JoCo Librarians Fact Check Presidential Debate." *KSHB-41 Action News Kansas City*. Last updated October 22, 2012. http://www.kshb.com/news/political/joco-librarians-fact-check-presidential-debate.

Weiner, Sharon Gray. "The History of Academic Libraries in the United States: A Review of the Literature." *Library Philosophy and Practice* 7, no. 2 (2005): 1–12. http://digitalcommons.unl.edu/cgi/viewcontent.cgi?article=1057&context=libphilprac.

Wells, Andrew. "Agile Management: Strategies for Success in Rapidly Changing Times—An Australian University Library Perspective." *IFLA Journal* 40, no. 1 (2014): 30–34. doi:10.1177/0340035214526539.

Westbrook, Lynn. "Unanswerable Questions at the IPL: User Expectations of E-Mail Reference." *Journal of Documentation* 65, no. 3 (2009): 367–95. doi:10.1108/00220410910952393.

Whitmire, Ethelene. "A Longitudinal Study of Undergraduates' Academic Library Experiences." *The Journal of Academic Librarianship* 27, no. 5 (2001): 379–85. doi:10.1016/S0099-1333(01)00223-3.

Wilson, Renee. "Ask a Librarian: Now Virtually Everywhere!" *Behind the Scenes* (blog). *National Library of Australia*. May 7, 2014. http://www.nla.gov.au/blogs/behind-the-scenes/2014/05/07/ask-a-librarian-now-virtually-everywhere.

Wise, Sharyn, Maureen Henninger, and Mary Anne Kennan. "Changing Trends in LIS Job Advertisements." *Australian Academic and Research Libraries* 42, no. 4 (2011): 268–95.

Wojcicki, Susan. "The Eight Pillars of Innovation." *Think Newsletter*. July 2011. Accessed June 23, 2014. http://www.thinkwithgoogle.com/articles/8-pillars-of-innovation.html.

York, Amy C., and Jason M. Vance. "Taking Library Instruction into the Online Classroom: Best Practices for Embedded Librarians." *The Journal of Library Administration* 49, nos. 1/2 (2009): 197–209. doi:10.1080/01930820802312995.

Yu, Holly, and Margo Young. "The Impact of Web Search Engines on Subject Searching in OPAC." *Information Technology and Libraries* 23, no. 4 (2004): 168–80.

Yunusov, Elena. "Winners Announced for Toronto's Startup Weekend: Library Edition." *Betakit Canadian Startup News and Emerging Technology*, April 4, 2014. http://www.betakit.com/winners-announced-for-torontos-startup-weekend-library-edition.

Zhang, Jie, and Nevin Mayer. "Proactive Chat Reference: Getting in the Users' Space." *College and Research Libraries News* 75, no. 4 (2014): 202–5. http://crln.acrl.org/content/75/4/202.full.pdf+html.

Zickuhr, Kathryn. "Innovative Library Services 'In the Wild.'" *Libraries in the Digital Age* (blog). *Pew Internet and American Life Project*. January 29, 2013. http://libraries.pewinternet.org/2013/01/29/innovative-library-services-in-the-wild.

Zickuhr, Kathryn, Lee Rainie, and Kristen Purcell. "Library Services in the Digital Age." *The Pew Internet and American Life Project*. January 22, 2013. Accessed February 26, 2014. http://libraries.pewinternet.org/files/legacy-pdf/PIP_Library%20services_Report.pdf.

Zickuhr, Kathryn, Lee Rainie, and Kristen Purcell. "Younger Americans' Library Habits and Expectations." *Pew Internet and American Life Project*. June 25, 2013. http://libraries.pewinternet.org/2013/06/25/younger-americans-library-services.

Zickuhr, Kathryn, and Aaron Smith. "Home Broadband 2013: Trends and Demographic Differences in Home Broadband Adoption." *Pew Research Internet Project*. August 26, 2013. http://www.pewinternet.org/2013/08/26/home-broadband-2013.

Zweizig, Douglas L. "With Our Eye on the User: Needed Research for Information and Referral in the Public Library." *Drexel Library Quarterly* 12, nos. 1/2 (1976): 48–58.

Index

academic libraries, 2, 6, 9, 10, 11, 13, 16, 27, 28, 34, 36, 37, 38, 57, 58, 58–59, 78, 79, 81, 97, 98, 106, 111
Academy of Certified Archivists, 3
accountability, 10, 17, 59, 66, 122
adaptability. *See* flexibility
American Association of College and Universities, 38
American Library Association (ALA), 3, 4, 38, 59, 66, 73, 88, 97, 98, 121, 124
Answerland, 83
Arapahoe Library District (Colorado), 79
archives, 1, 3, 15, 38, 84, 86, 97, 98
Ask.com, 29
Aspen Institute, 73
assessment. *See* evaluation and assessment.
Association of College & Research Libraries (ACRL), 15, 27, 38, 57, 58, 59, 73, 98, 118
Association of Research Libraries (ARL), 15, 27

Bill and Melinda Gates Foundation, 73
Brandeis model. *See* tiered reference.

Capella University, 36
change: covered in Library and Information Science curricula, 88; success factors, 116–117; leadership, xi, 60, 64, 112, 113, 114, 115, 117; management, xi, 60, 64, 88, 113, 116, 119, 122; obstacles to enacting, 111–112; resistance to, xi, 60, 111, 114, 117, 118, 119, 122; restructuring human resources, 118–119
chat reference. *See also* virtual reference: software, 9; trigger-initiated, 78–79

classifications of questions. *See* question types.
college students, 12, 13, 31, 37, 87
competencies, 6, 14–17, 38–39, 49–61, 62, 63–66, 64, 77, 83, 88, 120, 122, 124
competitors to reference, 16, 28–30, 96, 99, 112
consultations, research, 5, 15, 25, 30, 36–37, 40, 78, 79–81
content creation, 4, 39–40, 52, 106, 118
convenience, 10, 12, 13, 14, 32
counseling model of reference, 61–62
cultural competency, 55
curriculum. *See* education, LIS/library.
customer service, 7, 17, 54, 95

data curation. *See* data management.
data management, 16, 49, 56, 58–59, 64, 120, 122, 123
Deschutes Public Libraries (Oregon), 34
design thinking, 112
Digital Public Library of America, 87, 105
digital reference. *See* virtual reference.
Douglas County Libraries (Colorado), 34
Druker, Peter F., 74

East Texas Baptist University, 78
education, higher, 2, 38, 97, 116
education, LIS/library, 63–66, 88–89, 122–124
education, public, 1
email reference, 8, 28, 29, 30, 83, 85
embedded librarianship, 34–36, 75; relationship to instruction, 39
entrepreneurship, definition of, 74, 88
environmental scanning, 15, 17, 79, 88, 94–106

About the Authors

Laura Saunders is an assistant professor at Simmons College Graduate School of Library and Information Science, where she teaches in the areas of user instruction, reference, intellectual freedom, and academic libraries. Her research interests include information literacy, assessment, and social justice aspects of information access and literacy.

Lillian Rozaklis is an independent consultant in user research, learning analytics, and information services, with prior roles as a reference librarian in public libraries and as a research analyst in higher education. She received her Ph.D. in Information Studies from Drexel University's College of Information Science and Technology and an M.S. in Library and Information Science from Syracuse University's School of Information Studies.

Eileen G. Abels is dean and professor at Simmons College Graduate School of Library and Information Science. Her primary teaching areas are reference, business information, and special libraries. Her research interests include information access, the future of libraries, and the future of library and information science education.